PARENTING THE CRISIS
The cultural politics of parent-blame

Tracey Jensen

First published in Great Britain in 2018 by

Policy Press
University of Bristol
1-9 Old Park Hill
Bristol
BS2 8BB
UK
t: +44 (0)117 954 5940
pp-info@bristol.ac.uk
www.policypress.co.uk

North America office:
Policy Press
c/o The University of Chicago Press
1427 East 60th Street
Chicago, IL 60637, USA
t: +1 773 702 7700
f: +1 773-702-9756
sales@press.uchicago.edu
www.press.uchicago.edu

© Policy Press 2018

British Library Cataloguing in Publication Data
A catalogue record for this book is available from the British Library

Library of Congress Cataloging-in-Publication Data
A catalog record for this book has been requested

ISBN 978-1-4473-2506-2 paperback
ISBN 978-1-4473-2505-5 hardcover
ISBN 978-1-4473-2508-6 ePub
ISBN 978-1-4473-2509-3 Mobi
ISBN 978-1-4473-2507-9 ePdf

The right of Tracey Jensen to be identified as author of this work has been asserted by her in accordance with the Copyright, Designs and Patents Act 1988.

Cover design by Qube Design Associates, Bristol
Front cover image: www.alamy.com
Printed and bound in Great Britain by CMP, Poole
Policy Press uses environmentally responsible print partners

Contents

About the author

Tracey Jensen grew up in the coastal badlands of Essex, grew wise in the edgelands of south London and is now happily ensconced in Lancashire. She is a lecturer in Media and Cultural Studies at Lancaster University, with particular interests in social justice and equality, the politics of representation, and the welfare state.

Acknowledgements

This book is the result of several years of research, thinking and writing. Like all books, it was made possible through the support of friends, family and colleagues, who have sustained me in so many ways over the years and without whom I would never have found my words, or finished my sentences.

Thank you, always, to Ros Gill and Helen Lucey for the formidable intellectual training and friendship, and to Bev Skeggs, Gail Lewis and Meg-John Barker for advice, guidance and for so much encouragement. I am very grateful: to Lisa Baraitser and Sigal Spigel for inviting me to be part of the MaMSIE network and the *Studies in the Maternal* journal, and for encouraging me to present early work at the 'Mother Trouble' conference at Birkbeck, University of London; to Ellie Lee, Jennie Bristow and all involved in the events and discussions of the Centre for Parenting Culture Studies at the University of Kent; to Val Gillies and Ros Edwards for inviting me to present at 'The New Politics of Parenting' at London South Bank University; and to Martin Power, Kristina Alstam, Jo Littler and Alison Winch, Lisa McKenzie, Jenny Thatcher, Katy McEwan and Dan Silver for inviting me to present research and ideas at various stages. And my thanks to Shannon Kneiss, Jessica Miles, Rebecca Tomlinson and Helen Davis at Policy Press for their support throughout.

Many of the ideas in this book were incubated elsewhere first. Roberta Garrett and Angie Voela were wonderful co-editors on *We Need To Talk About Family*, which informed key themes here. Charlotte Faircloth invited me to write a chapter for *Parenting in Global Perspective* and organised an inspiring discussion event with contributors. Claire Maxwell gave me the chance to develop a case study analysis in a chapter for *Privilege, Agency and Affect*. Kim Allen and Sumi Hollingworth invited me to respond to the 2011 riots in a special section of *Sociological Research Online*. Mark Carrigan invited me to contribute a series of formative blogs to *The Sociological Imagination*. Thank you to everyone who contributed to a Special Issue of *Studies in the Maternal* on 'Austerity Parenting', which was generative of the principal arguments in this book. My thanks too to Les Back, Rob McDonald, Tracy Shildrick and Stephen Crossley – your work has been inspirational.

Thank you to all my colleagues at Lancaster University for extending warm welcomes, especially Debra Ferreday and Kate McNicholas Smith for sharing celebrity attachments, chip butties and quality feminist pop culture chat. I am grateful to Michaela Benson and Kat Jungnickel, who held my hand through the first writing retreat. Thank you also to everyone who organised and attended the writing retreats in Arnside and Kendal, which provided a much-needed (and breathtaking) space to push forward with, and complete, this book. Kim Allen and Sara de Benedictis have been enduring pals throughout our shared projects and have provided outstanding GIF-game and support when progress has felt slow. Monica Moreno-Figueroa, Hettie Malcomson, Carolyn Pedwell, Anne Graefer, Joanne Kalogeras and Molly Andrews have been kind and wise friends. Hat-tip to all the feminist academic freestylers who, in their academic practice and personal politics, illuminate another, kinder way to critically engage with the world and each other. A special thanks to Kim Allen, Sara de Benedictis and Clare Waterton, who read and commented on draft chapters. Extra special thanks to Imogen Tyler, who encouraged/instructed me to write this book, read the entire manuscript and offered wise counsel throughout, and who has been an unfailingly top mate, dog-walking companion and cider associate.

My fam and friends have waited for me to emerge from the writing chrysalis; thank you to the gent Bruce Bennett, Thembi Mutch, Jenny Weir and Euan the boy wonder, Jess and James Moxham-Lynch, Chris and Kate Bellis-Wright, Joanna 'Flash' Holland, Sara Davidmann and my oldest pal Cassandra Hollis, for being supreme mates. Big kisses, pats and hugs to my dear Mum, John, my bruvs Glen and Dean, the gorgeous Anna, who produced my beautiful nephew in the final stages of the bookwriting, the handsome Thijs, my nan and grandad Sheila and Sid, who remind me to smell the flowers, my big sis Tracy and little nieces Bella and Louisa for their love and laughter, and Aaron Madiot, my French spouse, who will always be the best of the best. My beautiful, inventive and hilariously entertaining daughter Milly has been extremely patient and uncomplaining while I wrote this book, and has provided lots of daft energy and affectionate silliness whenever I have been flagging. And finally, my sweet Alison, my rock and my beloved one, has fed me, nourished me, tended to my every need, reassured me and worked so hard to keep things going. I probably will have to agree to a third dog after this. This book is for her.

Preface

Parent-blame, which holds individual parents wholly accountable for the life trajectory of their children, emanates from multiple sources and sites, and manifests and settles within us in complicated ways. The machinery of parent-blame is initiated in pregnancy advice, childcare expertise, promotional literature for nursery childcare, on social media discussion forums, over hushed gossip and rumour, in a raised eyebrow at the school gates. I could fill a book with anecdotes, both amusing and disturbing, about moments where I have been made into a blameworthy object, a bad mother causing her child to be sent into an orbit of dysfunction and failure.

It can often feel that merely existing as a separate being – with a complicated emotional life and desires beyond the demands of social reproduction – is sufficient to be ascribed as being 'bad'. Once you add into this mix the weighty cultural expectations around parental perfection, the fetishistic glamorisation of pregnancy and post-birth bodies, and the insistence that every moment with a child be characterised with patience, sensitivity and moral direction, and stir, you have quite a heady and flexible cocktail of blame. Entire genres of confessional literature about parenting have told powerful stories about how even the act of acknowledging ambivalence about one's children and parenting life can feel dangerous. Psychoanalysts have described the twin poles of denigration and idealisation that parents are caught within and governed by – required to magically disappear from view in the processes through which children become autonomous, separate beings in the world, and blamed for being too present, too distant, too involved, not involved enough. Motherhood, in particular, has been described as a psychologically threatening experience, with mothers expected to be:

> container, mirror, receptacle for intolerable feelings, a body with bits attached or with supposedly vital bits missing, an object to be repudiated, hated or feared, the one who bears destruction and abandonment ... she who must to some degree be left, or more forcefully abjected or killed off (Baraitser, 2009: 5).

This is a book about parent-blame but specifically it is a book about mother-blame, and how the maternal captures and governs mothers in a political economy of parenting that genders the work of social reproduction, inscribes powerful cultural norms around childrearing, and catches parents within psychic landscapes of anxiety, guilt and disgust, which separate us from one another. At different, and often quite unremarkable moments, I have felt captured by what feels like unending requirements and obligations, exasperated, and exhausted by the powerful commonsense of the maternal that insists that mothering should come 'naturally' and 'effortlessly'.

The work of this book began with my desire to make sense of how and where I was placed by others in a landscape of maternal fantasies and idealisations; and to think through how and where I was placing myself. The purpose of this book was renewed time and time again, in unexceptional and entirely routine moments, where I was made a figure of failure and blame, by culture, in policy, across media, in interactions with state representatives, family members, friends, colleagues and strangers. I was always surprised by how willingly and enthusiastically we apportion blame and interpret the double binds of parenting as emanating from the failures, always, of mothers.

Researching and writing a book on the machinery of parent-blame did not protect me from sanctimonious lectures and unsolicited advice. My fieldwork and personal diaries detail the minutiae of difficult incidents that would have receded into the haze of experience – but which *became* disturbing through the interruptions of other adults. I had my own strategies for dealing with tantrums, defiance and other struggles (or, more often, no strategy at all), but I was always unprepared for the speed with which bystanders would deploy their accusations and allegations. On more than one occasion, 'offers' of advice would become tirades of abuse: a kindly-looking man screamed that I was 'a slag' and 'a terrible mother', when I politely rebuffed his concerns about my momentarily irritated child; a woman screeched to a halt in her car, nearly causing a crash and blocking traffic, to scold me for allowing my daughter to go ahead of me, safely on the quiet suburban pavement, on her scooter. Many parents will have similar stories. These are the everyday and unremarkable moments of hostility and antagonism, through which the machinery of parent-blame works.

This book is less about the mundane moments and experiences of 'failure' (real and imagined) and more concerned with how parent-blame has been produced, recycled, operationalised – and, ultimately, weaponised – in media, in public debate and in state policy. It explores how encounters with blame are 'taken inside' us and made 'commonsense' in the pursuit of broader political agendas that seek to make families responsible, aspirational and autonomous. In mapping the cultural politics of parent-blame, *Parenting the Crisis* aims to provoke wider questions about welfare reform, gendering and inequality. It tracks the socialisation of neoliberal ideas in parenting culture over recent decades and, specifically, the production of a 'parenting crisis' in neoliberal Britain across successive governments.

Although the 'death-knell' of neoliberalism has been allegedly sounded, especially after the financial crisis of 2008-09 and the enthusiastic embrace (and failure) of austerity, we are witnessing even now an intensification across policy making, media and cultural space and public debate of neoliberal accumulation and punitive disentitlement and disinvestment strategies. The pace of change has been dizzying. These changes are effecting unbearable pressures on the most marginalised and precarious families – families who are divided across national borders, migrant and refugee families, large families, single-parent families, families with disabled parents and/or children, families who are unemployed or in irregular employment. Child and maternal poverty is accelerating.

Despite the rapid rise of anti-austerity movements, the enduring hegemony of neoliberalism continues to be reinforced – often through symbolic familial markers, such as 'the hardworking family', and in disturbingly authoritarian directions (Tansel, 2017). Where neoliberalism was once described as the only 'viable' possibility, it now increasingly appears as the only 'imaginable' one (Fisher, 2009). As this book aims to show, the production of a 'parenting crisis' has been a central vector, through which the dismantling of social security and welfare institutions, and the pre-emptive disciplining by state apparatus, of those who are already most impacted and squeezed, has been legitimated.

Tracey Jensen, December 2017

ONE

Introduction

> There is a major problem in our society with children growing up not knowing the difference between right and wrong [...] In too many cases, the parents of these children – if they are still around – don't care where their children are or who they are with, let alone what they are doing ... [t]here is no one step that can be taken. But we need a benefit system that rewards work and that is on the side of families. We need more discipline in our schools. We need action to deal with the most disruptive families. (David Cameron, statement to the House of Commons following riots, 11 August 2011)

On Thursday, 4 August 2011, Mark Duggan, a 29-year-old man and father of four children, was shot and killed by specialist firearms officers in an altercation in Tottenham, London. The Metropolitan Police would take almost two full days to inform Duggan's family of his death. Their failure to adequately mediate the situation led to a vigil outside Tottenham police station on Saturday, 6 August of around three hundred people, including relatives, friends and neighbours, demanding an explanation. There are multiple accounts of what followed, but most agree that engagement with the police remained limited, that speculations and rumours filled this vacuum within the vigil, and that, following clashes between some protesters and police, tensions erupted around 8pm, leading to the burning of two police cars. Around 10.30pm, a double-decker bus was also set alight and some sections of the protest became mobile. Around 11pm, the first incidents of looting began. The violence and looting soon escalated and would continue for three days across the capital and spread to other cities across the UK. A spectacle of violence, burning buildings and looting was replayed across televisions, newspapers and social media for many days. The English riots of 2011 would eventually lead to more than three thousand arrests, five deaths, and property and business damage costing in the region of £200 million (Riots Communities and Victims Panel, 2012).

It would take the Independent Police Complaints Commission three and a half years to complete an inquest into the Duggan shooting. All officers were eventually cleared of any criminal intent, though the report called for urgent improvements in the accountability procedures and communications processes of firearms incidents. Mark Duggan's family and supporters have not accepted the report and continue to highlight inconsistencies and irregularities in officers' versions of events, particularly with regard to whether Duggan was holding a handgun when he was shot dead. Pam Duggan, Mark's mother, called the Independent Police Complaints Commission report 'a slap in the face' and vowed to keep fighting for a full explanation of his death. After a subsequent judicial appeal was overturned, Mark's aunt, Carole Duggan, said in a public statement, 'we feel we're being held responsible for the uprisings of 2011' (quoted in Dodd, 2014).

Social research conducted in the aftermath of the riots would demonstrate that there were clear connections between the Duggan shooting and the subsequent social unrest. A collaborative research study, *Reading the Riots*, conducted 270 interviews with people who had participated in rioting and concluded that the shooting of Mark Duggan was a catalyst that compounded more longstanding grievances against the state, including distrust of the police, resentments about racialising stop and search procedures that disproportionately targeted young black men, and experiences of marginality and dispossession (Roberts et al, 2011).

Criminologists have placed the 2011 English riots within a broader historical and social context of aggressive policing and racial discrimination, and sought to problematise the various 'moral panics' (street gangs, alienated consumption, social media use) that rapidly surfaced in media and public discussion of these events (Briggs, 2012). Cultural theorist Imogen Tyler frames the riots as an expression of anger towards 'the intrusive and excessive penal activities of the state' (Tyler, 2013: 196). Such activities have normalised policing practices which work through the invasive surveillance and harassment of young people in British cities, subject them to a penetrating and stigmatising gaze, and treat them as surplus populations of waste.

However, there was initially very little interest from politicians and public commentators in examining or understanding these grievances, or how they connected with the escalations of looting and violence, or in reflecting upon the strained relationship between the Metropolitan Police and the communities it served. Indeed, the very *idea* of sociological investigation into the riots prompted derision and dismissal. As video footage of crowds moving through British cities circulated on 24-hour rolling television coverage and across social media, politicians and news broadcasters struggled to make sense of what was happening and fell into repetitions of particular key phrases – what Tyler terms 'a torrent of underclass appellations' (Tyler, 2013: 180), with the favoured pejorative being, simply, 'scum'. The day after the final night of rioting, the then London Mayor Boris Johnson addressed a self-appointed 'riot clean-up' army in Clapham and told them: 'I have heard too much sociological explanation and not enough condemnation' (Davies, 2011). Before the dust had even begun to settle, Johnson demanded simple answers and clear lines of condemnation. The direction of this condemnation had, in fact, already stretched out towards the institution of the family, and in particular towards the figure of the bad parent.

'Where are the parents?'

On 11 August 2011, Home Secretary Theresa May, echoing the contempt for anything resembling 'sociological justification', stated with certainty that the rioters were displaying 'sheer criminality, pure and simple'. The same day, the then Prime Minister David Cameron, having finally abandoned his holiday and returned to the capital city, made a statement in the House of Commons about the disturbances. Dismissing the significance of Duggan's death to subsequent events as 'preposterous', Cameron went on to describe the riots as driven by the 'mindless selfishness' of 'opportunistic thugs in gangs … a hard core of young people'. He went on to identify those at fault – the *parents* of those who participated in the riots, whom he declared to be either absent or neglectful, and as such to have incubated 'the problem … a complete lack of responsibility, a lack of proper parenting, a lack of proper upbringing, a lack of proper ethics, a lack of proper morals' (Cameron, 2011a).

In the House of Commons discussion following Cameron's statement, other MPs would echo Cameron in blaming Britain's 'broken society' and specifically its failing parents. Theresa May demanded that parents keep their children at home that night. Education Secretary Michael Gove described the events as reflective of a 'culture of rootless hedonism'. The MP for Tottenham, David Lammy, suggested that the rioting had a straightforward cause: parents have become afraid to smack their children. As MP for the constituency where the rioting started, Lammy became a cause célèbre over the course of August 2011, offering anecdotal 'evidence' across multiple platforms, claiming that he had predicted the riots and, a few months later, publishing *Out of the Ashes*, a 'part-memoir, part political essay' (Lammy, 2011), elaborating on his hypothesis that ineffective parenting had created the right conditions for rioting. On 29 January 2012, Lammy repeated this claim in an interview on LBC Radio, stating that anti-smacking legislation enforced under the Children Act 2004 had made parents afraid to chastise their children in case social services were called, and that parents 'no longer feel sovereign in their own homes'.

The cause of this alleged violent, disrespectful cultural malaise, rapidly laid at the door of parents, solidified a powerful explanatory thread – a crisis of parental responsibility – which would quickly become a convenient alibi for politicians struggling to explain civil unrest. 'Where are the parents?' was a question rhetorically posed by Cameron, which soon became an accusatory question and political soundbite, accumulating strength with each utterance. Cameron's statement in the House of Commons began with the immediate issues of policing and public order, but quickly expanded into a wider discussion of a lax benefit system, the normalisation of worklessness, lack of discipline in schools and the 'problem' of disruptive families. His comments would come to license an extended discussion of 'the underclass', the dominant frame through which poverty and inequality are understood in British culture and politics. The riots, we heard repeatedly throughout 15 August 2011, were not about poverty and nor were they political; rather, they were about a 'culture of poverty', a dysfunctional and chaotic base that lacked morality and responsibility, that was unable to govern and control its children, that had been expanding and that was now contaminating the very rules of urban civility.

In subsequent days and weeks, the Prime Minister's certainty about a crisis of parenting seemed only to fortify over time, documented through his increasingly florid prose. On 15 August 2011, now speaking from a youth centre in his Witney constituency in his first public speech since the unrest, Cameron's explanation of 'poor parenting' had become more specific: it was the breakdown of the family and fatherlessness that were probably to blame for the events of August:

> I don't doubt that many of the rioters out last week have
> no father at home. Perhaps they come from one of the
> neighbourhoods where it's standard for children to have a
> mum and not a dad, where it's normal for young men to
> grow up without a male role model, looking to the streets

for their father figures, filled up with rage and anger. (Cameron, quoted in Slater, 2011)

Without providing any data or evidence, and apparently exonerated from the burden of proof, Cameron states that *he has no doubt* that fatherlessness and family breakdown caused the riots. His comments have the authority of commonsense; they draw, like so much post-riot commentary, on older, familiar, *unquestionable* narratives of 'broken families', of single mothers, fatherlessness and 'feral' children. This key explanatory thread of fatherlessness needed no evidence to support it, because it is a statement that 'goes without saying', that panders to knee-jerk prejudices and anecdote.

Beyond the House of Commons chamber, the underclass explanation took hold and the longstanding motif of 'Broken Britain' began to materialise (see Allen et al, 2013) across media commentary. Alongside politicians, 'experts' and commentators across the political spectrum rushed to identify the 'underclass' parents who had allegedly incubated and raised an army of rioters. Writing in the *Daily Mail*, columnist Melanie Phillips (2011) declared that 'we are not merely up against feral children but feral parents', and insisted that the 'willed removal' of fathers from families had resulted in the 'mayhem' of lone-mother households that could only generate 'feral savages'. In the *Telegraph*, Mary Riddell lamented the 'Hobbesian dystopia' of a 'ruined generation' (Riddell, 2011). David Goodhart, the director of the Policy Exchange think tank and writing for *Prospect*, blamed the 'nihilistic grievance culture of the black inner city' that was fanned by the 'sullen disaffection' lionised in popular and celebrity culture (Goodhart, 2011).

This narrative of a broken moral compass, caused by and through the poor parenting of the underclass, was not limited to right-leaning news publications. In an article for the *Guardian*, titled 'Being liberal is fine, but we need to be given the right to parent', journalist Amelia Gentleman quotes a string of Tottenham residents, whose contradictory proclamations about potential contributory factors to the riots ranged from casual sex, idleness and greed as potential contributory factors (Gentleman, 2011). Mark Easton penned an article for the BBC news pages, titled 'England riots: the return of the underclass' (Easton, 2011), which quoted the warnings from Secretary of State for Work and Pensions Iain Duncan Smith; namely, that a 'menacing underclass' has created 'a new generation of disturbed and aggressive young people doomed to repeat and amplify the social breakdown disfiguring their lives and others round them' (Easton, 2011).

I begin with the 2011 riots because they illuminate how rapidly frightening episodes of social unrest can be tethered to longstanding, pathologising ideas about the failing, chaotic and dysfunctional family. Let us remember the very real grief of Mark Duggan's family and community – left for almost two days without even official confirmation of his death from the police who shot and killed him. Let us reflect on the frustrations and resentments of young people who have been repeatedly stopped, searched, dispersed, criminalised, surveilled, stigmatised and abjected by intrusive policing and statecraft. We do not need to romanticise their rage to acknowledge that these riots, like all riots, were political events. As Chris Grover (2011) reminds us, it is no coincidence that rioting always accompanies periods of acute economic hardship, nor that, across history, those most likely to participate in riot events and social unrest are also most likely to be drawn from the most economically marginalised of society.

Indeed, since the events of August 2011, *there has not been one shred of evidence* to support the pithy narrative that 'poor parenting' was to blame in any way, much less that rioters streamed out from lone-mother households, or had no father figures at home. What the research, most notably *Reading the Riots* (Lewis et al, 2011), *has* shown is that those who took part in rioting *were* significantly more likely to be in poverty, to have a special educational need and to live in the most deprived neighbourhood wards. Yet the 'commonsense' that solidified in the immediate political debate and media coverage, as we have seen, did not coalesce around 'poverty', but rather 'a culture of poverty'. Such moralising and individualising explanations may, as Grover (2011) acknowledges, have a certain simplistic popular appeal. But this conceptual frame can only solidify the very processes of derision and humiliation that inscribe marginalised people as *the* problem – a surplus population, a residuum. In Tyler's terms, 'stigmatising discourses of the underclass produce the "wasted populations" they describe' (Tyler, 2013: 183).

The refusal to name the wider context of poverty and economic dispossession in which these riots happened, or the police actions that triggered the first disturbances, is indeed illuminating. These riots were *made meaningful* as evidence of social decay and immoral behavioural choices. They were transformed into media spectacles, which would, in turn, come to legitimate punitive measures for 'Troubled Families'. Reflecting on this narrative inevitability at a community meeting in Tottenham, on 15 August 2011, cultural theorist Paul Gilroy stated that:

> The media have a 'golden hour' after the story breaks, in which they can fix the story, and then that fixed story grows, like a snowball rolling downhill. What we need to understand is that this doesn't happen by accident. These things are techniques for making information meaningful, and we need to learn from them. (Gilroy, 2011)

In a published elaboration of his comments, Gilroy argued that such episodes of public disorder have been reframed as nothing more than a 'brisk sequence of criminal events and transgressions' that could be made intelligible *only* as issues of 'personal conduct' (Gilroy, 2013: 555). As Gilroy suggests, it is in this reframing – of disorder as 'misconduct', of grievance as 'immorality' – that demonstrates precisely the depth of neoliberal revolution in Britain.

Crisis talk and crisis figures

This book takes its theoretical cue from the work of the Birmingham School of Cultural Studies, the birthplace of British cultural studies. Members of the School produced a hugely influential range of interdisciplinary research, which used poststructuralism, feminism and critical race theory to open up critical dialogues between the machinery of politics and the culture of the everyday, connecting up the places where state power is exercised and where we take these workings of power into our lives, conversations and exchanges. The Birmingham School triggered a reflective 'cultural turn' across many disciplines of study, both establishing popular culture as an object for academic inquiry, and demanding that academic research recognise how central mediation processes are for producing consensus.

In particular, I draw on the stimulating ideas presented by Stuart Hall, Chas Critcher, Tony Jefferson, John Clarke and Brian Roberts in *Policing the Crisis: Mugging, the state and law and order* (1978). This landmark study remains one of the most thorough, powerful and persuasive accounts of how 'public consent' for new forms of statecraft and state reform is manufactured. The authors examine the emergence of a new authoritarian form of policing, in which the anticipatory powers of the police are extended and toughened: increased surveillance and information-gathering, dawn raids, heavy questioning, restrictions on the freedom of assembly, strong policing of demonstrations, free use of warrants, 'sweeping' population segments and fewer restrictions on the collection of private documents. These extended powers were used disproportionately in black communities, and they represented a new direction in disciplining political dissenters and organised labour – what Hall et al termed 'policing by consent'.

Why would people consent to this sharpening of the repressive legal instruments of the state, to more aggressive policing? The answer is to be found in the crafting of a new folk devil, around whom a moral panic could bloom – the 'mugger'. In August 1972, the first reference to 'mugging' was made in the headline of a British newspaper. By September of that same year, British courts were overflowing with 'mugging' cases. A new institutional definition for an old crime of street robbery was shaped and defined by the energies, attention and resources of mass media, judiciary and the police. *Policing the Crisis* painstakingly details how these agencies actively and continuously shaped a moral crisis that they were ostensibly 'reacting to': 'amplifying the deviancy they seem to committed to controlling' (Hall et al, 1978: 55). Hall et al mapped out the emergence of a new criminal figure and repetitions of mugger discourse – across news media, courtrooms, public commentary, everyday conversation, gossip and other formal and official sites of disquiet – through which, they argue, a new 'commonsense' consensus around authoritative policing is solidified and public consent is procured.

What made *Policing the Crisis* so innovative was that it recognised that this shift to more authoritarian policing could not have happened without public consent. It recognised that the political terrain of Britain itself was being transformed and that popular authority was essential to this. It recognised that a whole range of social institutions are needed in order to structure 'social knowledge' of street-crime, and to create and nurture a moral panic around the figure of 'the mugger'. 'The mugger' emerges as a new cultural figure, upon whom street crime is racialised and against whom social anxieties around youth, urban space and control become projected. In the second edition of *Policing the Crisis*, the authors reflect on the novelty of the conjunctural analysis they developed - mapping out public and official disquiet, 'trying to catch public opinion, unawares, in the very moment of its formation' (2013: preface, xiii) – was breathtakingly novel. Looking conjuncturally enabled the authors to painstakingly map the trajectory of 'the mugger', his sociocultural imprint becoming more firmly stamped on public consciousness with each repetition of mugger discourse, across news media, courtrooms, public commentary, everyday conversation, gossip and other formal and official sites of disquiet. The mugger, as they show, comes to have a figurative life, which solidifies a new 'commonsense' consensus around authoritative policing and race relations. It is through mugger discourse that young black urban men become the 'bearers' of crisis in the 1970s – and that consensus around social protection became dismantled and supplanted by an advancing new consensus of aggressive policing in localised (black) neighbourhoods.

Parenting the Crisis begins with this premise. It is concerned with mapping the emergence of the figure of the 'bad parent' as a 'bearer of crisis' and tracking how this figure came to populate public debate, popular culture, policy documents and political speech, everyday conversation, social media and media culture at the turn of the 21st century. This book will argue, following Hall et al, that such figures are essential at times of crisis, when new formations of 'commonsense' are condensing. Our current crisis – economic and political but also cultural, organised around the concept of austerity and the 'virtues' of restraint vis-à-vis the welfare state – is a crisis that is rapidly condensing upon figures of *family failure*.

Neoliberal crisis: policing to parenting

Stuart Hall often acknowledged his intellectual debt to the work of Antonio Gramsci, particularly how Gramsci's *Prison Notebooks* (1971) had transformed his thinking about politics. In a 1987 essay, 'Gramsci and us', Hall outlined the importance of Gramsci's concept of hegemony for understanding how social architecture can be re-made and how transformations in statecraft serve to restructure society. The analysis of *Policing the Crisis* traced the early rumblings of such a transformation: the displacement and reversal of the post-war political settlement, 'the historic compromise between labour and capital that had been in place from 1945' (Hall, 1987: 21).

Hall famously coined the phrase 'Thatcherism' to refer to the potent political project overseen by Margaret Thatcher during her tenure as Prime Minister, and argued that the groundwork for this project had begun as early as 1975, when she became leader of the opposition. In 'The Great Moving Right Show' (1979), Hall urged that we 'think in a Gramscian way' about Thatcherism and, in doing so, recognise that Thatcherism sought to reverse the commonsense of the welfare state, which had permeated British consciousness. Thatcherism, for Hall, was a hegemonic project; one that capitalised on the economic crises of the 1970s to undermine and dismantle the social settlements of welfarism.

The following four decades would entrench the Thatcherite project. Although this project acquired different names over this period, it was a project of neoliberalism. Neoliberalism is not a homogenous or discrete policy programme, and the wide designations of ideas and policies as 'neoliberal' has led to some dismissing the usefulness of the term, or even denying that neoliberalism underpins contemporary statecraft (for a cogent discussion of these debates, see Gilbert, 2013). As Jeremy Gilbert demonstrates, neoliberalism has been designated as a discursive formation, a governmental programme, an ideology, and the manifestation of specific group interests. Similarly, John Clarke (2008) compellingly argues that neoliberalism can be 'named' everywhere; its omnipresence and promiscuity can indeed serve to dilute useful analysis (Clarke, 2008).

Neoliberal deniers aside, scholars have tended to agree that neoliberal logic argues for the installation of competitive markets into all areas of life (Birch, 2015), the liberalisation and deregulation of finance markets, and the privatisation of public services and state assets. Bob Jessop (2014) describes neoliberalism as the undoing of the post-war Keynesian settlement between capital and labour, in favour of the interests of capital. Neoliberal economic policy, in Jessop's analysis, is motivated by a desire to undo and reverse regulations and restrictions that inhibit market freedom – such as labour laws, union rights and international trade tariffs – as well as to reduce government spending on welfare and social services in order to offer attractive tax rates for those with capital to invest in markets. David Harvey (2007) similarly describes neoliberalism as a 'class project', which aims to restore the wealth of the elite class, whose economic power was threatened by the redistributive logic of post-war social democracy. Harvey traces neoliberal philosophy back to the work of Friedrich Hayek and his contemporaries in the 1930s, who collectively argued that markets are the most efficient way to allocate resources and whose principles, now implemented, have formalised the enclosure of public goods and social services.

Margaret Thatcher was an enthusiastic disciple of Hayek, and their friendship was cemented through correspondence and advice. In 1984, Hayek sent Thatcher a leather-bound copy of his book *The Road to Serfdom*, which warned that state protections of labour would lead to us all becoming 'slaves of the state'. Thatcher treasured her copy and considered it compulsory reading for her ministers (Thatcher, 1996). When she was elected Prime Minister in 1979, Hayek sent her a congratulatory telegram, thanking her for 'the best present on my eightieth birthday anyone could have given me' (Weaver, 2015). Hayek's model of laissez-faire neoliberalism was enormously influential in determining the broad and ambitious programme of privatisation and union repression pursued by Thatcher across her tenure in the House of Commons.

Crucially, Thatcher was able to transform the multiple crises of the 1970s into a crisis of Keynesian statecraft. Her emphasis on 'law and order', her repeated calls to the British citizen to be 'responsible', to aspire to homeownership, her rejection of the concept of entitlement; all these spoke, in Hall's words, to 'something else, deep in the English psyche: its masochism' (Hall, 1987: 4). The phrases she employed addressed and solidified the collective fantasies and the anxieties of a nation in the middle of a crisis of capitalism, and cemented what Hall called 'authoritarian populism'; a new kind of commonsense that resonated with ordinary aspirations, recouped subordination and redefined the national project as one of 'iron times; back to the wall; stiff upper lip; get moving; get to work; dig in' (Hall, 1987: 4). The figure of the 'mugger', as mapped out in *Policing the Crisis* (Hall et al, 1978), was crucial to the emergence of this authoritarian populism. So too were other figures who were designated as the 'bearers of crisis' – the collectivist striker, the entitled welfare recipient.

The analysis of 'public opinion' machinery offered in *Policing the Crisis* (Hall et al, 1978), and across Hall's connected writing, is timely within the current context of welfare reform debates. As Hall et al compellingly demonstrated, public opinion, far from being 'spontaneous' or 'organic', is powerfully structured and editorialised via cultural sites. The authors heard, in the mugging crisis, 'the ugly sound of an old conjuncture unravelling' (Hall et al, 2013: xviii) and the subsequent panic around black proletarians formed a key route for securing popular legitimacy and compliance. What ugly sounds can we hear now? What old conjuncture is unravelling? What public opinions are being orchestrated today? In the almost forty years between *Policing the Crisis* and *Parenting the Crisis*, the 'open, frontal attack on social equality, shameless advocacy of elitism and complex refurbishment of the competitive ethic' (Hall et al, 1978: 307) seems to have succeeded in almost all dimensions. Two thirds of the current British government Cabinet are millionaires, presiding over tax cuts for the wealthy and the further dismantling of the social security net for the poor. Since the Welfare Reform Act 2012, a latticework of austerity policies has effectively shrunk the welfare state and extended the punitive and sanctioning capacities of an increasingly surveillant welfare apparatus.

Public consent for such policies of immiseration, however, has been surprisingly high. In previous periods of recession, social attitudes towards people claiming social security benefits of all kinds have usually been compassionate. Since the 2008 financial crisis and subsequent recession, however, social attitudes have hardened. In general, the British public seem to be in favour of welfare reforms and retrenchments (for a discussion, see Baumberg et al, 2012; Hills, 2015). These hardened attitudes must be contextualised within a context of repeated primetime television, newspaper coverage, political debate and social commentary about welfare claimants, 'scroungers', failing families and bad parents. These articulations of crisis perform a parallel function around punitive and restrictive welfare reform to that performed by 'mugging' around authoritative policing. The reinvention of crisis continues; a different time, a different crisis, but the same familiar lurch to the populist authoritarian right. Replace 'crime' with 'welfare' in the following 1978 quote from Hall and his colleagues, and we could be talking about the 'welfare crisis' today:

> Public opinion about crime does not simply form up at random. It exhibits a shape and a structure. It follows a sequence. It is a social process, not a mystery. Even at the lowest threshold of visibility – in talk, in rumour, in the exchange of quick views and common-sense judgements – crime talk is not socially innocent … the more an issue passes into the public domain, the more it is structured by the dominant ideologies about crime. (Hall et al, 1978: 136)

Just as *Policing the Crisis* took a fine comb to the sociosymbolic landscapes of the 1970s – the anti-immigrant, anti-welfare and racist ideologies that would shortly after its publication prove to be fertile ground for neoliberalism under Thatcher – so too does *Parenting the Crisis* track the cultural landscape in which figures of family crisis are orchestrated, editorialised, animated and circulated.

The 'parenting crisis' was not invented by David Cameron when he asked 'where are the parents?' in the days following the 2011 riots; its embryonic roots (and subsequent symbolic and political weight) run like a golden thread through a much longer history of neoliberal politics. Indeed, Thatcher herself identified the responsible family as the central pillar of neoliberal commonsense. Her most quoted refrain – 'there is no such thing [as society] – there are individual men and women and there are families' – was uttered during a fascinating interview published by *Woman's Own* in 1987 (Keay, 1987). The fuller answer, from which this quote was taken, consisted of Thatcher expounding at length on why welfare entitlements create a 'tragedy' of irresponsibility and encourage claimants to 'manipulate the system'. She concluded her remarks in this part of the interview by describing the fostering of irresponsibility in families as 'the greatest sin'.

The very emergence of the reactionary modernisation under Thatcherism is thus marked already by powerful ideas about failing families – irresponsible, grasping, their demands for governmental support far outstripping their obligations to society. The definition of a 'parenting crisis' today resonates with Thatcher's remarks in 1987, but it must also be contextualised within the broader and longer project of neoliberalism, which has secured consent for itself by normalising precarity, dismantling the pro-welfarist commonsense of the Keynesian era of social democracy, and generating perpetual competition and division between families.

Neoliberal citizenship and the eugenic imagination

Through examining the attachment of a complex period of social unrest (such as the 2011 riots) to an alleged 'crisis of parenting', we can begin to illuminate how and why 'bad parenting' has had such a profound significance in the political present. These public statements around bad parenting at the moment of the August 2011 riots mark the peak of an accumulating 'parenting crisis' in neoliberal Britain. This crisis is named and attached to 'troubled' or 'problem families', and articulates long-simmering public and policy concerns around: children growing up without a father; families who are out of paid work and claiming benefits; parents who are having 'too many' children; and an alleged decline in discipline and morality that is to be inscribed via the family.

Historians will recognise in these concerns the reproduction of the concept of the 'underclass', a pejorative term favoured across political, policy and popular culture that ostensibly names and describes a 'residuum' population, distinct from the working class and disconnected from the bulk of society. In his historical analysis of the 'underclass', John Welshman (2006) notes the periodic reinvention and renaming of this population and the conclusions from researchers who have attempted to define and measure 'the underclass' empirically – namely that the concept is 'hopelessly imprecise', that it conflates structural and cultural definitions of poverty, and that it is a 'potent symbol' rather than a 'useful concept' (Dean and Taylor-Gooby, 1992, quoted in Welshman, 2006: 4).

Welshman's analysis brilliantly maps the *discourse* of the underclass, and illuminates the moments when a vocabulary of the underclass erupts into public debate. One particularly salient period for underclass discourse was during the decade of the 1980s, when the debate between structural and behavioural explanations for poverty became particularly heated. Welshman notes that the current policy preoccupation with 'Troubled Families' has deep historical resonances with the irredeemably flawed concept of 'underclass', a fact that many politicians, press and commentators have seemed unaware of. The 'Troubled Families' initiative formally began in 2012, with the aim of making targeted interventions into the lives of families who had been identified as 'troubled' by local authorities. It included the formation of a Troubled Families Unit in the Department for Communities and Local Government, and the commitment of £448 million to 'turn around' such families. The targeted interventions on offer demonstrate precisely the behavioural explanations for poverty and disadvantages that are deployed in the political present. In 2016, an interim evaluation of the scheme's successes, conducted by the National Institute of Economic and Social Research, found that it had had 'no significant impact' (NIESR, 2016). Despite these damning findings, the scheme was extended for a further five years at a potential estimated cost of £900 million.

The launch of the 'Troubled Families' initiative was made in December 2011, four months after the August riots. As Stephen Crossley (2016) notes, the riots were crucial in legitimating the new forms of neoliberal statecraft that would accompany the 'Troubled Families' initiative; without the riots, it is unlikely that there would have been such widespread support for such an ill-conceived (and, as it would turn out, inefficient and ineffectual) project.

The commitment to a problematic project like the 'Troubled Families' scheme – even after it has been discredited by evaluators – demonstrates the continuing potency of 'underclass' symbols, which hypothesise that poverty and inequality can be explained through 'culture'. Such 'culture of poverty' explanations conceive of disadvantages as something *transmitted* from one generation to another, not by structural or material inequalities, but by choices, behaviours and attitudes. Such explanations were re-animated in the final decade of the 20th century, when, under a New Labour government, a period of intense scrutiny on the choices, behaviours and attitudes of parents contributed to a profusion of ideas about what 'good parenting' might be able to secure.

A whole policy apparatus aimed at 'supporting parents' was built by New Labour between 1997 and 2010. They produced a series of strategy documents, launched public consultations on how to help parents and commissioned evidence reviews to find out 'what works' for families. Underpinning this new interest in family life was the idea that social exclusion, poor health, deprivation, educational underachievement – and a whole series of other social problems – could be explained in reference to what individual parents do (or do not do), and that targeting parents to change the way they parent could unlock the potential of children destined to 'repeat the cycle' of poverty. A National Family and Parenting Institute was established by New Labour to promote 'best practice' in parenting and family life. An extensive programme of early intervention, Sure Start, was launched, to target families in areas of high deprivation and to promote 'good parenting'. The short-lived Department for Children, Schools and Families (DCSF) (2007-2010) reflected the significance of intimate family life in this period of policy making; while new forms of public pedagogy and popular culture, which direct and instruct parents, form the cultural arm of this policy making.

Although ostensibly this turn towards 'supporting parents' was framed as being empathetic and compassionate, there were punitive undercurrents for those who were unable or unwilling to comply with the neoliberal requirements to be enterprising, autonomous and self-sufficient. As *Parenting the Crisis* will document, the hypervisibility of 'parenting' served to legitimise a more individualistic approach to addressing socioeconomic inequalities that were once considered structural social problems. Consequently, it was the individual family that was hailed as the cause of such problems, and the individual family that became pathologised as 'in crisis', suffering a 'deficit' of parental skills and capacities.

As Imogen Tyler (2013) has cogently argued, the discourse of 'the underclass' that haunts these policy projects returns us to 'the other citational history of the underclass: eugenicist thinking' (2013: 191). As Tyler details, eugenics was built upon racist ideologies of social hygiene, and this ideology was shaped by beliefs that, first, 'deficiencies' were hereditary in origin and second, that social policy should endeavour to engineer the proliferation of groups understood to be without deficiency, and reduce or eliminate those held to be deficient. Eugenicist social policies of the 20th century sought to decrease the fertility rates of those deemed deficient – in Tyler's terms, the 'moral abjects' at the borders of citizenship – the poor and those held to be 'mentally defective' or 'feebleminded'. Citizenship, as she demonstrates, is not simply a description of status, but a productive concept that pivots on the distinctions between deserving and undeserving categories of people. In participating in such vocabularies of moral hygiene and deservingness, and by rearranging its longstanding concerns with 'equality' into the moralising discourse of 'social exclusion' (see Levitas, 2005), New Labour, like the Conservative government that preceded them and the Coalition government that would follow them, extended and reinvented these classification processes.

Tyler argues that the eugenicist discourses of underclass concepts are deployed to legitimise the processes of neoliberalism. Her work identifies a range of 'national abjects', such as migrants, welfare claimants, who work as 'ideological conductors', imagined as parasitical drains on state resources, transformed into political and popular figures of stigma that can generate the public consent necessary for neoliberal projects and policies. Extending Tyler's insights, I argue in this book that 'bad parents' work as yet another ideological conductor. Throughout the book, I locate the construction of 'parenting crisis' within a broader context of neoliberalism, which positions the freedoms of the individual above social obligations to one another, and circulates a commonsense of liberty over collective solidarities. The figure of the 'bad parent', as this book will show, is absolutely central to the 'commonsense' of neoliberalism. In the first decade and a half of the 21st century, British welfare reform has been increasingly geared towards 'responsibilising' the family; a euphemism for reducing welfare spending and public services, and replacing economic interventions (reducing family poverty) with parental pedagogy (training parents to be 'good parents').

Neoliberalism is associated with the triumph of individualism over traditional social bonds and relationships, the extension of economic imperatives into personal and intimate realms, and the supplanting of cooperation and mutualism with virulent competition, contractualisation and the rules and norms of the market. We can see the profound ways in which neoliberalism has extended into intimate life and how parenting has been thoroughly 'neoliberalised', albeit in contradictory and complex ways. 'Parenting' – articulated as moral and personal conduct and choices about how to raise one's children – is positioned as being *the most important factor* in determining a child's life chances, more important than income, security, access to decent housing, healthcare, education, and so on. This *moral* narrative around good parenting distorts wider debates about widening social and economic polarisation and stagnant social mobility. The moral narrative around good parenting extends the explanatory power of neoliberalism, which holds that dispossession, disenfranchisement, poverty and precarity are the consequence of the failures of individual families.

The neoliberalisation of parenting, as *Parenting the Crisis* will show, disguises and obscures the structural processes and excesses that are widening social inequality and deepening the poverty of those marginalised at the bottom. We should be alarmed by empirical data that documents the recapture and consolidation of the economic power of the most wealthy at the beginning of the 21st century (Piketty, 2014). We should be troubled by the unjust and dysfunctional state and market mechanisms that have facilitated the remarkable 'return of the rich' and the restoration of wealth and income inequalities not seen in over a century (Sayer, 2014). While the wealth trickles upwards (again), those punished most harshly by austerity measures and rollback of welfare are precisely those whose entitlements have always been most precarious and who have been marked as morally suspicious – single parents, families with disabled parents and children, and those in insecure work or on low pay. The production of a 'parenting crisis', as this book will show, is a deeply political project at the very heart of neoliberalism, congealing new forms of 'commonsense', which seem sensible and self-evident, with older eugenicist projects that hold poverty as something to be caused by a type of person.

Gendering parent-blame

> 'It takes *so little* to be considered a great dad, and it also takes *so little* to be considered a shitty mom. People praise my husband for coming to all of my doctor's appointments with me. Guess who else has to go to those doctor's appointments? Me! I'm the star of the show! There's nothing for the camera to see if I'm not there, but he's the hero for playing *Candy Crush* while I get my blood drawn.' (Wong, 2016)

This book examines the cultural politics of parent-blame – but perhaps more precisely, it is concerned with tracking *mother*-blame. The manufacture and circulation of 'bad parents' is part of a social, cultural and political rubric that is at once gendered and gendering. While there has been a preference in contemporary political and public debate for the gender-neutral term 'parenting' – with good reason – the adoption of the term 'parenting' can disguise and obscure the gender politics of parent-blame. Comedian Ali Wong's biting observations about the different pressures and expectations that circulate around good mothering and good fathering reflect longer-held commonsense assumptions about who will be 'holding the baby', and gendered assumptions about who has the best temperament to do so.

Historical analysis has problematised the idea that fathers were either 'authoritarian' or 'absent' and suggested that, like mothers, they were expected to be 'present', to cultivate and educate their children and to morally instruct them (Lupton and Barclay, 1997). Contemporary scholars of parenting culture have argued that fathers are more monitored and scrutinised than past generations, and are now routinely addressed and targeted by parenting expertise (Lee et al, 2014). But the intensity and texture of these paternal addresses remain shaped by wider gender relations and roles. Charlotte Faircloth (2014) notes that while there has been an extension of 'good parenting' precepts and instructions to fathers, men are still presented as a 'special case' with particular needs. The call to 'dad-proof' family services and parenting, for example, might appear to centre gender equality between parents, but it does this by implicitly framing fathers as less capable, more distant and less burdened by parenting.

Esther Dermott's (2008) research on the discourse of 'new fatherhood' suggests that it remains a vague concept and there may be some distance between the commitment that fathers express towards their families and the practical contributions that they make. This is echoed in Tina Miller's (2010) examination of the 'micro-politics' of fathering practices, which finds that fathers' commitments to gender-balanced parenting are often undermined by the constraints of welfare models, workplace cultures and their own hard-to-shake 'patriarchal habits'. In short, although the way we *talk* about parenting suggests that we are moving towards more gender-symmetrical family formations, the advent of children in practice continues to mark the beginning of familial *asymmetry*, whereby 'parenthood crystallises a gendered division of labour largely by reshaping wives' and not husbands' routines' (Sanchez and Thomson, 1997: 747, cited in Miller, 2010).

In terms of parent-blame, the parameters of 'good' fatherhood are, as Miller proposes, less clearly drawn than those of good motherhood, and circle around notions of emotional involvement and financial provision. Discourses of bad fatherhood tend to attach to being either 'absent' or 'feckless'. In contrast, the vocabularies that are available around mother-blaming are rich and complex; there are so many ways for mothers to fail. Ladd-Taylor and Umansky review some of the 'bad mother' subjects that are animated in custody disputes, political speech and popular culture. They list the accusations: 'welfare mothers, teen mothers, the career woman who has no time for her kids, the drug addict who poisons her foetus, the pushy stage mother, the overprotective Jewish mother, and so on' (Ladd–Taylor and Umansky, 1998). Mothers are key figures through which 'the nation' is imagined and animated. The figure of the mother illuminates the classificatory logic of the national body politic: who is desirable, who is to be excluded, who presents a risk to order and security, who is valued. It is via the figure of the mother that enduring dilemmas around work, worth and value are staged.

Parenting the Crisis aims to examine the cultural, politcal and economic purpose of parent-blame in Britain today. It begins with the premise that, first, parent-blame is potently gendered; and that, second, parent-blame manifests, in part, through the sacralisation (making sacred) and idealisation of some mothers. Ladd-Taylor and Umansky (1998) track the impressive flexibility of mother-blame in American culture, from overprotective mothers 'causing' their sons to become homosexual, working mothers blamed for juvenile delinquency, and black mothers blamed for welfare dependency. They point to how discourses of 'good mothering' signalled an advance for the women who had most chance of embracing such an ideology – principally white, middle-class and heterosexual – and how the production of a 'woman's sphere' of mothering defined the place of women in the project of nation-building as being 'a mother's place'. Precepts of 'good mothering' granted (some) women the *possibility* of being defined as 'good'; but even those mothers might be recouped as blameworthy, if they engaged in paid employment, were welfare claimants, divorced the fathers of their children, or failed to be self-sacrificing, intensive and to devote the majority of their time and energy to their children.

Which mothers are to blame? Reimer and Sahagian (2015) begin their collection on 'the mother-blame game' by asking this question and, in doing so, reflect on the roots of what they call 'the dysfunctional cultural rubric that never fails to find mothers lacking' (Reimer and Sahagian, 2015: 2). While Reimer and Sahagian argue that these roots are patriarchal, I want to complicate the analysis and propose a more intersectional answer to the riddle of the mother-blame game. In particular, *Parenting the Crisis* acknowledges that all mothers (and some fathers) are potentially 'bad', some mothers are always/already more deeply inscribed with the etchings of failure. Mother-blaming has, as Ladd-Taylor and Umansky posit, always been a sharper machine when directed at poor mothers, single mothers, welfare-claiming mothers. Mother-blaming can be thus conceived of as a stigmatising repository for social ills, 'the cipher of the bad mother standing in for real confrontations with … poverty, racism, the paucity of meaningful work at a living wage, the lack of access to day care, antifeminism' (Ladd-Taylor and Umansky, 1998: 23). This book aims to translate these insights to the current neoliberal moment in Britain, in order to ask: how is the 'parenting crisis' being scripted and constructed in the here and now, and with what effects? How is the machinery of mother-blame shaping our (necessary) debates about work, welfare and value?

In the economy of social reproduction, without which capitalism would buckle, the question of who does domestic labour, tending to children, providing food, maintaining private space, and the myriad of other unpaid and unrecognised services that supplement the public world of paid work, is crucial. Feminist philosophers have insisted that we centralise these forms of labour in order to better understand exploitation and inequality.

Indeed, as Nancy Fraser (2013) has cogently argued, the progress of liberal feminism has relied absolutely on these forms of labour remaining *invisible*. While some women have been able to reduce their labour requirements around social reproduction, to forge professional careers alongside motherhood and to succeed in creating that most elusive of holy grails, a 'work–life balance' – ostensibly symbolising the success of liberal feminism and 'having it all' – such 'successes' are often achieved by outsourcing such tasks to other women. The labour of these 'other' women – working-class and migrant women – are central to the feminist narrative itself. We have to think critically about how to ensure that gender equality extends to all women and does not operate in the interests of some and to the cost or detriment of others.

We can already see how precarious the claims of liberal feminism are, when we consider the rapid speed with which the public services that are most used by mothers have been eviscerated under the project of austerity. Such services are among the first to be branded 'unaffordable' and positioned as a luxury that we can no longer afford in an era of accelerated austerity. The speed at which social infrastructure (libraries, holiday playschemes, after-school facilities, breakfast clubs) has been dismantled is paralleled with the acceleration of childcare costs. It is well documented that, once childcare costs are taken into account, many women are participating in employment for very paltry wages indeed. It is crucial that we dismantle the fantasy figures that govern our sense of 'good motherhood' – the stay-at-home, attentive and engaged mother, the ambitious working mother, for example – and think critically about how such figures are situated within normative systems of whiteness, class privilege and heterosexuality.

The structure of this book

Parenting the Crisis tracks the manufacture and circulation of ideas of bad and poor parenting across policy and media. It considers how categories of parent failure are reproduced, contested and attached to particular bodies and lives, condensing and concretising imagined pathologies as the failures of individual families to self-govern and to manage themselves according to the cultural logics of neoliberalism. The argument of this book is that the production of this parental 'commonsense' serves to legitimate new punitive forms of statecraft, undermining the very concept of entitlement, and withdrawing and dismantling different forms of social security and welfare support, in the name of 'responsibilising' families.

The forms of parent pedagogy that populate British culture today have a long lineage. Historians of this pedagogy have identified archives of advice that stretch back to at least the 17th century. But the content of this advice, and the receipt of it, has varied wildly from one moment to the next. In Chapter Two, I explore the shifting 'structures of feeling' (Williams, 1961) around parent pedagogy and review key historical accounts. These accounts have tended to either celebrate the rise of the 'empowered parent', who is able to adopt a consumer lens to shop around for a parenting philosophy that suits her; or they have interpreted parent pedagogy as a vehicle that undermines the 'natural' or 'instinctual' knowledge and wisdom that mothers are presumed to have access to. Considering the case of parenting website Mumsnet, I propose that the dominant 'structure of feeling' around parent pedagogy and advice is antagonistic and defensive, inviting mothers into a fragmented and incoherent politics of parenting, which is premised on generating moral value for one's parenting choices. Far from being 'empowered' by the proliferation of parent pedagogy, Mumsnet illustrates the imperative to morally author oneself as competent within a climate of doubt and uncertainty.

In Chapter Three, I explore the emergence of new political vocabularies around families and parenting that attempted to create distance with the New Right's preoccupation with narratives of 'decline' and its use of the family as a moral barometer. Under Thatcher in Britain and Reagan in the United States, 'combative and militant' familist strategies sought to pathologise (respectively) homosexuality and single parent families, and to undermine the right to abortion (Barrett and McIntosh, 1982: 14). The New Labour government that took power in 1997 used a more inclusive language around 'families' to ostensibly embrace greater variations and diversities of household and to signal that it was what families *did*, not what they looked like, that mattered. New Labour also popularised a new vocabulary of meritocracy in its vision for making Britain a 'classless' society, and placed good parenting at the centre of this vision. An intense period of 'parent upskilling' policy coincided with the phenomenal success of parenting pedagogue Jo Frost, whose television programme *Supernanny* promised to 'train' parents in techniques of discipline and consistency.

In this chapter, I unpick how encounters with *Supernanny* showcased an emotional politics of classification and distinction that was premised on ideas of parenting 'science' and 'expertise'.

Chapter Four focuses on the emotional politics of parenting culture – specifically, the importance of the idea of the 'pure relationship' in the manufacture of a crisis of parenting. Under the 'pure relationship', parents are presumed to act as autonomous, reflexive agents and to incubate and foster relationships that are underpinned by democracy and debate. As much critical scholarship has argued, the 'pure relationship' disguises and euphemises the unevenness in which parenting is accomplished, and silently marks middle-class intimacy practices as 'normal' and 'desirable'. I examine the contradictions and complexities in how 'tough love' became manufactured as the solution to the 'parenting crisis'. This chapter asks what kinds of parental feelings become acceptable, how feeling itself becomes governed, and how the turn to moral regulation around feeling, spectacularly realised in television parent pedagogy, legitimated an extended interventionist turn in families deemed to be 'troubled'.

Extending on these fantasies of 'tough love' as a method for incubating the character of children, Chapter Five reviews the explanatory power afforded to the 'warmth' of parenting over the 'wealth' of parents. Such discourses both reflect and confirm shifts away from structural explanations of the causes of inequality and towards behaviourist explanations. Following the financial recession of 2008–09, an austerity culture emerged in Britain and the United States, which prized and celebrated the virtues of restraint and 'making do' with fewer resources. This chapter tracks the movements of these austerity cultures and how they stitched ideas of good parenting to being thrifty, resourceful and resilient. It explores how the hidden labour of thrift connects to the invisible labour of social reproduction, and how austerity culture occasioned a retreatist set of fantasies that sought to move mothers from the workplace back into the home.

Chapter Six represents ideas and analysis developed in collaboration with Imogen Tyler (a version of this work has been published as Jensen and Tyler, 2015), and examines how, in a state of apparently permanent austerity, new forms of hostility are fuelled towards those seen as wasteful, irresponsible and a parasitic drain. Such groups have become constituted as objects of disgust, repeatedly paraded across circuits of media spectacle such as newspapers and television programmes. Of particular salience is the figure of the 'benefit brood' family, large families who are constructed as disgusting via their excessive fertility and welfare dependency. This chapter begins with a case study of one such 'benefit brood' family, and explores how such narratives become weaponised in a broader ideological project that seeks to construct an anti-welfare commonsense.

TWO

Mothercraft to Mumsnet

The history of 'mothercraft' – the 'craft' of raising children – is both a history of different parenting practices and philosophies, and a history of shifting expectations around how to sift through such expertise and to decide on and adopt a childrearing philosophy. Expert-led 'good parenting' discourses work as a crucial dimension of 'mother-making', in which parents engage in struggles over what constitutes good, better and best parenting practice and seek legitimation for their own navigations through it. Such knowledge is always contested, and parents must negotiate a route through different, often conflicting forms of expertise.

This chapter reviews how the 'scientific motherhood' of early mothercraft – concerned with hygiene, moral development and domesticity, written largely by male physicians and a vocal group of elite pioneer mothers (Hardyment, 1995) – came to colonise new disciplines and to create new forms of knowledge. Some theorists have interpreted parent pedagogy as a patriarchal erosion of female authority in the sphere of maternal life (Rich, 1976; Ehrenreich and English, 1979). Others have considered parent pedagogy to be a significant space for mothers to politically organise themselves (Ladd-Taylor, 1994), or have argued that parents have been empowered by the gradual displacement of clinical authority, the proliferation of different childrearing philosophies and the growing consumer-power of autonomous parents who can 'shop around' for a parental pedagogy (Hulbert, 2003; Apple, 2006).

This chapter traces some of the key shifts in mothercraft and parent pedagogy, and reviews what 'counts' as good parenting, who is recognised as a legitimate expert, the different disciplines and fields from which parent advice springs, and the registers in which it is spoken, at different historical moments. Significantly, this chapter explores the changing relationship between parent and parent pedagogue, from authority to ambivalence, and from confessional to comic. An orchestration of parent pedagogy was first limited to pamphlets, but gradually extended to include books, magazines, radio, television, weblogs and digital media such as Mumsnet. The dominance of Mumsnet forms a case study at the end of this chapter, which reflects on the formations of professional maternity at play in contemporary culture.

'The mother of all elections'

During the months of campaigning that preceded it, the 2010 UK general election became widely known in the British press as the 'Mumsnet election' (Merrick and Brady, 2010: 11) – an election that, in the words of journalist Beth Neil, would be won or lost 'at the school gates' (Neil, 2010: 7). Neil described the founders of Mumsnet, Justine Roberts and Carrie Longton, as 'the most powerful women in Britain', and it was widely claimed that as many as 40% of the website's users were 'floating voters', undecided and thus forming a crucial (virtual) constituency. Incumbent Prime Minister Gordon Brown described Mumsnet as 'a great British institution', with more readers than many newspapers, and took part in a live Mumsnet web chat (together with David Cameron of the Conservative party and Nick Clegg of the Liberal Democrats) in an apparent courting of the 'parent vote'. The 'Mumsnet election' epithet served to position parents (and particularly mothers) as having a new and profound degree of influence and voice in Parliament. Reviewing the media commentary around the 2010 General Election today, it is hard not to be struck by an enormously optimistic tone that the needs of parents would be at the centre of social reform.

Mumsnet remains to this day Britain's most populated parenting website, attracting up to seven million a month and with an estimated six hundred thousand registered users. It was set up in 2000 by Roberts and Longton, mothers who met one another in antenatal classes. Although both have often claimed to be digital 'novices' before setting up Mumsnet, they each had extensive media experience, networks and knowledge in their respective careers as television producer and journalist. On its homepage, Mumsnet describes itself as 'the UK's busiest social network for parents', and in 2013, national radio programme *Woman's Hour* placed its founders in the top ten most powerful women in the UK.

Angela McRobbie (2013) describes Mumsnet as part of the network of feminine mass media – along with BBC Radio 4's *Woman's Hour*, the *Femail* section of the *Daily Mail* newspaper, daytime television such as *Loose Women* and a broad range of lifestyle, gossip and celebrity magazines. These media, McRobbie proposes, work to 'invent a repertoire of woman-centred positions which will confirm and enhance the core values of the neoliberal project' (2013: 167). Such media broadly endorse modern, liberal values and, in doing so, offer a more 'attentive address' to the concerns of women, and particularly mothers. Dissecting the actual parameters of Mumsnet's political influence is outside the scope of this book; rather, I want to explore what *kind* of parental constituency does Mumsnet imagine and address? And what might this imagined Mumsnet constituency tell us about the construction of 'good parenting' today?

There is little consensus from the parenting culture landscape about what 'good parenting' looks like in contemporary Britain, although some scholars of this landscape have described it as intensive, paranoid and beset by a consciousness of 'risk' (Lee et al, 2014). Mumsnet does not offer a coherent model of best parenting, but its reach and ubiquity can reveal something about the 'structures of feeling' (Williams, 1961) that shape emerging consciousness, and the kind of parenting subject that might come into being through engagement with parenting culture.

Finally, by prising open the discourses of choice and individualism that structure Mumsnet, this chapter seeks to open up questions around the biopolitics of the family and of childrearing expertise. The emergence and accumulation of knowledge and techniques to raise children sought to divide and classify women into respectable and unruly, and to train the former to take diligent pride in her role as protection against the excess of the latter. The organisation and management of intimate family life, including child rearing, has from mothercraft to Mumsnet been a mechanism of governmentality – classifying, ordering and disciplining families (Foucault, 1977; Donzelot, 1979; Rose, 1990). These mechanisms invite women into respectable femininity, through a latticework of productive power-knowledges about 'being a good mother'.

While the content of these knowledges is periodically reinvented, the subject-making procedures that they dramatise have remained constant. The discussion threads of Mumsnet illustrate the 'compulsory individuality' (Cronin, 2000; Skeggs, 2004) of late-modern subjecthood, in which parents are required to position themselves in dialogue with consumerist discourses of choice, enjoying agency over their life transformation and mobility, exhibiting extensive evaluative capacities, willingly self-monitoring, and always reflexively exploring the consequences of one's choices. Indeed, the very architecture of Mumsnet echoes the conversational environments that have solidified around 'elite mothercraft' over two centuries, and, as we will see, dramatises the postfeminist and neoliberal sensibilities of contemporary parenting advice. (Neo)liberal motherhood remains underpinned by expectations that mothers will be self-reflexive about childrearing and that they will seek to optimise and consolidate their resources through social reproduction.

The rise of mothercraft

> If we buy a plant from a horticulturalist we ask him many questions as to its needs, whether it thrives best in sunshine or shade, whether it needs much or little water, what degrees of heat or cold; but when we hold in our arms for the first time, a being of infinite possibilities, in whose wisdom may rest the destiny of a nation, we take it for granted that the laws governing its life, health and happiness are intuitively understood, that there is nothing new to be learned in regard to it. (Elizabeth Cady Stanton, quoted in Apple, 2006: 25)

Stanton, a 19th-century reformist who argued for 'science' to turn its attentions to child rearing, was one of the first mothercraft pioneers. Mothering, for Stanton, was a complex and fragile business, and raising children ('beings of infinite possibilities') required great diligence and care. In *Perfect Motherhood*, Rima Apple (2006) explores the lives and writings of mothercraft pioneers and charts the evolution of 'scientific motherhood' through manuals, magazines and pamphlets. Scientific motherhood, conceived of as the unsteady marriage of 'science and love', supplanted ideas of motherhood as a 'natural' and instinctual ability to care for children, to a *skill*, requiring study of medicalised expertise. This expertise expanded in reach and ambition, from controlling the environment, cleanliness and nutrition, to protection from infectious diseases, through advances in nutrition, to emotional and psychological health, to scales and tables of developmental 'normality'. Yet the 'ideal' mother at the centre of this expertise, Apple argues, has remained constant, as has the foundational premise that mothers need medical and scientific help to raise their children. In addition, technological change, declining family size, delayed marriage and less experience with younger siblings results in lives that do not resemble those of mothers and grandmothers, and so advice and knowledge about child rearing has to come from elsewhere.

In *Raising America,* historian Anne Hulbert (2003) similarly charts the establishment of 'scientific motherhood' in the United States, emerging in the early 19th century from educated pioneer mothers' demands that science find standardised answers to the riddles of parenting. Hulbert's part-genealogical, part-biographical study outlines the generational recycling of conflict between parenting expert 'odd couples', each positioned on a spectrum of 'hard' and 'soft' approaches. The 'hard' camp of experts emphasise the importance of compliance, obedience and parental authority, circulate fears about weakened citizens produced by maternal indulgence, and advocate parent-centred childrearing methods that generate inner moral discipline and good habits. On the other side of Hulbert's expert scale are those from the 'soft' camp, who tend to emphasise the innate capacities of the child and advocate child-centred parenting methods that foster creative individuality and encourage growth and discovery.

Hulbert argues that expertise is elastic, contradictory, and therefore always political. Every generation of her 'odd couple' experts expressed private reservations and ambivalence about the parenting methods they advocated, but nonetheless participated in manufactured public debates that tapped into and fed the loyalties of their supporters and champions. Hulbert also shows how the 'hard and soft' camps of expertise are often put to unexpected ends; for example, 'hard' expertise has often been promoted as convenient and workable for time-pressed working mothers and served progressive ends for women seeking entry to the labour market. Similarly, liberal 'soft' childrearing methods require a child-centred intensiveness that has often reproduced normative gender requirements for mothers to always remain at home and provide exclusive care.

The hard and soft camps of parenting expertise were animated throughout the British parent pedagogy climate too. Here the complexity of childrearing debates were often flattened to a choice between 'discipline' and 'love'. Christine Hardyment's *Perfect Parents* (1995, originally published as *Dream Babies*, 1983) remains one of the most comprehensive histories of British baby and childcare advice, tracking the emergence of new philosophies through moments of economic depression, and imperial affluence. The 'terse little booklets written by enlightened doctors' (Hardyment, 1995: 36) of the mid-18th century were pragmatic and defeatist, necessarily and narrowly focused on questions of hygiene and physical wellbeing, and saying little about moral upbringing and education. As Hardyment reminds us, more than half of children would die before their second birthday.

As physiology, disease and anatomy became better understood, practices of purging, applying leeches and tight swaddling became unfashionable, and 'mothercraft' extended into moral and spiritual development, discipline, religious instruction and building 'character'. New forms of baby and childcare technology were invented and popularised as liberating conveniences; the perambulator, harnesses, leads and walking aids, as well as equipment and toys for play activity, which would stimulate mind and imagination. Many pedagogues instructed parents to encourage lively curiosity in their children and to ensure that they had plenty of fresh air and exercise. Yet the continued liberal use of laudanum, calomel and opium syrup – prescribed as 'quietness' – and the preference in many middle- and upper-class families to 'receive' children for a limited time in the evening demonstrates the continued restrictions on child liveliness.

The turn to 'scientific motherhood' in the 20th century invited elite mothers to observe their children with curiosity and to prioritise routines, formulas and the formation of good habits. Wealthy mothers were able to employ the services of a new genteel class of nurses and governesses, while maternity and infant welfare legislation and a new infrastructure of health visitors and baby clinics did much to popularise classificatory technologies such as 'milestone' charts, regular weighing and diary keeping. These, together with the emerging popularity of behaviourism and its habit-forming approach to training children, and the nation-building 'social renaissance' promised by eugenic thinkers (whose desires to grow superior citizens would underpin parent pedagogy for much of the 20th century), contributed to a broader professionalisation of childrearing. Producing happy, compliant and convenient children required standardised and 'scientific' practice, and was considered crucial to reproducing the nation and the citizens of tomorrow.

The production of 'scientific motherhood' transformed and extended the moral responsibilities that were attributed to mothers. Prior to the 19th century, matters of moral instruction had emanated from religious sources of authority; under the new mood of scientific motherhood, childrearing (at least in middle-class families) became an issue to be investigated, quantified and studied by knowledgeable professionals with appropriate training and expertise. The same professionalised mothers who imbibed this knowledge and applied it to their families – charting children's progress, monitoring their behaviour and keeping abreast of new developments in the field – would go on to use it in their charitable and philanthropic work.

These activities could be turned to productive, and punitive, directions. In *Policing the Family*, Jacques Donzelot (1979) tracks the ways in which mothers are transformed into agents of the state, assisted by philanthropy, social work, mass education, family courts and psychiatry, showing how educational, judicial and medical discourses in France come to increasingly regulate and proselytise the normal and desirable family image and experience. Through such policing, the institution of the family becomes a crucial site for the extension of state power over workers and produces new figures in need of social control: such as the delinquent or 'problem' child. Significantly, Donzelot highlights how such regulatory regimes have different consequences for working–class and 'bourgeois' children – equally surveilled by penal authority, but the latter have access to extracurricular activities and investments, which help to guarantee the reproduction of privilege from one generation to the next. The family, then, is anything but a private institution; rather, it is a key site of biopolitical power – in Donzelot's words: 'a protector of private property, of the bourgeois ethic of accumulation, as well as the guarantor of a barrier against the encroachments of the state' (1979: 5). Mothers who became employed in early state-welfare and assistance programmes at the turn of the 20th century would draw on the knowledges associated with such parenting science to scrutinise the habits and behaviours of poorer women who claimed charitable assistance.

State interventions in family life became an inescapable part of the procedures for assessing moral deservingness. In her analysis of welfare policy in the United States, Molly Ladd-Taylor (1994) documents how poor mothers were constructed as the 'enemy of the child' and how this paved the way for eugenic programmes of mass sterilisation. Pat Starkey (2001) tracks similar eugenic sentiments in Britain at the same time, and examines how newly confident social workers in the first half of the 20th century drew on mothercraft knowledges to identify families they deemed to be 'at risk' because of perceived incompetence or neglect. The medicalised knowledge of mothercraft that was used in these cases enabled state workers to remain quite blind to, and uninterested in, the economic and social conditions of the families who were considered 'deficient'.

Feminist anger at the experts

There is little feminist consensus around how to theorise motherhood. Feminist philosophers have approached it as: a cause of oppression; a source of identity; a uniting experience; a dividing experience; an institution that creates misunderstanding, hostility and oppression between women; a form of political activism that can alienate women who are not mothers, don't like being mothers or don't want to be identified primarily as mothers; *and* a social position that some women secure by oppressing other women (DiQuinzio, 1999).

Some first-wave humanist activists, such as Charlotte Perkins Gilman (1903), sought to liberate women from reproduction and developed rich critiques of motherhood as a prison and a pedestal that trapped women in stifling sexual-economic arrangements. Others, such as Ellen Key (1909), saw 'motherly love' as crucial in creating future citizens, and supported suffrage and domestic equality for women, at the same time as retaining the special indispensability of the 'female principle'. Simone de Beauvoir (1949) saw motherhood as a vulnerabilising status that was part of the apparatus that could only ever grant women a partial, divided and fragmentary subjectivity. The feminist politics of mothering has thus always been paradoxical, dramatising the enduring feminist dilemmas of individualism and difference, equality and identity, redistribution and recognition.

Second-wave feminism interrupted the post-war wave of prosperity across Western Europe and North America, and in Britain made a powerful challenge to the gender blindness of a social democratic model of capitalism that had only imagined redistribution across class lines. Nancy Fraser argues in *Fortunes of Feminism* (2013) that this second-wave developed its 'insurrectionary spirit' in conjunction with other international, radical movements, including those opposing the Vietnam War and racial segregation. This insurrectionary spirit took aim at materialism, consumerism, sexual repression, sexism and heteronormativity, and in particular at the ideology of the bourgeois family and the tyrannies of social reproduction.

While there is an often repeated 'commonsense' that second-wave feminism was anti-children, anti-family or anti-mothers, the feminist landscape was far more complex than this. Certainly, many second-wave feminists identified the nuclear family and the romantic fictions of motherhood as a crucial site of oppression. Millett (1971) stated that the nuclear family worked to frustrate and stall revolution; Firestone (1970) described pregnancy as 'barbaric' and detailed her utopian vision for artificial reproduction that would liberate women; Friedan (1963) examined the wordless unhappiness – the 'problem with no name' – suffered by suburban housewives and considered mothering to be an obstacle to autonomous selfhood.

But these powerful critiques of the nuclear family as a source of oppression did not translate into a wholesale rejection of mothering. Many strands of cultural feminism in the second wave sought to celebrate women's difference, and to reclaim the creative and productive possibilities of mothering through practices such as co-mothering and communal living (Segal, 1997). In her powerful exploration of motherhood *Of Woman Born* (1976), Adrienne Rich firmly locates the difficulties and anxieties experienced by mothers within the matrices of power that are produced by patriarchy. Drawing on Engels' theorising of the nuclear family as domestication through economic need, Rich argues that the institution of motherhood divides women into house units, institutionally separating the domestic sphere from the public world and transforming motherhood into 'powerless responsibility'. Leaving aside her somewhat rosy idealisation of pre-patriarchal life, Rich's work ossified a valuable division between the *institution* of motherhood and its *experience*, which could be celebratory. Rich compellingly argued that the modern doctrine of continuous and unconditional mother-love and denial of anger and ambivalence (repeated throughout mothercraft manuals), along with exhortations to embrace 'natural' instincts for mothering through femininity, create a toxic environment for mothers. Rich usefully plotted the historical contingency of supposedly 'natural' aspects of motherhood and, in doing so, denaturalises maternal identity as neither automatic nor natural but, rather, as a difficult process that is always/already marked by the potential for failure. Motherhood, far from being a private enterprise, is always, endlessly, exhaustively public, involving the medical establishment, legal institutions and the state. The mantra 'the personal is the political', a fundamental rallying cry for second-wave feminist thought and activism, simmers through Rich's blistering critique. For women who fail to live up to the romanticised vision of the self-sacrificing, boundlessly loving woman, the diagnosis offered by parenting experts is relentlessly individualised. As Rich remarks:

> Reading of the 'bad' mother's desperate response to an invisible assault on her being, 'good' mothers resolve to become better, more patient and long-suffering, to cling more tightly to what passes for sanity. The scapegoat is different from the martyr; she cannot teach resistance or revolt. She represents a terrible temptation: to suffer uniquely, to assume that I, the individual woman, am the 'problem'. (Rich, 1976: 277)

Rich has, rightly, been critiqued for neglecting to attend to the racial and classed axes of difference between mothers (Collins, 1994; Reynolds, 2005). Nonetheless, her sensitivity towards the part that discourses of 'good' and 'bad' mothering play in opening up divisions *between* women remains crucial to understanding how the institution of motherhood operates, and to what purposes, and her insights around the 'terrible temptation' continue to resonate within contemporary parenting pedagogy.

Also complicating the feminist politics around motherhood, Ann Dally (1982) illuminated the gaps between ideals of motherhood – specifically, the vision of the self-sacrificing martyr – and the experience of mothering. Dally argues that 'scientific' parenting models have produced a narrow vision of motherhood, which presumes and relies on a heterosexual, legitimate, monogamous, financially secure family. In particular, she tasks the mythical 'mother-love' within psychoanalysis and child development studies as creating impossible demands, which set women up to fail. Researchers such as John Bowlby popularised an intensive model of mother-love, positing that maternal deprivation of *any* kind would have profound and irreversible effects on the ability of children to form relationships and become autonomous adults. Such models insist on exclusive and unbroken maternal care, sideline the importance of fathers and other caregivers, and claim that caring has real benefits (and few costs) for women. Dally argues that these pressures have had dire personal and psychological consequences, and that the doctrine of mother-love *damages* both mothers and children, stating: 'Unbroken and exclusive maternal care has produced the most neurotic, disjointed, alienated and drug-addicted generation ever known' (Dally, 1982: 10).

These feminist insurrectionary texts thus seek to explain maternal unhappiness, not through individual pathology or inadequacy, but as a sensible response to patriarchal social structures that isolate women into nuclear units. Specifically analysing scientific expertise produced for women, Barbara Ehrenreich and Deirdre English, in *For Her Own Good* (1978), argue that multiple advice industries work as a force that removes power from women and pathologises the complexities of their everyday lives. Their furious history tracks the rise of 'expertise' across the realms of health and wellbeing, gendered and sexual 'sickness', germs and cleanliness, relationships and 'lifestyle' and maternal pathologies. Expertise, they argue, manufactured by ministers, doctors, psychiatrists, clinicians and life coaches, offered with the solemn and intimidating authority of 'science', works to ratify ancient prejudices: namely that women's bodies are fraught with peril and that the sensible solution is a life of quiet domesticity. The emergence, and in the 20th century, extension, of 'scientific expertise' has, in their analysis, created an obliging string of sexist pronouncements for mothers. Mothers are required to respond to their child's every need as urgent, forbidden to share or delegate childcare to others under fear of disrupting children's emotional wellbeing, and at the same time are denigrated as too passive, too crazy, too castrating – and certainly unable to rely on their own judgement. Ehrenreich and English are unequivocal in their conclusions: the science of parenting has been nothing less than the misogynist disenfranchising of women from their own reproduction and childrearing capacities, and the production of an individualising pathology, which cleaves women from one another and makes broader collective social change unthinkable. The task becomes merely to transform oneself.

Celebrating the advised mother

The palpable anger that textures second-wave accounts of the institution of motherhood – and the parent pedagogy that reproduces and scaffolds this institution – became somewhat tempered by the idea that expertise *could* be democratised, and that clinical and medical authority over childrearing could be loosened, if women applied their critical intellect to the debates and adopted a 'radical scepticism'. Indeed, Ehrenreich and English concluded the foreword to the second edition of *For Her Own Good* with the following words: '*Our* advice still holds true: no matter how many degrees the experts dangle in front you, no matter how many studies they cite, dig deeper, value your own real-life experiences, and think for yourself' (Ehrenreich and English, 2005: vi, original emphasis).

This notion that parents should adopt a position of radical scepticism towards advice is perhaps the *only* point of consensus in contemporary pedagogy. In *The Mommy Myth*, Susan Douglas and Meredith Michaels (2005) point out that in the final two decades of the 20th century, some eight hundred books on motherhood were published. Far from disappearing, parent pedagogy has proliferated at a dizzying pace. One central legacy of feminism's damning critiques of motherhood and marriage was the proliferation of a new wave of expertise, which came from the lay knowledge of mothers themselves.

Many of the early 'mothercraft' treatises were written by men, who themselves had no immediate experience of baby care and childcare at all. Although mothers have always been parent pedagogues, they have often been in the margins. Hardyment (1995) details how one of the most consistently vociferous contributory groups to mothercraft (directly or indirectly) were mothers. The growth of domestic and personal pedagogy coincided with the growing public authority of a new category of author – mothers – taken seriously as writers and, through their motherhood, able to inject immediacy, experience and a sense of personal purpose into their writing. Indeed, a key part of feminist consciousness-raising was discussing the everyday experiences of being a woman, including childcare, and these discussions were often then archived and published as lay expertise.

The proliferation of parenting advice from the 1980s onwards, and the routine appearance of mothers themselves as lay experts and parent pedagogues, might be interpreted as answering feminist calls to make the mothering labour visible and to reinstate mothers as experts in their own lives. Three social historians – Anne Hulbert (2003), Rima Apple (2006) and Julia Grant (1998) – make precisely this claim, seeing the intensification of childrearing advice as a progressive empowerment of mothers, a broader transfer of authority from clinician to parent, and the new capacity for parents to 'choose' their expertise and their childrearing philosophy within a marketplace of advice.

Anne Hulbert (2003) argues that the 'hard/soft' expert continuum in earlier mothercraft has been supplanted by a broader commercialised parenting advice, diversified into a range of media formats that has eroded the paternalist authority of the mothercraft pioneers. The movement of authority, from expert to consumer, is a shift that she terms 'by-the-book' to 'buy-the-book'. In 'shopping around', this marketplace of ideas has, crucially, embedded *uncertainty*, for how can we know we have made the wisest 'purchase'? The plethora of available advice and contradictory childrearing philosophies has formalised a new kind of doubt, as we can see in the now obligatory reassurance routinely presented by parent pedagogues: 'Trust yourself – you know more than you think you do' (tagline on Dr Spock's *Baby and Child Care*); 'Use it to guide, not to dictate. To augment your instincts, not supplant them. To build your confidence, not tear it down. To empower you, not paralyse you' (Murkoff, 2000).

Indeed, it is by acknowledging uncertainty that many parenting philosophers 'stake their place' in the marketplace of advice. It is *de rigeur* for any writer offering parenting advice today to begin with an almost identical disclaimer; there is 'too much' parenting advice on offer, it has confused and undermined parents, is bossy and patronising, and that this particular offering will be 'different' (see Murkoff, 2002; Doherty and Coleridge, 2008; Skenazy, 2009). In light of proliferating advice and the invitation by experts to 'trust yourself', it is not surprising to see parents more readily scrutinize or reject advice, and adopt positions of scepticism.

What is novel in parent pedagogy today is the widespread proclamation that 'parents know best' and that they should find and follow whichever model suits best. The repeated message is: trust your instincts, this is your child, and you decide which parenting orthodoxy you prescribe to. It is no coincidence that the parenting manual that has outsold all others, and which has been reprinted time and time again, is Dr Spock's *Baby and Child Care* (first published in 1945 and now in its ninth edition, Spock and Needlman, 2004). Spock was the first parent pedagogue to situate the mobile, consuming, empowered and informed parental unit at the centre of advice, and the first to disseminate the message that parents know best. His book sold half a million copies in its first six months – and to date an incredible fifty million copies. Parent pedagogues today try to replicate his warm conversational tone and reassuring address. Parenting clinician Dr Tanya Byron probably best approximates the Spock style, and her book *Your Child, Your Way* (2008) was marketed as an antidote to the 'excess' of parenting books that advocated, above all else, that parents trust their own instincts.

Social historians have interpreted the normalisation of scepticism as a triumphant shift in the pendulum of power from clinician to parent. In *Perfect Motherhood,* Rima Apple (2006) charts the evolution of 'scientific motherhood', which she defines as rewriting 'motherhood' from a natural and instinctual ability, to a skill requiring labour, study and input from medical experts. For Apple, this history is neither a story of women's oppression through medicalised motherhood, nor of the triumph of maternal love, nor of continual, steady, medical progress. Rather, she describes it is a story of 'women's search for the best childcare practices … coping with the trials and tribulations of the daily grind of childrearing', which 'documents the ways in which women accepted, rejected and reshaped medical and scientific pronouncements in order to ensure the health and wellbeing of their children' (2006: 3). Like Hulbert's 'elite mothers', Apple's 19th-century mothers were 'active women, typically middle-class women, women with agency, searching for the best means of raising their families' (Apple, 2006: 8). In the early 20th century, expertise shifted in tone and presumed a passive mother, who would take direction from a physician, rather than evaluate knowledge herself. By the late 20th century, the proliferation of childcare advice – and particularly its extension across digital formats – has 'swung the pendulum back' from physicians and doctors, to mothers. These mothers, Apple argues, are increasingly empowered to negotiate, contest and reject different models of childrearing. She offers examples of changing grassroots mother groups, such as the La Leche League, as demonstrating how the dyad of 'subservient mother and authoritative physician' has been overturned and supplanted by respectful cooperation.

Finally, in *Raising Baby by the Book* (1998), Julia Grant argues that experts have never had a monopoly on 'expertise', but rather have proposed parent pedagogy within complex webs of knowledge and authority. Grandmothers and other (mostly) female relatives have offered influential wisdom which gets enmeshed, rejected and negotiated within and alongside other discourses, some purporting to be scientific or objective. Other women – friends, colleagues, acquaintances – also take a central place in Grant's analysis, serving as sounding-boards for navigating through pedagogy and shaping decisions about how to 'raise baby'.

These historical accounts admirably seek to place maternal agency back into the history of childrearing advice and to complicate the top-down, second-wave feminist accounts of parent pedagogy, which did not always attend fully to the motivations and investments in parenting by women. Hulbert, Grant and Apple challenge the script that mothers are passive, disempowered receptacles for childcare advice pushed upon them by medical experts, clinicians and psychologists. Instead, the mothers in these accounts become reconfigured as managers of 'expertise', sometimes demanding (and producing) such expertise. Social-historical approaches are useful in rethinking and complicating how expertise and authority work, and augmenting expertise histories with a sense of the active choices that mothers make.

In other ways, however, these histories – in reversing the direction of authority between mothers and experts, in celebrating parents' capacity to shop around for their expertise, and in assuming that consumption equals empowerment – have a somewhat flattening effect on parent pedagogy. Under neoliberalism, subjects (including parents) are required to make sense of their lives through discourses of choice, freedom and empowerment. We need an approach that can orient us critically towards how 'buying the book' is a problematic freedom that does not reverse the effects of moralising forms of maternal value: indeed, it exacerbates them. The invitation to 'buy the book' and to approach parent pedagogy with the spirit of enterprising and consumerist calculation exhorts parents to think of themselves as risk-taking and autonomous individuals. We need to theorise these exhortations within a broader context of individualisation. We need a fuller engagement with how the processes of commodification and commercialisation have *themselves* transformed the intensity of parenting culture. We need a deeper theorising of the differences *between* mothers, some of whom live lives that are already inscribed with social and cultural value and some of whom are already pathologised as lacking or deficient.

Mothering sits within wider struggles to emulate desirable lifestyles and to create (and be recognised as having) value in a classificatory system that divides women into unruly and respectable, desirous and disgusting, deserving and undeserving. These real and imagined differences between mothers have driven the engine of a wider moralising politics of maternal value. Most significantly, we need to think critically about how the *marketisation* of parent pedagogy has itself legitimated and animated the idea of 'choice', a central organising principle in liberal society. This privileging of 'the market' as an ethical mechanism that can guide human action, constitutes subjects as self-managing, calculating, autonomous and enterprising, and is a key dimension of neoliberal governance.

Postfeminist parent pedagogy

> With intensive mothering, everyone watches us, we watch ourselves and other mothers, and we watch ourselves watching ourselves. (Douglas and Michaels, 2005: 161)

The introductory assertion in much parenting advice, which posits that there is 'too much advice', is not simply deeply ironic. It also demonstrates how advice marketplaces incorporate and capitalise on critique. In some senses, it also illuminates the *postfeminist* texture of parent pedagogy, whereby the critique offered by feminism has become co-opted by a new generation of parent pedagogy.

The term 'postfeminism' has been used in many ways: to indicate a backlash against feminism, blamed for incubating unattainable desires in women (Faludi, 1993); to gesture to the practice of reclaiming misogynist words (Wurtzel, 1999); and as a strategy to broaden feminist debate beyond the alleged whiteness or middle-classness of the second wave (Modleski, 1991; Hoff-Sommers, 1994). In popular discourse, the term 'postfeminist' is used to state that the goals of feminism have now been reached, that feminists are 'out of date', 'selfish' or are themselves 'the problem' (Tyler, 2007).

Feminist theorists have unravelled these competing definitions of postfeminism and explored how and where they have been deployed. Ros Gill (2007) positions postfeminism as a distinct cultural *sensibility*, which invites and inscribes a particular set of expectations for women (and men) in their relationships with one another, with culture and with themselves. A postfeminist sensibility, she argues, invites subjects into processes of self-surveillance, and requires that they monitor and regulate themselves and their practices of living. It expects that subjects will willingly enter into 'makeover' paradigms of transformation and improvement, and that they will seek out and evaluate advice pertaining to this improvement. A postfeminist sensibility is saturated with individualism, and imagines that old structures and constraints have faded away and been replaced with endless possibilities to 'invent yourself'. We can see the resonances of this sensibility, in 'parent-knows-best' parenting advice that obligates you to choose. Whatever parenting philosophy you choose, you certainly need to choose one; and that choice envelopes you in an architecture of postfeminist individualism.

Feminist scholars have further sought to unravel the seductions of the postfeminist vocabulary of 'choice'. Angela McRobbie (2004) argues that this vocabulary inscribes women within ever more insidious forms of normalising power, whereby they must 'choose to be subjected' to norms and constraint. Postfeminist culture requires that women 'dis-identify' with feminism. Feminist politics is thus erased and becomes unspeakable, and the vocabularies of sexism, gender norms and structural oppression are supplanted by a triumphant female individualisation, which McRobbie terms 'an anti-feminist endorsement of female individualization' (2004: 257) that sutures the principles of feminist change with an absence of its political language. Individual ambition replaces collective politics, or in other words, the grammar of psychological improvement replaces the language of injustice and oppression (see Walkerdine, 2003).

Media and cultural forms, such as television makeover programmes, celebrity and gossip magazines, 'female-oriented' tabloid newspaper supplements and digital discussion forums, all serve as barometers of this postfeminist climate. These feminine mass media forms generate and legitimate new forms of antagonism and judgement *between* women, licensing new virulent forms of cruelty on those who are held to have done inadequate work on themselves, to have failed to aspire highly or competently enough. McRobbie (2004) develops a useful critique of discourses of 'empowerment' through the concept of 'postfeminist symbolic violence', showing how the very premise of choice and transformation further erodes the possibility of solidarity between women. Indeed, it is useful to track how neoliberal forms of motherhood work to extend and intensify women's investments in norms of middle-class life and respectability. Part of McRobbie's analysis is to map the importance of imagined 'other mothers' (too young, too old, benefit-claiming, unpartnered, not sexually desirable, and so on) in the production of culturally intelligible 'good mothers' (see McRobbie [2013] for an expanded discussion).

Postfeminist sensibilities require mothers to adopt surveillant and self-regulating approaches to their intimate lives, to manage their families like corporations, to vigilantly invest in the labour of staying sexually desirable, in order to achieve affluent, middle-class maternity. Feminists once tried to account for parental 'impossibilities' by attending to structural issues such as the gender politics of the family, the incommensurability of care and employment, the unattainability of idealised motherhood, and the cultural scripts that require and expect constant availability from mothers (while excusing fathers from the labour of social reproduction). These kinds of structural explanations have not only receded from popular view under postfeminism, but have become constructed as part of the problem. In a stunning sleight-of-hand, feminist critique is positioned as itself causing women's unhappiness: causing women to want what they 'cannot' have – meaningful social and structural change (see Tyler, 2007).

Postfeminist and neoliberal forms of motherhood are unable to account for, or even to see, the uneven and brittle social terrain in which family life is conducted, supposing that mothers are always empowered by exercising the choices that they have allegedly already been gifted. The lack of choice facing mothers is itself defended against with a language of choice. Mothers who find themselves unable to combine the requirements of work and care, for example, or who experience maternity discrimination and lose their jobs as a result of pregnancy, narrate the pain of withdrawing from the labour market as a positive 'choice' to stay at home and raise the kids.

Such postfeminist obligations further solidify chasms between women, and oblige them to divide into ideologically opposed groups of breastfeeders, bottlefeeders, co-sleepers, attachment parents, tough love disciplinarians and free rangers. The common issues that face all mothers, whatever their parenting philosophy, disappear from view.

Mumsnet and neoliberal motherhood

I want to move beyond celebratory optimism and think critically about how Mumsnet, in its very architecture and in its tone of address towards its users, generates postfeminist sensibilities. These sensibilities precisely illuminate the contradictory combination of female individualisation with anti-feminist endorsements that McRobbie detects in popular culture. The architecture of Mumsnet also scaffolds a neoliberal feminism that uses the 'husk of liberalism' (Rottenberg, 2013) to calculate 'smart' motherhood choices (how to calibrate 'work/life balance', how to time the arrival of children, how to choose schools), while saying nothing on the structures of impossibility that shape the uneven terrain of mothering.

In this final section, I consider what kind of 'maternal public' (Tyler, 2008) is convened and assembled via Mumsnet. Like all 'publics', maternal publics have to be called into existence and summoned. How is this done, and who is invited to be part of it or excluded from it? And how does the architecture of the site (see www.mumsnet.com) produce these invitations and exclusions?

A salient lesson from the so-called 'Mumsnet election' is that Mumsnet does not represent parents in any constitutional sense (despite the media narrative), but rather it assembles and constitutes what Cvetkovich (2003) terms an 'archive of feelings', encompassing the struggles, failures, anxieties and triumphs of parenting. Such archives are not simply repositories of ready-formed emotions, but are themselves part of the machinery and the practices that encode and preserve feelings. In assembling its maternal public, Mumsnet – along with other forms of mass media, which create cultural repertoires of feminine address – illuminates neoliberal forms of motherhood, which flexibly weave together themes of family values, individualism, social conservatism and middle-class parenting norms. Mumsnet demonstrates how mothers become socialised into neoliberalism in their interactions with other mothers – and importantly, it documents the significance of imagined 'other mothers' in this process, the familial figures onto whom ideas of parent crisis and deficit are condensed.

In her insightful account of different formations of 'the public', Richenda Gambles (2010) argues that the Mumsnet public overlaps personal, political and privatising orientations and generates a complex 'structure of feeling' (Williams, 1977). As Gambles proposes, the 'official consciousness' of parenting becomes tangible in moods, sensibilities and atmospheres; simultaneously experienced as 'structures' (shaping, obstructing and constraining), *and* as fleeting and difficult to pin down. Gambles defines Mumsnet as both a popular cultural representation of parenting and an invitation to participate in a specific constellation of 'structures of feeling'. These structures of feeling hold parents more responsible than ever before for the economic, social and educational successes of their children (Gillies, 2005, 2011). They require devotion to the development of children in ways that are expensive, time-consuming and require the interventions of experts (Hays, 1996; Lareau, 2003). And they incite women to invest in their post-pregnancy 'yummy mummy' bodies and to perform the labour needed to maintain sexual desirability (Littler, 2013). These 'structures of feeling' around responsible, attentive, autonomous, affluent and professional parenting have sharpened considerably within the wider 'structures' of social reproduction, characterised by further privatising (and contracting) the care economy, dismantling various forms of social and welfare support for parents, and imposing new forms of conditionality on family welfare support (Gillies, 2001; Jensen and Tyler, 2012; Shildrick et al, 2012; Patrick, 2017).

The structures of feeling that underpin parenting culture also frame and make intelligible different practices, experiences and identities principally through the rhetoric of 'choice' (Thomson et al, 2011). In their multigenerational empirical study on contemporary cultures of motherhood, Rachel Thomson, Mary-Jane Kehily, Lucy Hadfield and Sue Sharpe (Thomson et al, 2011) track the fragmentations in the politics of motherhood, resulting in a generation of mothers who are newly visible in culture but also socially polarised. As they demonstrate, motherhood is a crucial site of social division; divisions produced and experienced overlapping layers of age, occupation and, most significantly, social class. By exploring the narratives produced by mothers as they embark on their maternal journeys, and the quite different narratives produced by *their* mothers, Thomson et al (2011) are able to map out the present sociocultural terrain of motherhood and the 'mothering projects' that women endeavour to produce and occupy. They demonstrate how the motherhood of today operates with 'a sustained and dynamic stretch of the commodity frontier' (Thomson et al, 2011: 18), with material culture and consumption taking a central position in ways that were not present for mothers of earlier generations (see also Taylor et al, 2004).

In particular, mothers now are compelled to constantly evaluate their maternal experiences in relation to the 'choices' they are making, to monitor how and where they are 'getting motherhood right' (or wrong) and making the 'right' choices. This exhaustive rhetoric of choice resonates across maternal consumer culture, and as we have seen, in the explosion of moralised parenting pedagogy across cultural sites (Hardyment, 2007; Jensen, 2010). Mumsnet contributes powerfully to these neoliberal, postfeminist maternal formations in a number of key ways.

Registering as a Mumsnetter

First, upon registering to use the site, the Mumsnetter is immediately required to personalise her journey as a consumer, and asked to provide a home address (in order to be connected to local service providers), age and gender details of any children, and to state whether she is pregnant. The rationale offered for this remarkable data collection is that the weekly Mumsnet email can be individualised to include 'developmental bulletins, tailored to your own child's progress', 'pregnancy e-mails tailored to each stage of your pregnancy', 'our weekly e-mail round-up of parenting news' and to access discounts on a variety of family and parenting products and services. From the very moment of registration, Mumsnet is scaffolded by expectations that motherhood is an experience 'to be displayed and consumed' (Thomson et al, 2011: 126) and to be mediated through technical (developmental psychology, obstetrics, paediatrics) as well as consumer discourse.

Once registered to the site, members can 'opt in' to receive regular invitations to test products, review services and evaluate the family friendliness of various businesses as a 'mystery shopper'. In order to do so, members must disclose additional information to Mumsnet 'on behalf of its clients', including household income, employment status, number of family holidays a year, online shopping habits, supermarket of choice and preferred products. This aspect of the site is voluntary, but it significantly extends the constitution of maternal culture as a site of consumption and of Mumsnet as an interface between its 'clients' and the market research possibilities of its registered users. Mumsnet is big business: in 2016, it made almost £7 million in profit from harvesting user data to sell to its advertisers.

The conversational environment

A second, significant manifestation of the fragmentary politics of parenting on Mumsnet unfolds in connection to regimes of parenting 'expertise'. The website is implicitly situated as non-pedagogical, inviting members to exchange opinion and experience, rather than to solicit or offer expertise. However, in practice Mumsnet absolutely replicates the pedagogical texture of parent culture and invites evaluation of the advice that members have been offered by parenting experts, health visitors, midwives and schoolteachers.

The architecture of the site invites members to think of themselves as 'professional parents' and to approach their parenting lives as a set of informed choices, requiring intellectual attention and practices involving training. Mumsnet provides a reflexive conversational environment, with permanent discussion forums titled 'Am I being unreasonable' that invite members to narrate their decisions, solicit support, demonstrate how they are informed by sources of authority such as parenting 'science', display their knowledge and competence, scrutinise the decisions of others and contest one another.

Indeed, Mumsnet discussion boards prompt incredible amounts of reflexive and evaluative discussion, with some threads generating hundreds or even thousands of replies. Some scholars have conceptualised these exchanges as illustrating the web's potential to disrupt normative relationships between experts and mothers (Mungham and Lazard, 2010) or a 'democratising' of knowledge. The relationship between Mumsnetter and parenting expert can, of course, be antagonistic, and can reveal itself as uneven and hierarchical in key moments. In 2006, parenting author Gina Ford, whose *The Contented Little Baby Book* (1999) advocates strict babycare routines, threatened Mumsnet with legal action after multiple defamatory remarks. Although the Mumsnet team initially protested, claiming that the site was a 'conversation between its users' and 'neither pro- nor anti-Gina Ford', they eventually relented and deleted the posts (Muir, 2006: 11; see also Jensen, 2013).

Yet the ability to 'speak back' to parenting advice is also uneven and is itself an enactment of different forms of privilege, entitlement and a sense of oneself as competent. Mumsnet offers a conduit for parents to 'test out' how they might speak back and to accumulate the knowledge to do so. The website encourages, and incubates, these reflexive subject positions in its frequent staging of webchat Q&A sessions between 'parenting experts', including behavioural specialists, psychotherapists, writers, and parent pedagogues, inviting members to bring questions to roundtable discussions. Discussion threads are 'sandbox' spaces, where evaluative skills can be both exhibited *and* generated.

Class antagonisms

A third dimension to the structures of feeling around parenting that manifest on Mumsnet is in the social polarisations and divisions that open up between its members. The online conversational environment of Mumsnet is pseudonymous, rather than anonymous, and is loosely governed by rules of affective sociability.[1] The website provides some general 'netiquette' guidance around courtesy, trolling and spamming. It also offers some foundational rules of courtesy when posting on the talkboard,[2] but discussion posts are not subject to any moderation process and are only subject to scrutiny (and possible deletion) if a registered member reports on the grounds of harassment, libel or containing 'racist, sexist, disablist or homophobic' language (as defined by Mumsnet). This 'mumsnetiquette' (Jensen, 2013) makes appeals and exhortations to the ideal Mumsnetter – her 'good manners' and 'common sense' and her imagined reflexive competency – as central to helping to 'police' the site and limit disturbances.

Despite this counsel, even a brief perusal of the 'talkboard' threads reveals discussion punctuated with frequent provocations and soaked with affective antagonism. Many exchanges become petty, spiteful and bullying. Importantly, the 'mumsnetiquette' rules do not make mention of class discrimination, class hate terminology or class pathologising. This absence of 'classism' in the mumsnetiquette rules is significant, because it is precisely around social class that Mumsnet antipathies most often erupt. The generation of classist remarks on Mumsnet includes expressions of disgust and anger at classed figures such as 'chav' mums (caricatures of 'the underclass', see Tyler 2008) and 'benefit breeders' (Jensen and Tyler, 2015), as well as envy and irritation at 'yummy mummies' (Littler, 2013).

The unspeakability of social class – and its centrality to the antagonisms of Mumsnet – documents wider denials and euphemisms around class formation, the disappearance of vocabularies of class exploitation and the denigration of working-class culture and the pathologisation of working-class life (Skeggs, 2004). As Bev Skeggs brilliantly shows, class is formed in dynamic systems of symbolic exchange, which fix working-class subjects into place and morally code them through evaluations of dirt, waste, contagion, disorder, deficiency and pathology. On Mumsnet, the constant unspeakability of class inequality and its materiality is matched only by the constant symbolic repetition and circulation of classed spectres and imagined 'other mothers', against whom the Mumsnetter must define and defend herself and from whom she must claim a moral distance.

Thomson et al (2011) brilliantly capture the guilty thrill of the Mumsnet voyeur and reflect on the simmering undercurrent of potential classed provocation, which can (and does) rapidly magnify and enflame. In particular, they remark on the complex *pleasures* of these antagonisms, describing time spent browsing Mumsnet talkboards as 'a pornographic experience, generating a scopophilic rush that is dirty and compelling at the same time … the vicarious highs of a hyper-real display of the obscenity of middle-class sensibilities' (Thomson et al, 2011: 147). Indeed, there are contradictory pleasures to be had in reading and participating in these catalogues of petty irritation, confessions of ambivalence and annoyance, gossip and the minutiae of morality. The casual browser does not have to look far to find affective exchanges concerned with inscribing, classifying and demarcating the moral boundaries of class formation. One thread, which is quite typical, discusses toddlers and television, and begins with suggestions for easy activities to do with small children, but quickly develops an undercurrent of resentment and antagonism, summarised here:

'[W]e can't all have little angels that play by themselves whilst we cook and clean lol. And we can't all b Mother Earth and spend every second with our kids'

'[I] wouldn't listen to some of the know it all militant mums on here'

'[B]eing pregnant is no reason to be a lazy parent to your toddler. But sure, if you think an hour a day of completely passive, useless sitting and staring is harmless, then have at it.'

'[H]ow judgey some people can be about a bit of tv.'

'At least the toddler isn't strapped into the buggy in front of the t.v with a packet of crisps and a bottle of coke for company.'

'Nowt wrong with a packet of crisps and a bottle of coke'

'[E]xactly, so long as they're organic'[3]

The invisibility of class and classed privileges on the Mumsnet 'netiquette' page is instructive; it reproduces the discourse of 'classlessness' – itself a classed discourse, which permits the injuries of social class to be evaded (Reay, 1997; Sayer, 2002). This evasion of social class is crucial to the liberal parent pedagogies that underpin Mumsnet and the production of an ideal Mumsnetter; imagined as self-monitoring, reflexively exploring the consequences of her choices and engaged in discussion with others approaching their parenting projects in similar ways. In the exchange reproduced earlier, Mumsnetters engage in symbolic struggles to define what constitutes good, better and best parenting practice. They are 'making class' – establishing and seeking legitimation for their parent practices from other parents and, in doing so, seeking recognition in the field of parenting culture.

No mother is able to (always) conform to the demanding visions of maternal 'perfection', but at least on Mumsnet she can acquire some social value from others, by presenting her parenting practice as always driven by knowledge, executed with choice and by acknowledging where she is cutting corners with wit and self-deprecation. Indeed, Mumsnetters defensively ward off the 'perfect mothers' ('Mother Earth', 'militant mums'), who they imagine would hold them in contempt for failing to be perfect, in the earlier example for letting their children watch television. In this exchange, the spectre of maternal failure, that members are playfully positioning themselves in relation to, is profoundly classed: the mother who not only lets her child watch television but also 'straps' them to a bottle of Coke and a packet of crisps. The semiotic trilogy of television, Coke and crisps catalogues a litany of imagined classed pathologies, through which these Mumsnet users can gently mock their own classed pretensions ('as long as they're organic'), to neutralise through humour the accusation that they are lazy, and to demonstrate the reflexive compromises behind parenting decisions. Thus they can morally authorise themselves (for example, letting one child watch television in order to breastfeed the other). Exchanges such as these illuminate the simultaneous dual sense of agency and constraint produced through contemporary parenting culture.

The production of the 'Mumsnetter' offers a fascinating example of how forms of neoliberal, postfeminist motherhood are produced, in dialogue with consumerist discourses of choice, transformation and social mobility, and what critical feminist scholars of class have termed 'compulsory individuality' (Cronin, 2000; Skeggs, 2004). The evasions around social class do not mean that class has disappeared – quite the opposite. Classificatory processes continue to inscribe bodies and behaviours into categories of 'deviant' and 'disciplined', police the borders of fragrant respectability, and incite women to invest in marriage, motherhood and domesticity – and on Mumsnet, powerfully so. It is precisely through accounting for oneself, narrating oneself as always choosing, and conforming to moral conventions around choice and governance, that middle-class selves come into being (Skeggs, 2004). The corollary effect is that constraints and structures become unspeakable and the self is experienced as an act of self-determination. In the words of Anthony Giddens, 'we are, not what we are, but what we make of ourselves' (1991: 75).

Moral motherhood

Mumsnet, in the invitations and incitements it makes, and the inscriptions that are produced in its conversational architecture, is not a place for collective organising around maternal dissatisfactions with the requirements of global neoliberalism or conditions of precarity. Rather, the maternal public it assembles works more as a meeting place, where Mumsnetters can exchange knowledge about how to morally authorise themselves. In so doing, it reproduces the principal tenets of privilege, permitting class privilege in particular to remain invisible. Mumsnet endeavours mean different things to different participants – but the architecture of the site is organised around becoming a subject of value (Skeggs, 2004), a good mother. Through engaging in the Mumsnet space, the Mumsnetter is engaging in a range of symbolic struggles to authorise her experience and perspective and, in doing so engaging in the production of a particular form of personhood: the reflexive, individualised mobile individual of reflexive modernity.

The interpellation of the Mumsnetter, through the architecture of the website, is made manifest through discourses of consumption, engagements with pedagogical sources of authority about issues of parenting, and through a substitution of class politics with discourses of reflexive individualism. As argued in this chapter, it is in the structure of the website and the invitations it makes to its users, that a particular classed set of desires and affective sensibilities around parenting is produced and circulated. These sensibilities, produced within the architecture of the site, position the Mumsnetter as a subject of agency: the website itself initiates and petitions its contributors to approach, account and understand their family lives and parenting 'choices' as classless, meritocratic and underpinned by expertise that has been carefully reflected upon. The invitations/requirements to enter into dialogue with other Mumsnetters about potentially any aspect of one's parental life (parental 'choices') rehearse and extend this powerful discourse of neoliberal motherhood. In doing so, Mumsnet also frames *out* (as 'unspeakable) the structural, gendered and economic inequalities that limit and inhibit choice. Far from being empowered by ever-conflicting bodies of childrearing advice, from their entry in record numbers into the labour market, or by the postfeminist invitations to 'invent themselves', mothers are damned if they do and damned if they don't, as Imogen Tyler notes:

> Young working-class mothers are still routinely demonised in political discourse and are stable television comic fodder, working mothers are routinely castigated for failing their children, mothers who don't work outside the home are rebuked for failing themselves, their families and the economy. (Tyler, 2009: 1)

As Tyler points out, the maternal has never been so hyper-visible, and yet so incoherent, as it is at this moment. Constraints around 'choice' shape experiences of mothering. The widely documented 'motherhood penalty' (Correll and Barnard, 2007) cumulatively reduces women's earning potential every time she has a child: mothers are perceived as less competent and less dependable in the workplace, they are less likely to be promoted and the recommended starting salaries for mothers are substantively lower. Maternity discrimination leads to an estimated 54,000 women losing their jobs every year in the UK as a result of becoming pregnant (Maternity Action). In 2015, the Department for Business, Innovation and Skills (with the Ministry of Justice) found that almost half of the women who have been awarded financial compensation for pregnancy or maternity discrimination by tribunals do not receive the money due to them.

Yet these scandals of maternal injustice are notably absent in the common culture of motherhood. We do not see rightful anger at the centre of this motherhood culture, but rather notions of good and bad mothering, and conversations about how to situate oneself within the former and avoid the latter, that continue to dominate popular cultural and representational fields. As this chapter has explored, recent social histories of parenting advice have also rehearsed a version of the newly empowered parents, choosing and consuming advice, and this fantasy figure has *itself* been incorporated into much contemporary advice, rendering its web of discursive power ever more insidious.

Neoliberal parenting culture both constitutes parenting as a newly intensified object for public concern and summons new subjects for/of public action. The figures of anxiety that have populated the landscape of parenting culture have ranged from the cold and distant mother, popularised by the work of John Bowlby (1951) and his thesis of 'maternal deprivation', to the technology-fixated child who is now imagined to be suffering the consequences of a 'toxic' addiction to 'screentime' and paltry quality 'family time' (Palmer, 2008). In the antagonistic landscape, exemplified on Mumsnet, new figures of anxiety continue to play out across parent pedagogy and parent culture, 'bodied forth' (Tyler, 2008) as overdetermined and caricatured expressions of imagined social crises. These include: 'the helicopter parent', whose inability to leave children alone is seen as contributing to their children's dependency and fragility (Bristow, 2014); 'the tiger mother' (exemplified in Chua, 2011), whose pathological and competitive obsessions with success are seen to come at the expense of affection and child autonomy; and the 'yummy mummy', whose glamorous sexualisation works to infantilise, fetishize and redomesticate motherhood (see Littler, 2013).

The Mumsnet website assembles a potentially radical maternal public, immediately diffused by its very architecture, which invites mothers into relationships of antagonism, into processes of social distinction and into an individualised and fragmented politics of parenting. It documents the 'symbiotic' relationships between neoliberal culture and liberal feminism (McRobbie, 2013) – a relationship which could potentially be disrupted, if its maternal public could orient itself to a broader constellation of concerns, beyond the tenets of professional, middle-class, neoliberal motherhood and moral respectability. McRobbie (2013) proposes that we revisit the demands for collectivised childcare and rediscover the bracing ideas of socialist feminism.

Certainly, we need to interrupt fantasies of parenting perfection with experiential accounts of the everyday experiences, struggles and anxieties of raising children (Baraitser, 2009) – which the talkboards of Mumsnet often do already – and to put front and centre stage the systems of discrimination and material disadvantage that so unevenly shape women's lives. We need to challenge the rhetoric of freedom, opportunity and choice that allows those systems and structures of maternal inequality to disappear from view. It is by speaking to wider concerns and constraints around welfare reform, custody battles, reproductive autonomy, maternity discrimination, racism and the hovering threat of state-ordered child removal that we can, in Imogen Tyler's words, find ways to support women to 'communicate what they already know in ways that will make a difference' (Tyler, 2008: 4).

Chapter Three explores how discourses of parenting deficit became mobilised and circulated by media producers and across political and public debate in the first years of the 21st century. These discourses recycle existing figures of parent-blame, and as we will see, manufacture new ones, in a spectacularly televisual form.

Notes

[1] 'Mumsnet talk' is a largely unmoderated discussion space, where registered users can begin or contribute to discussion threads that are grouped under a variety of categories. Members choose their own pseudonym and create personal profiles; other members can track their comments and threads via these profiles.

[2] The full list includes restrictions on the following: personal attacks; posts that break the law; 'trolling', goading or misleading; troll hunting; spamming (www.mumsnet.com/info/netiquette).

[3] www.mumsnet.com (accessed 10 January 2013).

THREE

The cultural industry of parent-blame

'I don't care about the camera. It's just another family that needs my help. It doesn't matter if it's one camera or thirty cameras. What's here – the space between me and you – is all that matters.' (Jo Frost, interview with Macaulay, 2010, for the *Telegraph*)

Supernanny, a reality television programme that promised to transform the lives of families struggling with parenting, was first broadcast by Channel 4 on British television in July 2004. The first episode featured the Woods family, whose two-year-old child Charlie was described by the programme's promotional material and accompanying voiceover as 'a raging toddler who's destroying and dominating family life with his out-of-control behaviour' ('The Woods', 2004). Within the first few minutes of the episode, viewers watched a tense and fast-edit montage of Charlie punching his father, emptying a packet of sweets over the floor, having a screaming tantrum and starting a fist fight with one of his siblings. Over the next 45 minutes, viewers watched the Woods family as they were visited, scrutinised, advised and berated by the 'Supernanny' Jo Frost, described by the programme voiceover as a 'professional nanny and parenting expert'. Frost introduced a 'routine chart' that detailed how the family were to manage their day, demonstrated a range of behavioural techniques to contain and discipline Charlie, and offered a mixture of encouragement, reassurance and scolding, when the Woods parents failed to stick fully to the techniques and rules she had prescribed.

It was television dynamite. The first episode was watched by 4.6 million viewers, and the first series of *Supernanny* would eventually come to command viewing figures of between 6 million and 7 million for every episode – almost a third of the primetime audience. Channel 4 would go on to broadcast seven series of *Supernanny* in total. The programme was an enormous commercial hit for television production company Ricochet. In 2005, following the first series, Ricochet would report pre-tax profits of more than £2 million, and that same year were bought by Shed Productions for £30 million in cash and shares

(Terazono, 2005). Ricochet retained secondary rights to *Supernanny* (and other programmes on its catalogue). It would subsequently export the programme to the United States in 2005 (still fronted by Frost), where it would run for seven seasons, as well as franchising the format across Europe and beyond, as far as China (broadcast on state television channel CCTV), Brazil (broadcast by SBT) and Australia (broadcast by GEM and Nine Network).[1] The official *Supernanny* website states that the English-language version of the programme is broadcast in 47 territories.

Prior to fronting the programme and her accompanying media career, Frost ran a childcare service and parent consultancy with some notable celebrity clients. In media interviews, she has described her *Supernanny* career as the result of responding to an open audition call after seeing 'an ad in the paper' (Roberts, 2007), though it seems likely that being employed as a nanny by a television producer had some bearing on her transition to reality star (Macaulay, 2010; Philby, 2013). However the *Supernanny* format was devised, its initially spectacular success heralded the eruption of a new genre of reality television that focused on family dysfunction and transformation that would quickly form a staple of primetime broadcasting.

Other television broadcasters would quickly imitate the *Supernanny* format, with programmes such as *The House of Tiny Tearaways* (BBC, 2005), *Brat Camp* (Channel 4, 2005), *Little Angels* (BBC3, 2004) and *Bringing Up Baby* (Channel 4, 2007). A poll of nearly four thousand parents, commissioned by the National Family and Parenting Institute, found that 55% of adults – and 72% of parents – had watched at least one parenting television programme, the most common example being *Supernanny* (Ipsos-Mori, 2006). Jo Frost's television career was briefly renewed after a brief hiatus, when she fronted *Extreme Parental Guidance* in the UK (Channel 4, 2010) and *Family SOS* in the US (TLC, 2013), but neither reached the giddy heights of the *Supernanny* ratings.

The media economy of popular parent pedagogy brought the television spectacle of 'families in crisis' into the nation's living rooms. This genre seemed to document an apparently unseen crisis in family life, presented by these reality and documentary television formats as both scandalous entertainment and as pedagogic exercise. Viewers were invited to be both appalled by the bad behaviour of children and the failure of parents to control them, as well as to take lessons for themselves about how to raise their own.

The parent pedagogy media economy created a number of celebrity pedagogues and lucrative media portfolios, including books, websites and consultancies, publicised alongside the television economies that produced them. The parent pedagogy narrative followed a clear staging: crisis, submission to a parenting 'expert', joyous family transformation. This was not only an extremely valuable franchise, but also a crucial media anchor in structuring and defining the wider perceptions of parent crisis. It was decisive in generating a powerful moral consensus that hidden numbers of parents were unable to discipline and control their children. In short, a lucrative cultural industry of parent-blame erupted in the UK, driven by the media, and taken up strategically in subsequent policy debates about family intervention.

Imagining a 'parenting deficit'

Supernanny might seem an unlikely television hit; why would so many tune in, week after week, to watch children and parents in upsetting and often disturbing conflicts? There was little consensus in the explanations proffered for its extraordinary popularity. Some commentators argued that all reality television represented a 'dumbing-down' of television's original remit to 'inform, educate and entertain', as imagined by the first Director-General of the BBC John Reith. Unnamed 'industry sources' lamented the domination of television schedules by reality television, describing it as 'salacious tabloid crap' that amounted to documentary television 'selling its soul' (Robinson, 2004). Some industry figures voiced their disdain publicly; broadcaster John Humphrys condemned reality television as "mind-numbing, witless vulgarity" (Humphrys, 2004). As Sue Holmes and Deborah Jermyn (2004) note, reality television has often been the most vilified of recent televisual forms.

Supernanny, too, has often been derided – by commentators, reviewers, journalists and television viewers – as incendiary, manipulative, sensationalist and contrived. Analysing another example of the 'formatted documentary' genre, *Wife Swap* (Channel 4, 2004), Holmes and Jermyn point to the more complex oppositional and ambivalent readings that can be opened up in viewer responses to such television, and they caution against interpretations that flatten this complexity. We will explore some of the viewer ambivalences opened up around *Supernanny* in more detail later in this chapter.

Government ministers were usually keen to problematise reality television. In 2003, for example, Culture Secretary Tessa Jowell was reported to have urged viewers to 'revolt' against 'cheap' reality television formats which were being 'flogged to death' (Arlidge, 2003). But they suspended criticism and interpreted *Supernanny* differently; several ministers publicly praised the programme's extraordinary ratings as useful indications to the government that there was indeed a public desire for parenting instruction. In the foreword to *Every Parent Matters* (DfES, 2007), Secretary of State for Education Alan Johnson stated that: 'Parents are demonstrating a growing appetite for discussion, information and advice, as we see from the increasingly vibrant market in television programmes, magazines and websites' (DfES, 2007).

In a 2006 media interview, Louise Casey, then head of the government's Respect Task Force, drew parallels between television crusades by celebrity chefs and the *Supernanny* audience: 'Jamie Oliver rightly landed on school meals and said "we are feeding children such bad food that they cannot sit down in the classroom" and I think the millions watching TV about parenting are saying the same thing to government' (quoted in Wintour, 2006).

In July of the same year, Children's Minister Beverley Hughes interpreted *Supernanny*'s success as indicating a British hunger for parenting intervention: 'Government too must extend the opportunities for parents to develop their expertise; the popularity of *Supernanny* exemplifies the hunger for information and for effective parenting programmes that parents often express to me' (Hughes, 2006).

Although ministers were quick to capitalise on *Supernanny* and link it to existing policy agendas to 'support parents', its commercial and ratings success need to be approached with caution. The *Supernanny* flashpoint exceeded a straightforward parental demand for advice. As we saw in the previous chapter, the parent pedagogy landscape has become bloated. Many scholars of parenting culture have tracked the exponential rise of parent pedagogy, noting that the parenting publishing industry has doubled under neoliberalism (Lee, 2014: 5) and estimating that between the mid-1970s and the end of the century, the number of books about motherhood increased seven-fold (Douglas and Michaels, 2005).

Clearly, the parent pedagogy industry has not been driven by a problem of scarcity – indeed, the reinvention of 'good mothering' across different periods demonstrates how elastic, and deeply political, the project of parent training could be. Why, then, did *Supernanny* in particular capture the public imagination at this specific moment? What made its narrative so compelling – in a cultural studies tradition, we should ask, *why this text now?* What did *Supernanny* do; what kind of cultural work did it do for the viewers who were watching it, discussing it, reflecting upon it? What can the explosive success of *Supernanny* tell us about broader cultural discourses of parent crisis in Britain at this moment?

Rather than interpreting the success of *Supernanny* as an indicator of what parents 'really' want, I want to explore the complicated ideological work that this programme did at a very specific cultural and political moment. Far from indicating a simple desire for advice, *Supernanny* (and its media peers) incubated new classificatory processes of identification, disavowal, taste and judgement. Across parenting culture, the struggle to define particular practices as desirable, and others as pathological, have become politically and morally charged. The most banal and everyday decisions about feeding, playing, disciplining and bedtime routines are made to map onto defining ideas about who we are, who we proximate to and who we wish to hold at a distance. A closer examination of *Supernanny* reveals the ambivalent and contradictory policing processes that are opened up by a fervent cultural economy of parent-blame. *Supernanny* dramatised parent pedagogy, and turned parental failure and success into a spectacle; in doing so, it invited viewers into the pleasures of judgement, and licensed a new turn in the cultural mediation of 'parent crisis'.

Vanessa Reimer and Sarah Sahagian (2015) outline the 'mother blame game' of contemporary culture, but the scope of their work sees blame games as lived primarily through gender and follows mother-blaming to its patriarchal roots. The blame game of *Supernanny* is certainly gendered, but it is also profoundly classed. The cultural industry of parent-blame animates multiple classifications of value and worth. As Bev Skeggs (1997) has powerfully argued, the emotional politics of class is 'fuelled by insecurity, doubt, indignation, and resentment – but also lived with pleasure and irreverence' (1997: 162).

Supernanny helped the British public to imagine a compelling sense of 'parental deficit'. The construction and circulation of this parent deficit did not need to map easily onto any empirical realities about family life. The actual amount of time, energy and resources that are devoted to children, monitoring their wellbeing and attending to their needs, became quite inconsequential to this incarnation of 'parent crisis'. As Rosalind Edwards and Val Gillies (2013) remark, while the construction of the family as a problem has a long history, the idea of a 'parenting deficit', in particular, is relatively recent. In their review of the archive of two research projects conducted by community researcher Dennis Marsden on family life in the 1960s, Edwards and Gillies find a curious lack of moral commentary on the parenting practices of the participating families. The research archive bears little trace of ideas of parental responsibility or the expectation that parents will assess and monitor risk, and neither parents (in interview transcripts) nor Marsden and his associates (in fieldnotes) discuss parenting as an activity requiring attunement, attention or reflection. Practices and values that would today be viewed as neglectful or abusive, such as leaving young children alone at home, leaving babies and toddlers in the care of their young siblings, allowing children to roam outside without supervision and late into the evening, were widely accepted and recorded in the research archive without remark.

Extensive research documents how parents now spend more 'quality time' with their children than ever before, are more engaged with their children's education, are committed to their emotional and intellectual flourishing, prioritise their needs, and are more anxious than ever about being (and being seen as) 'good' parents (Zelizer, 1994; Cunningham, 1995; Hays, 1996; Blum, 1999; Lareau, 2003; Gatrell, 2005; Warner, 2006; Hardyment, 2007; Nelson, 2010).

Charlotte Faircloth (2014) notes how the expected 'work' of parenting has expanded, extended and intensified, encompassing a growing range of activities, duties and obligations that were not previously considered necessary. Research shows we are 'better' parents – or rather, more accurately, that parenting has become more attentive and children more 'priceless' (Zelizer, 1994) and more likely to survive illness and to avoid accidents. Nevertheless, an 'ideological displacement' (Hall et al, 1978: 32) has occurred, in which *a new definition of the situation* has supplanted the simple set of facts. As Hall and his colleagues showed in *Policing the Crisis* (1978), it is through perceptions and beliefs that reality becomes ideologically (re)constructed. Hall et al show how the central apparatus of social control – the police and the courts – shape the ideological construction of crime and transform mundane and everyday incidents into a perceived 'wave' of criminality. These agencies, together with the media and other public institutions, articulate a rationale for action, by creating uniform and weighty definitions, structuring broader public definitions, generating a moral consensus, amplifying the dominant ideologies of the powerful and legitimating more authoritarian strategies. These same processes of definition, initiation of punitive policing and control campaigns, and public legitimation (via the media) form part of a circle of parenting crisis.

The 'circle of crisis' that has solidified around the figure of the 'bad parent', like the 'crisis of mugging', has a long pre-history. Old histories of mother-blame without doubt play a part in this machinery, whereby any mother who does not fit a middle-class nuclear ideal may be classed as a 'bad mother'. The alleged 'golden age' of good mothering, often considered to have fallen somewhere between the authoritarian Victorians and post-war 'anything-goes' liberalism (Squires, 2008: 20), rehearses the Victorian 'cult of womanhood' as pure, pious, domestic and submissive, and presents a sentimentalised version of sacrificial diligence (see Ladd–Taylor and Umansky, 1998). These discourses help to construct and shape contemporary narratives of 'parent deficit'; for example in allocating parent-blame to mothers who work outside the home and thus allegedly generate a 'time famine' in family life (Hochschild, 1997; Baraitser, 2017).

The imagining of contemporary parental deficit, as manufactured and structured by *Supernanny* and the wider industry of parent-blame, helped to generate a powerful moral consensus. This was that 'parenting' required extensive training and intervention by experts, and that there was a hidden problem of deficit parenting in Britain that needed to be exposed and monitored – by documentary television, by state organisations and social workers, and by parenting support initiatives.

Enter *Supernanny*

Domestic historian Christina Hardyment memorably suggested in her book *Perfect Parents* (1995) that mothers today are caught up in a complex web of self-surveillance, not simply doing the work of mothering but also 'watching ourselves be mothers' (1995: 298). It is perhaps through its spectacular re-imagining of parental failure as reality entertainment, and through its routinised surveillance of the most intimate domestic spaces, that *Supernanny* most powerfully transformed the industries of parent pedagogy and parent-blame.

Each episode of *Supernanny* followed Frost as she visited a family in crisis and diagnosed and prescribed transformative changes to their problematic routines and habits. The episodes are heavily scripted into chapters that barely deviate from one family to the next. The first section of the programme comprises a combination of *cinema verité* footage of the featured family at home and brief to-camera interview segments, where parents explain the issues they are struggling with. This is followed by a camera pan through the neighbourhood, as Frost approaches the family home and introduces herself at the front door. She (and the surrounding camera crew) silently observe family interactions for one or two days. The following day she revisits the parents (now without their children) and stages an intervention, stating, in the boldest terms, how and where they are incubating family problems through their interactions with the children. She demonstrates discipline and control 'techniques' and shows them how to implement them: there is an emphasis on consistency and boundary-setting. A period of a few days follows, where the camera crew are present but Frost is not. Frost then returns to the family, armed with camera footage that details where parents have deviated from the prescribed 'techniques'. After making new commitment to the techniques, a final section of the programme narrates parents' continuing resolve and happy transformation.

In detailing this script, I want to highlight what happens when parent pedagogy migrates from books, pamphlets and magazines, onto reality television. Family failure became spectacularly visual, and thus profoundly more immediate and pressing. Television scholar Helen Wheatley (2016) challenges notions that television engagement is characterised by inattentive 'glances' or distraction, and shows how its 'spectacular' dimensions can provide deeply pleasurable eruptions of excess, which fascinate and attract, and can hold, engage and enthral viewers. The presentations of 'real', ordinary parents suffering the effects of 'failure' right in front of the camera – the framing of the minutiae of domestic drama, the opening out of the subtleties of familial interaction to the scrutiny of the camera (and to the television audience) – these were decisive in defining, structuring and 'making sensible' the idea of a parental responsibility deficit that was already in circulation. The cultural studies tradition of media analysis has always sought to situate media texts within the *contexts* from which they emerge, and the broader cultural and political economies that generate, manufacture and anchor them.

Supernanny, anchored within a particular cultural moment of family crisis discourse, re-presents parent-blame; it catalogues, categorises and archives parent-blame into manageable and digestible hour-long narratives. In *Mediating the Family*, Estella Tincknell (2005) maps powerful mythologies of 'the family', remade across different broadcasting genres, and that can offer viewers pleasurable opportunities to fantasise, breathe life into existing anxieties (about working mothers, or monstrous children), ridicule and parody structures of power (such as patriarchy), and package dysfunctionality as entertaining pathology. Tinknell argues that these mythological representations of 'the family' work to circulate particular hegemonic meanings, such as domestic competence, competitive individualism, the stability of the nuclear family and nostalgia for consumer affluence. In doing so, these myths flatten out the classed, gendered and racial inequalities inherent in family life, and recycle individualised and depoliticised versions of the familial sphere.

Supernanny contributes to these mythologies of dysfunctionality, but its pedagogic and pseudo-documentary pretensions channel a cultural politics of the family that constructs and 'commonsenses' a specific kind of crisis discourse. 'We', the television audience, are invited to look on the unfolding domestic drama as witnesses and collaborators, but also perhaps as fellow failures. Jo Frost the Supernanny is unfailingly and panoptically present, and the complex web of watching and looking that unfolds in *Supernanny* interpellates the television audience in multiple ways. We are invited to witness scenes of bad behavior and parental failure alongside Frost, the camera positioned so that we look over her shoulder, or cued into outrage with a conspiratorial close-up of Frost tutting, rolling her eyes, or looking back at the camera wide-eyed and open-mouthed in shock or disgust. At crucial points in the narrative, in which parents are instructed to follow her 'techniques', the programme layers an additional frame of surveillance as *we watch Frost watching* events develop through *her* own television screen via hidden cameras, listening and coaching her protégés through an earpiece and microphone. We are invited to see what she sees, how she sees it and as she sees it, and to scrutinise as, when and how she does. This web of watching and looking, constructed as it is through heavy post-production editing, is not quite a window into 'the real', but rather, a window into 'the actual' (Kavka and West, 2004). 'Actuality' invites a (limited) reflexive awareness of the staging and editing of television production processes, but suspended through a fantastical sense of 'presentness', of proximity without presence, manipulating time, resuscitating a feeling of 'liveness' and promising immediacy with the drama that is unfolding on the screen.

Perhaps we 'know' that *Supernanny* has been scripted and carefully packaged – but nonetheless its panoptic web compels us to participate in its illusions. When *Supernanny* entered the landscape of parent pedagogy, it dramatised a spectacle of parental failure and offered this spectacle as both entertainment *and* instruction. Its layers of surveillance invited audiences to both enjoy the failures of others (over the shoulder of Frost) and imagine themselves as part of the spectacle, to imagine their own failures. *Supernanny*'s complicated invitations were to be both appalled by the failure of other families, and guilty at one's own failure to be a perfect parent.

The 'devil version of Mary Poppins'

Jo Frost the Supernanny was a media figure with complex appeal. The programme consciously toyed with a key figure in British cultural history: the nanny. Caitlin Flanagan (2005) reminds us that although the British nanny is often thought of as one of England's oldest institutions, she was actually relatively short-lived. Between the early days of Queen Victoria's reign and the end of the Second World War, the combined effects of industrialisation and a population explosion brought together different social classes in 'a highly regimented and hierarchical servant culture' (Flanagan, 2005: 4). Nannies occupied an intimate and sometimes troubled (and troubling) place within this servant culture; not quite as formalised a role as the governesses or tutors employed by aristocratic families (though nannies sometimes oversaw some elements of child education) and not quite servants, nannies were both not of the household and simultaneously central to it. Despite the relative brevity of her reign, the nanny has come to occupy a particularly fond place in British culture.[2] For Flanagan, this is principally due to the groundbreaking epoch of children's literature published in the first half of the 20th century, produced by writers remembering (and misremembering) their own childhoods. In particular, the 'Mary Poppins' stories by P.L. Travers, which would later be rescripted by Walt Disney and turned into an award-winning film, have been foundational in extending the cultural life of the nanny, and these were central to the *Supernanny* franchise and the modes of parent-blame that it popularised.

The nanny of Travers' Mary Poppins stories – 'formally trained, bred to the job, imperious, unflappable, and immaculately turned out' (Flanagan, 2005: 7) – was a deeply ambivalent figure. In her biography of Travers, Valerie Lawson (1999) suggests that Poppins has something of the sadist in her, in spite of her moments of tenderness. She scolds the children, belittles and humiliates them, threatens and frightens them, and allows events in the supernatural realms they visit to become strange and terrifying, and then denies scornfully that anything magical has happened at all. The character of Mary Poppins was softened by Disney in his sentimental rewrite and casting of the sweet-natured, well-spoken and ever-singing Julie Andrews for his 1946 musical film version. The struggles between Disney and Travers to cement the character of Poppins are well documented (and these struggles have themselves become the subject of a 2013 film, *Saving Mr Banks*). The haunting dimensions of Travers' original Poppins character remain as compelling as ever.

In both Travers' books and Disney's film, the Banks children come to love and adore Mary Poppins, stern and disciplinarian as she is. They ask her when she will leave, and implore and beg her to stay with them. But Mary Poppins is impermanent; just as she blows in with a hurricane, she tells the children she 'will leave when the wind changes', and makes no apologies for the heartbreak they suffer when she leaves abruptly. Farah Mendelsohn (2008) sees Poppins, like all nannies, as an upwardly mobile, working-class woman. Unlike governesses, who were almost always downwardly mobile and professionally trained genteel women, nannies occupied a complex position in the household; expected to be docile servants, yet love the children, able to wield limited power over their charges, yet remain obedient to their employer, who represents bourgeois power that they may simultaneously long for and despise.[3] Being among other things 'prim, spick and span', Mendelsohn sees Poppins as a 'classic caricature' of the upwardly mobile woman, whose roots lie in the tidy respectability of working-class life.

Other critical readings of the Disney version of *Mary Poppins* (which Travers so despised) have suggested that we often misremember the main message of the film: in Caitlyn Flanagan's words, "fire the nanny!" (Flanagan, 2005: 3). Disney's Poppins, as Flanagan reminds us, never intends to work permanently for the Banks family: indeed her principal aim is to transform Mr and Mrs Banks themselves and, in doing so, make herself superfluous. The initially distant and sullen Mr Banks, under Poppins' benevolent intervention, becomes an affectionate and engaged playmate father, while suffragette activist Mrs Banks abandons her feminist work at the film's finale and uses her 'Votes for Women' sash to make a tail for the children's kite. Walt Disney knew that employing a full-time servant to raise one's children would make no sense to an American audience in the 1960s, so it was necessary to invent a need for Poppins to enter the Banks' household. The Banks family (at least in Disney's rewrite) must be presented as dysfunctional – a father who is physically present but emotionally absent and a mother who has lost sight of her maternal vocations. As Flanagan expounds, memories of the *Mary Poppins* film would come to actively shape the nanny culture of the latter half of the 20th century, fuelled by the global movement of cheap female immigrant labour and by the incommensurable demands of parenting and paid employment. Poppins is therefore a curious figure with a complex life; a vehicle for Travers to rewrite her own unhappy Australian childhood in an imaginary version of London, reinvented by Disney as part of his advocacy for family life to be traditional, nuclear and conformist, serving as an anchor for 'nanny culture' throughout the 20th century, and reinvented again for reality television by the *Supernanny* format.

Through reviving these cultural histories of the nanny – which are so intimately bound to the character of Mary Poppins – the *Supernanny* television series glimpses a number of distinct, but connected, periods of family life, parenting pedagogy, crisis and childcare cultures and practices. *Supernanny* invokes the emotional politics of servant culture, with its congealed layers of longing, dislike, disdain and obedience and the contracts and techniques of control that held the rules of domestic service in place (for an astonishing intellectual history of servant culture, see Steedman, 2009). *Supernanny* also playfully echoes the servant status of the Edwardian nanny. Visually, the nod to Poppins is clear – Frost appears immaculately turned out in a tailored suit, an overnight bag and an umbrella. Like Poppins, Frost will 'stay until the wind changes' – each *Supernanny* episode filmed over a period of two weeks – her visit is finite and functional. In some episodes, Frost appears to delight in creating a Poppins-like magic for children, weaving extensive illusions and inventing fables such as the 'Nappy Pirates' and the 'Dummy Fairy'.

Perhaps the sharpest nods to Poppins, to servitude and domestic hierarchy, and to ideas of Britishness, form around notions of 'good manners' and in training children to follow rules of civility and being socially appropriate. This was echoed in television parent pedagogy that sought to capitalise on the success of *Supernanny*. In the US, for example, *Nanny 911* (Fox, 2004–2007, CMT 2007–present, United States) featured several nannies, a head nanny and even a butler as childrearing experts, all in full Edwardian period dress, who promised not only to deal with temper tantrums, but also to teach 'social etiquette'. Frost herself acknowledged the significance of her Britishness, when beginning filming for the American version of *Supernanny*:

> What I did notice is that the Americans have a very high regard for the British nanny, and the standards and the etiquette that we have. That's very much respected over there, added to which, of course, they love the accent. (Calhoun, 2005)

But where the fictional Poppins always acquiesced to the servant hierarchy she belongs to and deferred compliantly to her employers, effecting changes in the Banks' family through subterfuge and trickery (and, of course, magic), Frost boldly criticises parents and lists their failures in often-excruciating scenes. The camera lingers on reaction shots of parents' faces, frequently on their tears of shame (the 'money shot' of reality television – see Grindstaff, 2002). These scenes are often disturbing and painful to watch, and have generated a range of public, media and academic responses, which have criticised Frost as bossy, incendiary and punitive. When the *Supernanny* format was first exported to Australia, anthropologist Stephen Juan described Jo Frost the Supernanny as a 'devil version of Mary Poppins', stating that:

It is the outmoded view of the controlling parent. It is so
destructive psychologically. It seems to be so anti-children.
It puts the needs of parents first ... This show is about
taming rather than understanding. You will not be the
helping parent. You will be the controlling parent and
when the child gets older they can't be controlled any more.
(Quoted by Edwards, 2005)

This evaluation of the *Supernanny* as oppressive, dominating and
over-controlling repeats across multiple accounts of the programme.
Juan's criticisms cast the 'good parent' as one who seeks to understand,
to express empathy and patience, and to develop children's sense
of self. These interpretations resonate with how childcare practices
become inscribed with the meanings of class, and how working-
class women become pathologised as repressive and insensitive to
children's needs (Walkerdine and Lucey, 1989). As we will see in the
subsequent sections, Frost's very 'working-classness' is a central pillar
in these interpretations. Many reviews of the programme gleefully
sexualised Frost and highlighted the 'dominatrix' stylings of *Supernanny*
(MacDonald, 2004), one journalist suggesting in his interview with
Frost that her trademark 'naughty step' must indicate her 'fetish for
punishment' (Duerden, 2007). The parallels, real and imagined, between
Supernanny's child-training techniques and the puppy-training methods
used in reality television canine equivalents, such as *It's Me or The Dog*
(2005-08), have been extensively documented by journalists reviewing
the programme (English, 2006; Atkins, 2009). Some academics have
described Frost's techniques as 'threatening' and involving a 'submission
element' (Hendrick, 2016). Additionally, the expertise offered up by Jo
Frost has been challenged in public commentaries and reviews of the
programme, precisely because she has not acquired it through being
a parent herself. Through the broadcast years of *Supernanny*, Frost
was unfailingly interrogated by journalists about 'when' she planned
to have children. In a 2013 *Daily Mail* profile of Frost, her child-free
life and her child expertise are presented as a 'central irony of her life'
(Das, 2013) and a *Mirror* profile the following year described the 'loud
ticking' of her 'biological clock' (Pietras, 2014). In my own research,
I found that while watching *Supernanny*, parents frequently sought to
contain Frost by making reference to her 'childlessness', thus casting
doubt on the source of her expertise (Jensen, 2010).

This ambivalent treatment of Jo Frost, and of the programme, by
journalists certainly forms one pillar in the classificatory processes
of value and worth at the heart of parent pedagogy. Such media and

cultural commentary provide cues for parents seeking to dismiss or hold Frost and her programme at a safe distance, by casting her and her techniques as inappropriate, 'unscientific', disturbing or threatening to children. The transformation of parent-blame into primtetime entertainment initiated a complex set of readings and responses. How, then, did parents themselves interpret and make sense of the often disturbing and painful television content of *Supernanny*?

Standing up to (and sitting down with) *Supernanny*

> The first time I ever watched the hit UK TV series *Supernanny*, I spent the entire hour shouting at the TV. Who did this woman think she was, barging into complete strangers' lives, bossing them around, patronising them, talking about them behind their backs to an audience of millions? And who were these people, who asked this woman into their homes, presented themselves for verbal castration, and embraced the humiliation of exposing the chaos of their private space? ... The second time I watched *Supernanny*, I cried. ... What upset me the most was that this time, I felt I understood its appeal. Who invited Supernanny home? We did. Why? Because we feel so inadequate as parents. (Bristow, 2009: 11)

In her book *Standing Up to Supernanny*, Bristow (2009) captures the generalised and intensive anxiety that is incubated in the cultural economy of parent-blame, reflecting on her own complex experiences of watching *Supernanny* and of moving between feeling enraged, humiliated and indignant. Parenting culture has undermined parents' confidence in their own abilities, while simultaneously holding them responsible for every aspect of their child's futurity; in Bristow's words, it 'sets expectations that are both unreasonably high, and insultingly low' (2009: 17). Bristow's book is a bracing and fortifying tonic in a wider climate of parent-blame. But what it leaves perhaps less interrogated is how encounters with parent pedagogy *themselves* work as mechanisms of classification. We have already seen some of the complicated responses to the programme. When we encounter *Supernanny* and feel angry or inadequate, what kind of productive classificatory *work* do these emotions do? How do evaluations and assessments of *Supernanny* by *Supernanny* viewers – the interpretive work of engaging with media culture and representations that we are all, always, engaged in – enable such viewers to place themselves in a moral economy of parenting?

Indeed, Bristow's very invitation to 'stand up to *Supernanny*' (the title of her book) is itself a classificatory position that operates through (for example) rejecting the *Supernanny* behaviourist pedagogy, disavowing mass media entertainments, or taking a critical position against reality television.

In empirical audience research with *Supernanny* viewers (Jensen, 2010), I wanted to better understand the moral economies that circulate through parent pedagogy and the part they play in authoring parental subjects. This research attended to textual encounters and used the illuminating 'text-in-action' method, developed by Helen Wood (see Wood, 2009), to explore how audiences 'talk back to' (and talk with and talk over) television. This method helps to open up the ambivalence and pleasures of television and to map the multiple responses audiences have when they react to media in all its spectacular and incendiary pleasures. Mapping audience reactions to *Supernanny* also enabled me to complicate the somewhat dry media survey data produced around parenting television (for example, Ipsos-Mori, 2006), which polled viewer preferences. Although this survey data was enthusiastically embraced by politicians seeking to legitimate national parenting initiatives, it could not illuminate the troubled and anxious layers of parent-blame in television pedagogy, nor the incredibly rich and complex moments of viewing that have been illuminated by qualitative media research, particularly that informed by critical feminist traditions (see Skeggs and Wood, 2012; Wheatley, 2016; Moseley et al, 2016).

When we pay attention to how parents encounter parent pedagogy, we can start to track how class is made, signalled through moral euphemism and produced through the work of interpretation and association, in conversation with representations of good and bad parenting. Parental encounters with parent pedagogy television are not rational, cognitive events. They are bodily, emotional and affective. The parents who participated in this research laughed and gasped with the horror of recognition; they moaned, groaned and sighed in sympathy with the spectacle of weeping parents; they tutted, rolled their eyes and shook their heads in disbelief at the conduct of the families on the television screen. They talked over the voiceover, refuted the explanations presented and offered their own analysis to me, shouted at the Supernanny; and at crucial moments, fell silent, clasped hands to mouths and covered their eyes. Some became angry with the boldness of Jo Frost's parental critique, others challenged the legitimacy of her authority, and others spoke quietly of the burning shame of recognition. These were complex and at times painful encounters with a cultural economy of parent-blame that could only be partly dismissed, made safe and held at a distance. Watching *Supernanny* – and indeed interacting with all kinds of parent pedagogy – creates complex investments, identifications and loyalties. To understand these, we need to draw on methods of 'damp sociology' (Munt, 2007) that are attuned to the affective dimensions of cultural life.

I interviewed parents, alone and in peer groups that they assembled, about their parenting lives and their connections and engagements with parenting pedagogy. I used Wood's (2009) text-in-action method; watching, recording and analysing their encounters with an episode of *Supernanny*, followed by reflective discussions. This combination of methods enabled me to map the ambivalence around parent pedagogy and parent-blame, and to explore the affective movements of (dis)identification with figures on the screen. The rich texture of the viewing encounters complicated – and often contradicted – the diplomatic and considered narratives of expert-led parenting that participants offered during interview. Parents sought to erect reassuring barriers between themselves and the parents on the screen, and between themselves and 'other' *Supernanny* viewers. At crucial moments in the episode, they acknowledged the permeability of these imagined barriers. They spoke of feeling insulted by the advice offered, and of identifying with the unreasonable demands placed upon the *Supernanny* families. They articulated their discomfort with the scrutinising gaze of Jo Frost and found ways to dismiss her.

These encounters with *Supernanny*, in short, were crucial sites, in which social class was made. In the following section, I summarise some of the ways in which class circulates and becomes animated through cultural values, premised on morality, judgement, evaluation and the production and exchange of value (for a fuller account, see Jensen, 2010 and Jensen, 2012).[4]

Distinction through parent pedagogy

We have already tracked some of the debates that have been staged, recycled and reinvented between different parenting experts. Sifting through, weighing up and assessing advice and making evaluative comparisons between different bodies of parent pedagogy are part of the work of 'intensive parenting' as explored by Sharon Hays (1996) in her seminal book *The Cultural Contradictions of Motherhood*. What parenting orthodoxy will you follow: what *kind* of parent will you aspire to be? Parenting culture studies (Ellie et al, 2014) have conceived of these obligations to choose between parenting 'styles' and orthodoxies as part of the generalisation of risk, uncertainty and paranoia about social life. Key studies have conceived of the process of attaching oneself to categories or styles of parenting as part of identity work, for example mothers describing themselves as 'attachment parents' or 'lactivists' (Faircloth, 2013), as 'Tiger mothers' (Chua, 2011) or as 'free-range parents' (Skenazy, 2009). But what has been less developed in these accounts is how parenting culture works as part of the culturalisation of class, and how class is increasingly 'spoken' through culture; through practices, values and morality. Bev Skeggs (2004) has powerfully articulated how culture has become a form of property invested in the (middle-class) self, and shows how central culture is to increasing one's volume and composition of capitals and thus one's overall exchange value. Parenting culture matters because it is a central vector in the distribution, accumulation and consolidation of value. In evaluating and selecting parenting styles, orthodoxies and pedagogies, parents are choosing a repertoire of the self and producing themselves as classed subjects.

We can see these processes of class formation at work in encounters with *Supernanny*. Both in interview and during viewing sessions for this research, parents constructed a cultural hierarchy of parenting advice, within which *Supernanny* was ambivalently cast. Although all but two of the participating parents had watched *Supernanny* before, several consciously accounted for this viewing as accidental and casual in almost identical phrases:

> 'We only watch it when it's on ... we've never done that purposively, just sort of stumbled across it.' (Helen, interview)

> 'I don't make a *point* of watching it. Just if it's on and I happen to catch it.' (Louisa, interview)

> 'I haven't watched it *religiously* ... just when it's on and I catch it.' (Clara, interview)

These remarks were complicated somewhat by the subsequent viewing sessions, where parents seemed highly engaged and familiar with the scripts of the programme, offering predictions and providing ironic commentary. These evasions about viewing are strategies for holding the format at a critical distance. They also echo classed ambivalences about watching television in general (Silverstone, 1994; Skeggs et al, 2008) *and* produce distinctions with other imagined audiences – the parents who 'need' *Supernanny* and are considered to be the 'real' audience. The participants in this research displayed their critical skills, by drawing attention to the artifice of the programme at key moments, demonstrating that they were 'savvy' about television production and editing processes and could participate in its pleasures without succumbing to its illusions (Andrejevic, 2004; Couldry, 2010; for a closer analysis of these moments, see Jensen, 2013).

By making unfavourable comparisons between *Supernanny* and other preferred examples of television parent pedagogy, parents were able to productively mark out and display their cultural knowledge and, in doing so, confer, or withhold, legitimacy. Parents accessed a range of cultural resources to display their understanding of parenting debates. They demonstrated an ease and familiarity with existing critiques of *Supernanny*, drawing on their knowledge of other models of parenting expertise and public commentary about Frost, and referring to other television programmes about children and parenting, to appraise and 'review' the episode as we watched:

> 'We've watched some of the Professor Winston one. Er, was it *Child of Our Time*? He's less sort of … prescriptive. And dictatorial.' (Phillip)

> 'There's some reality television that I love … I just feel that there's some integrity about them. I'm sure *Child of Our Time* doesn't have such a big audience. They're not being made just for entertainment. It's done with so much more integrity, it just has a much more positive view of children and their parents.' (Amy)

These comments are not just about viewer preferences; they also represent opportunities for social distinction around what kinds of programmes you watch and enjoy, and what those choices say about the kind of person (and parent) you are. Although there were many ambivalent or hesitant accounts of whether and how often they watched *Supernanny*, often littered with provisos, these parents found it easier to profess their love and loyalty of other parenting programmes, which were described in comparatively glowing terms. Not all reality television or parenting television was deemed problematic; indeed, Amy's comments about the smaller audience commanded by more 'highbrow' programmes such as *Child of Our Time* reproduces hierarchies of cultural value, between mass entertainment and more exclusive forms. Susan, too, spoke of other parenting programmes 'resonating' with her:

'I related quite a lot to Tanya Byron, and *Little Angels* and all that. I just thought, whatever she was saying, just sort of resonated with me, I thought, yes that sounds right, and I took that on board ... anything with Tanya Byron.' (Susan)

Susan's comments draw on and reproduce a specific juxtaposition in a great deal of parent pedagogy cultural commentary, which contrasts *Supernanny* with more 'highbrow' parenting programmes made by Dr Tanya Byron. Byron's television output on parenting includes *House of Tiny Tearaways* (BBC, 2005-07) and (as Susan mentions) *Little Angels* (BBC, 2004). Several parents named Byron as a counterpoint to Supernanny Jo Frost, and Susan herself referred to Byron repeatedly, drawing comparisons between the two experts in terms of their qualifications and experience. Susan attempts to describe her 'problem' with *Supernanny*, by asking the other mothers in the viewing session 'right, what are her qualifications?' and noting that 'she's not a child psychologist'. Expert knowledge is there to be contested; experts may be 'ordinary' or have acquired their expertise through experience. Ellie Lee (2014) usefully tracks the blurred and complex status of 'parenting expertise' as a marketable commodity. She highlights instances where mothers have restyled themselves as coaches, trainers and educators, extracting from their own parenting experiences and repackaging these experiences as legitimating sources of knowledge. Frost's claims to 'expertise' were a source of contestation; although 'experienced' as a nanny, her childlessness and lack of formal qualifications marked her expert status with suspicion.

Frost's and Byron's television programmes – and the logic that underpins each of their parenting models – are broadly similar. Both emphasise the importance of consistency, of employing 'age-appropriate' sanctions and of rewarding 'good' behaviour with warmth and praise. While their respective programmes are styled, packaged and promoted differently, received and reviewed differently in the media, both nonetheless use therapeutic and confessional narratives to organise episodes, employ similar behavioural strategies and are similarly paced in terms of editing. The same issues of voyeurism, children's consent and vulnerability and the problematic transforming of 'dysfunction' into 'entertainment' might be levelled equally at the television programmes that both Frost and Byron front. Yet they have been repeatedly constructed as being 'in opposition' across cultural commentary, in ways that illuminate the crucial significance of class in the cultural economy of parent pedagogy.

These class formations are perhaps best exemplified in two separate interviews conducted by journalist Decca Aitkenhead and published in the *Guardian* – one with Frost in 2006 and one with Byron in 2007. When read concurrently, Aitkenhead's interviews document (respectively) a remarkable contempt for and obsequious compliance with the machinery of parent-blame. Her hostile and vilifying interview with Frost in 2006 illuminates the ambivalence with which *Supernanny* was received in some quarters, and details a profound classed contempt towards Frost as a working-class woman. Aitkenhead constructs an account of parenting advice that is curiously static, and positions *Supernanny* as a sensationalist departure from established 'consensus'. Our historical alarm bells should be ringing! Frost herself is described as an 'unqualified nanny', who has 'never trained formally' and as being at odds with the 'science' of childrearing that Aitkenhead has diligently revised; as she remarks, 'she has never read – or even heard of – any of the leading theorists I mention'. Even more disconcerting than Aitkenhead's inaccurate portrait of harmonious 'parenting science' is her painstaking documentation of every instance of Frost's verbal tics and mispronounciations:

> "But I am," she says indignantly. "I am [curious about why children misbehave]. It goes without saying. I don't just want to know on the surface why. I need to know and find out exactly where the root of that lies. So in retrospective [sic] of that I do that mandatorially [sic] within the families" … "Nothing is ever set up or derived [sic]". I think she means contrived. (Aitkenhead, 2006)

The message to be taken from this interview is clear: Frost should be dismissed as uneducated and inarticulate, a 'parenting expert' whose expertise is illegitimate, a chancing grifter of no value to parents seeking 'science'. The contempt with which Aitkenhead portrays Frost is thrown into sharp relief, when compared with the interview she conducted the following year with Byron. The similarities between *Supernanny* and *Little Angels* are symbolically annihilated. Aitkenhead introduces Byron as 'the respectable face of parenting television' and sketches a fawning portrait of a 'calmly authoritative', 'compelling' and 'thoughtful' clinician, 'brilliant in her field', a 'polymath' who has combined education, professional success and domestic respectability:

> At 38, her CV is a paean to alpha-female achievement, with a doctorate in clinical psychology and her first child

at 27. She has been with her actor husband Bruce, DC Terry Perkins in The Bill, since she was 21, and they live with their two kids in a rambling north London house, which she shows me round with an unaffected charm. (Aitkenhead, 2007)

Byron herself withdrew from parenting television in 2007, making oblique comments about how it had become too 'well-marketed', had begun to 'go too far' and making reference to other 'experts' in suspicious quote marks. She implicitly referenced Frost's most infamous *Supernanny* technique, stating that she was 'not a fan of naughty steps' (see Mumsnet, 2007). Her co-clinician on *Little Angels* (BBC Three, 2004), Stephen Briers, repeated this in his book *Superpowers for Parents* (2008), promising that 'you won't find any naughty steps here'. These hierarchies of parenting science, pedagogy and educated professionalism were enthusiastically circulated by parents in viewing sessions. Several parents echoed Frost's infamous mispronounication of 'unacceptable' ('unasseptable') with delight, and spoke with contempt and irritation of her perceived 'bossiness', her lack of formal qualifications, her childlessness.

In these evaluations and dismissals, parents were engaged in complicated reflexive work, through which they sought to produce themselves as subjects of value in a parent pedagogy landscape that created layers of surveillance and blame. They sought to create a critical distance between their own parenting lives and the intrusions of *Supernanny*, by distinguishing themselves as critical and cautious viewers, who were quite separate from the 'real' audience, and by situating this programme at the bottom of a hierarchy of parent pedagogy. They sought critical mastery of *Supernanny*, by comparing and evaluating its advice alongside other celebrity-pedagogues, whose advice was considered more valuable, highbrow or qualified. As such, these encounters with parenting culture serve as potent symbolic spaces for the pursuit of social distinction (Bourdieu, 1979); these parent-blame audiences were engaged in processes of class-*making*.

We will turn now to the wider political climate, which also licensed a retreat from thinking about the material and lived effects of social class and inequality on families. In particular, longstanding concerns about structures of disadvantage were replaced with 'cultural' concerns about the behaviour and conduct of individual families.

New Labour's civilising project

The cultural industry of parent-blame hit its peak at the mid-point of New Labour's political tenure. After 18 years in opposition, the Labour Party (now rebranded 'New Labour') won the 1997 General Election with a parliamentary landslide, taking an additional 145 constituency seats with the biggest election 'swing' since 1945. Under the premiership of Tony Blair, New Labour made a commitment to eradicate child poverty, and positioned children and families at the centre of a complex set of policies which mobilised several government departments and ministries. On 18 March 1999, Blair delivered the Beveridge Lecture in Bristol, where he laid out New Labour's vision for welfare reform and where he pledged to end child poverty within 20 years, stating that: 'we have made children our top priority because … they are twenty percent of the population but they are one hundred percent of the future' (Blair, 1999).

During Blair's first term in office, New Labour brought in a range of initiatives oriented towards this goal, including the National Child Care Strategy (1998), the Children's Fund (2000) and the Children's and Young People's Unit (2000). During Blair's second term, New Labour launched *Every Child Matters* (DfE, 2003), a multi-agency policy initiative, and passed the Children Act 2004. In Blair's third and final term, New Labour dissolved the Department for Education and Skills (DfES) and, in June 2007, the same month that Gordon Brown would succeed Blair as Prime Minister, the newly formed (and, as it would transpire, short-lived) Department for Children, Schools and Families was officially launched. In 2007, *Every Parent Matters* was launched, which outlined 'the vital role of parents in improving their child's life chances' (DfES, 2007). The enthusiasm for targeted government spending on families with young children can be seen in Blair's remarks that, if he had an extra billion pounds to spend, he would spend it on the under-fives (see Parton, 2006).

Across its 13 years of government (1997–2010), New Labour would consistently place parenting at the heart of its project of social renewal. But this project was articulated, at least initially, with some hesitancy and a great many caveats and qualifications. New Labour sought to put distance between its emphasis on parenting and the earlier 'Back to Basics' Conservative campaign of the 1990s, and to distance itself from other New Right moral crusades against unmarried mothers, divorce, queer families and cohabiting couples with dependent children.

In recognition of the (fantasy) status of the institution of 'the family' as autonomous, conservative and private, we can discern a degree of discomfort with making family life such an explicit object of policy intervention. In the foreword to *Every Parent Matters*, the then Education Secretary, Alan Johnson, stated that 'traditionally parenting has been a no-go area for governments' (DfES, 2007), while Blair himself reassured readers of *The Sun* newspaper that 'no-one's talking about interfering in *normal family life*' (Blair, 2006, emphasis added).

The modernisers of New Labour sought to preserve conventional understandings of 'the family' as an autonomous, and sacrosanct, idealised institution. Their ambitious policy project was presented as a necessary and legitimate intervention into the conduct of (some) families, though the question of 'which' families was left deliberately fuzzy. The state has, of course, made constant intrusions into the lives of (some) families, and scholars have documented a long history of state-sponsored surveillance, monitoring and regulation of working-class families, and families claiming (some forms of) welfare (Jones and Novak, 1999; Starkey, 2001; Gillies, 2007; Crossley, 2017). New Labour would (re)classify families into categories of 'normal' – those from whom good parenting could be reassured, whose family life would continue to be 'no-go' and who could continue to enjoy autonomy – and in doing so, would draw new lines of distinction and value. The category of 'normal' would balloon to include some families who had not hitherto been recognised by the state. At the same time, this category of 'normal' would simultaneously contract in older and more familiar ways, to mark and target other families as continuing objects of concern and intervention.

New Labour were positioning themselves as a political party looking to the future and upholding progressive values about who could be considered to constitute 'a family'. Their policy documents at the time of their 1997 election sought to acknowledge a more diverse range of intimate formations, for example by repealing Section 28 of the Local Government Act 1988, which prohibited local authorities from 'promoting homosexuality' or what were termed 'pretended family relationships'. Section 28 was eventually repealed after several thwarted attempts through Parliament, but these parliamentary processes and debates exposed the politicised use of longstanding homophobia that would be strategically employed to pit Lesbian, Gay, Bisexual and Trans citizens against defensive fantasies of 'the family under attack'.[5] In 1998, the Home Office published *Supporting Families*, which set out proposals to tolerate and support a wider range of families than previous governments had done. In the words of the *Supporting Families* document: 'Neither a "back to basics" fundamentalism, trying to turn back the clock, nor an "anything goes" liberalism which denies the fact that how families behave affects us all, is credible anymore' (Home Office, 1998: 5).

The Supporting Families document represents an important shift towards talking about the right way to parent, rather than lecturing on who should be considered a family or what families should look like. In Rethinking Families, Fiona Williams (2004) details the ways that New Labour began to increasingly address parents rather than spouses – mothers and fathers, not husbands and wives – and how through this parental address, they staked their interest in the quality of parenting. As Williams states, 'parenthood began to be seen as something parents do rather than something they are' (2004: 31, emphasis in original).

While New Labour articulated its 'moral tolerance' towards the diversity of family forms, and increasing numbers of lone parents, step-parents, queer families and so on, this articulation nevertheless occurs alongside an alleged 'parenting deficit', decline in family values and concerns about the impact of absent fathers (Barlow et al, 2002). As Ben-Galim and Gambles (2008) point out, such 'moral tolerance' and *acknowledgement* of diversity operate alongside wider concern about *some* families, a continued (but muted) privileging of marriage, and a revival of debate about civic accountability and responsibility. As they remark, diversity is considered 'fine', but marriage is still considered 'best'.

In shifting the terms of discussion from family form to parental capacity, from 'being' to 'doing', New Labour began to vacate the centre-Left ground of policy debate – which focused on the ways that structures of inequality impact differently upon families positioned by class, race, geography, immigration status, and so on – and moved towards a much more atomised understanding of inequality, aimed at 'upskilling' individual families suffering from an alleged 'parenting deficit'. By intervening in such families, New Labour aimed to close the achievement gap between the children of the wealthiest and the poorest. Thus, New Labour philosophy locates social renewal tomorrow within early years interventions today.

Significantly, the 'parenting deficit' was considered by New Labour to have been caused, at least in part, *by* parenting diversity. Wider social transformations within the family – the rise of mothers working outside the home, the geographical mobility of the aspirational nuclear family and the breakdown of extended family and communities – became for New Labour the very reasons why Britain needs a programme of parental 'upskilling'.

Indeed, New Labour drew extensively on communitarian philosophy through the years of party renewal in the 1990s, particularly the work of Amitai Etzioni (1995), for whom the family, located within the local neighbourhood, is the significant force for social renewal (see Bevir, 2005). Etzioni considers the modern family to be newly unshackled from community ties that used to guarantee social order and morality. Families increasingly live in isolation from older generations and the extended family, as well as from their communities (seen through the decline of religious affiliation and community group membership). Communitarian philosophy frames the crisis as one of the 'indulged child', unmoored from their communities and morally directionless under the charge of permissive parents. Parents thus need more advice and more interventions by this logic, because they are isolated from *their* parents, the grandparents who would have taught the parenting skills to the next generation of childrearers. Such a 'parenting deficit' must therefore be compensated for, through civil re-education in matters of social morality and responsibility, assisted by parenting experts and parenting practitioners rather than grandparents and neighbours.

As Clarke and Newman (2004) suggest, this policy shift towards civil re-education demonstrates how New Labour's 'social renewal' project was marked by a 'thin multiculturalism'. Clarke and Newman argue that rather than engaging meaningfully with family diversity, New Labour required all families to perform in standardised ways, in order to satisfy 'responsibility tests', which framed citizen 'rights' as contingent upon commitments to be 'responsible'. This 'rights and responsibilities' framework ostensibly recognises diverse family forms, yet in practice it continues to create contradictions for families who do not satisfy a nuclear, financially autonomous, two-parent ideal. Duncan and Edwards (1999) highlight how lone parents, for example, are faced with an impossible tension between being financially autonomous workers and being 'present' for their children. As they rightly ask, which 'responsibility' should take precedence here?

Such civil re-education projects also rehearse and reproduce a gendered politics around the family. It is principally mothers who have usually been held morally responsible for generating future citizens and reproducing the nation, in ways that fathers are not. Concerns over the moral purity of women, and thus of the nation, have historically been inextricably bound up with concerns around the moral deficiency of the lower classes. Mothers are thus constituted as being central to the moral and civil health of the nation. The present vision of 'good parenting' has important roots in older discursive formations that established formal interventions into the family practices of working-class women and mothers. As Bev Skeggs (1997) demonstrates in her historical examination of the 19th- and 20th-century familial social policies:

> The concerns about the potentially polluting and dangerous working class were seen to be resolvable if mothers were educated to civilize, that is, to control and discipline themselves and their husbands and sons who were likely to be the cause of anticipated problems. It is part of a process in which the mother acts as an invisible pedagogue. (Skeggs, 1997: 43)

Despite its preference for talking about 'parenting' rather than 'mothering', New Labour's civil re-education project continued to obliquely address mothers. Although 'tolerating' diversity, New Labour's *Supporting Families* policy direction continued to interpret official statistics on key trends in living arrangements as a distressing indication of societal and moral decline (Chambers, 2000). Single-parent families remained a 'social problem'; Home Secretary Jack Straw described family stability as 'the single most effective crime prevention strategy available to the government' (*The Observer*, 25 October, 1999). Such 'tolerations' under 'thin multiculturalism' enabled New Labour to preach its commitment to diversity, even as in practice it positioned such diversity as the cause of parenting deficit. Under the guise of 'supporting families', New Labour initiated a process of 'recovering, revamping and reasserting' (Chambers, 2001) a vision of 'the family' that constituted 'parenting' as a set of hundreds of universal skills that can be taught – indeed that *must* be taught – in order for social renewal to happen.

It was into this policy context of thin multiculturalism, parenting deficit and parental 'upskilling' that Channel 4's *Supernanny* was first broadcast. The political context of New Labour's 'parent support' resonates clearly with the project of parent training offered in reality television at this time. A new 'commonsense' around families was consolidating across media and policy, which held that children's successes and failures were not caused by entrenched systems of inequality, but because their own parents were failing to prepare them for the world and failing to to instill the lessons of liberal citizenship, responsibility, aspiration and resilience. This commonsense imagined a crisis stretching out to future generations, reanimating a eugenic anxiety, whereby ineffectively parented children were presumed to be destined to reproduce inadequacies in their own children. The solution was for a kind of re-schooling, training parents in habit, conduct and behaviours *and* schooling children to obey, to be compliant and to be routinised.

The machinery of parent-blame was enthusiastically drawn upon by education representatives, who sought to explain educational inequalities through a framework of individual family deficit. In 2006, Lynn Edwards of the Professional Association of Teachers called for compulsory *parenting* classes for all 14- to 16-year-old children, which would include instruction around manners, road safety and what constitutes 'acceptable' behaviour (Smith, 2006). Mary Bousted, the General Secretary of the Association of Teachers and Lecturers, complained that parents were 'buying off' their children with consumer items and failing to instill discipline, routine and respect in them. In a newspaper article that she penned for *The Guardian*, Bousted wrote:

> Too many children start school without the social and verbal skills to be able to take part in lessons and to behave well. Too many are starting school unable to hold a knife and fork, unused to eating at a table, unable to use the lavatory properly. These children will not be living in absolute poverty. The majority will be living in homes with televisions, computers and PlayStations. What too many of them do not have are adults who are prepared to give their time and energy doing that difficult, but most essential of jobs: raising their children properly. (Bousted, 2009)

In 2014, Michael Wilshaw, head of Ofsted, went further and called on the government to grant headteachers the authority to impose financial penalties on parents they considered to be 'bad parents'. In an interview with *The Times*, he suggested that bad parents might be 'tracked' (and consequently fined) by recording non-submission of homework or non-attendance of parents' evenings; or even by tracking which parents do not read to their children. He stated that poverty should not be used as an excuse for failure:

> I would tell them they are bad parents ... I think headteachers should have the power to fine them. It's sending the message that you are responsible for your children no matter how poor you are ... If they love their children they should support them in schools. (Hurst, et al, 2014)

there was an appetite and an audience for these discourses of individual parenting deficit. In seeking to 'explain' different forms and degrees of engagement with education as evidence that some parents are not 'responsible', not willing to do the work of childrearing, or even not 'loving' their children enough, these comments document (and reproduce) a set of *classed* assumptions about what 'good parenting' looks like. These comments remark on the (assumed) presence of objects like televisions and computers in the family home; in so doing, they anticipate and ultimately reject, the 'excuse' of poverty ('how can they be poor when they have these things').

Public statements like these display a lack of understanding and curiosity about the logics of social class and how these logics shape dominant discourses of worth that some families are able to conform to and others are not. Why might some parents appear more engaged with the education system than others, be more likely to attend school events like parents' evenings and participate in homework activities and management of other curricular and extra-curricular activities? These forms of engagement are assumed to be neutral signs of 'good parenting', yet they are profoundly classed – and classing. School institutions hold different meanings for different families; some parents might seek to extract themselves from its surveillant systems, as a result of being marked and stigmatised as having been 'deficient' while at school themselves (Gillies, 2005).

Engaging with the education system in these ways not only requires resources – enough free time, for example, to be able to attend school events – but also presumes a particular cultural logic to childrearing. In *Unequal Childhoods*, Annette Laureau (2003) detailed the 'concerted cultivation' methods that middle-class parents used to raise their children and the synergies that this approach holds with the middle-class professionals of their school life. Not only were these parents able to comply with the demands of teachers, but they were also oriented towards education as an opportunity to consolidate class advantages. The cultural logic that underpinned their parenting, importantly, was recognised as legitimate by teachers; it had an institutional 'pay-off', through which they were validated as 'good parents' and others were cast as 'bad'.

The new vocabularies of meritocracy and aspiration that formed the backbone of the New Labour project licensed this retreat of interest from class systems of inequality. New Labour's 'thin multiculturalism' suspended rosy nostalgia for a 'golden age' of family (Coontz, 1992) in favour of a more pragmatic civilising project, one which would 'upskill' parents understood to be 'in deficit'. The allusions to failures, responsibility and moral discipline were accompanied by a broader consensus-making in policy and culture that there were 'bad parents' who could learn to become 'good parents' and, in doing so, realise the fantasy of a perfect meritocracy, a 'classless' Britain. The political vision of parent training, as set out by New Labour at the turn of the 21st century, was accompanied by a period of massive investment in what Sharon Gewirtz (2001) termed a 're-socialisation and re-education programme'. This aimed to eradicate class differences, by transforming working-class parents into middle-class ones, or at least transplanting middle-class habits to all parents. Importantly, these class differences were not anchored in a context of inequality, but rather were framed as differences of 'culture', behaviour and attitude – and therefore as capable of being remedied and corrected.

The production of a 'parenting crisis' across media culture provides figures of 'bad parenting', whom viewers can hold at a distance from themselves, and offers up celebrity-experts who provoke, irritate, are assessed and refused, or admired and applauded. The cultural industry of parent-blame that emerged alongside New Labour's civilising project sought to provide a spectacular vision of parental failure that individualised the struggles of family life. This industry constructs children as monstrous, demanding, insistent, uncontrollable, ungovernable and their parents as weak, resigned and ineffectual, thus licensing the proliferation of an extensive apparatus of popular pedagogy. Far from being a 'classless' activity, this populist parent pedagogy served as a crucial site for the reproduction of class difference. The cultural industry of parent-blame was very much a constitutive space, where parental subjectivities and identities are formed. Indeed, by failing to account for the foundational contexts of inequality in which parenting (and indeed all forms of social life and activity) are done, this cultural industry of parent-blame contributed to broader disinvestments in the vocabularies of social class and classificatory processes.

Importantly, the cultural industry of parent-blame 'prepared the ground' for the supplanting of a supportive welfare state with a punitive neoliberal state. The 'parenting crisis' constructed in British culture and policy as the 21st century loomed intensified through the 1990s, and authorised a new kind of statecraft that intervened in family life with more boldness in the early 2000s. The New Labour government oversaw a frenzy of policy initiatives, which centred on the conduct of parents and precipitated a new scrutiny of parent practices, to which we will now turn in Chapter Four.

Notes

[1]   *Supernanny* has been exported to at least two dozen countries, though some media profiles with Jo Frost put the figure at nearer to 50 countries, most often under the title *Supernanny* but occasionally under a variation or regional colloquialism, for example: *Les Nanny* in France; *S.O.S. Tata* in Italy; and *Mission Familie* in Germany. In addition to formal exports and franchises, many more formats have been produced that have taken inspiration from the original UK series.

[2]   Another fictional troubleshooting magical nanny that deserves a mention is Nanny McPhee, the central character of the films *Nanny McPhee* (2005) and *Nanny McPhee and the Big Bang* (2010). The films were set in, respectively, Victorian England and World War Two-era England, and construct deeply sentimentalised and bucolic versions of a rural idyll. The films were adapted from the *Nurse Matilda* books (written by Christianna Brand) by Emma Thompson, who also played McPhee in both films. Thompson's reputation (and 'Britishness') has been built over a lifetime of playing characters with restraint and dignity, often in 'heritage' settings. An interesting side note is that Thompson, as well as adapting books about nannies into screenplays (and playing the nanny herself), would also play the part of an author who wrote books about nannies, playing the role of P.L. Travers (author of the Mary Poppins books) in *Saving Mr Banks* (2013).

[3]   Nannies have always been part of the care economy, alongside other arrangements, but their intimate proximity and unmonitored sovereignty can also make them figures of anxiety and distrust. Sales of 'nanny-cam' surveillance spiked after the high-profile case of Louise Woodward, a British nanny found guilt of manslaughter of a young boy left in her care in Boston, United States, in 1998. In the same year, shock-documentary *Nannies From Hell* (1998, directed by Jessica Fowle) used incriminating hidden-camera footage, alongside interviews with regretful mothers (see Palmer, 2003), which successfully played on uncertainties about trustworthy childcare. But perhaps the truly extensive cultural life of the nanny unfolds in the genre of horror. Psychodrama film *The Hand That Rocks the Cradle* (1992) charted the growing influence of the softly spoken, villainous nanny Peyton Mott on the intimate life of her employers, the Bartel family. Mott slowly but chillingly ramps up her nanny sabotage, subtly undermining the authority of Mrs Bartel, secretly breastfeeding the Bartel's new baby, attempting to seduce Mr Bartel and murdering their closest family friend. The figure of the psychopathic nanny has been (less impressively) revisited in a range of low-budget and made-for-television films, including *While the Children Sleep* (2007) and *The Nightmare Nanny* (2013). There is a long cinematic history of women desexualised by their entry to motherhood and usurped by a young, sexually attractive woman originally hired as an au pair or babysitter, often showing little inventiveness around either plot or title; see, for example, *The Babysitter* (1969), *The Babysitter* (1980), *The Babysitter* (1995) and *The Babysitters* (2007). What set *The Hand That Rocks the Cradle* apart was the confidence with which it exploited multiple fears and anxieties about nannies and other forms of childcare provision. The parental fear that nannies will neglect or mistreat the children left in their care is overshadowed at key moments by a more significant seam of anxiety: that children will actually *prefer* the company of their nanny to their parents; that nannies will learn about and expose parental failures; and that they will be more effective, more authoritative and more emotionally nourishing at the work of parenting than parents themselves.

⁴   This research was conducted between 2006 and 2008. The full thesis is available via the British Library repository.

⁵   Most infamously, in 2000 David Cameron (at the time a Conservative party member) attacked the Labour party in a letter to the *Daily Telegraph*, accusing Tony Blair of being 'anti-family' for wanting to repeal Section 28. The following year, he was elected as MP for Witney and continued to campaign for the retention of the clause and voted against its repeal in 2003. By the time he had been elected Conservative leader in 2006, however, Cameron had apparently changed his mind and he began to court the pink vote (and the pink pound), by endorsing first civil partnerships and then equal marriage rights for LGBT people. Crucially, he framed this not as primarily an issue of equality, but rather as an issue of commitment, telling his party conference in 2011 that: "I don't support gay marriage despite being a Conservative. I support gay marriage because I am a Conservative … society is stronger when we make vows to each other". The 'pinkwashing' of the Conservative party was complete by 2016, when Cameron was controversially named 'Ally of the Year' by PinkNews.

FOUR

Parenting – with feeling

In 2007, the global humanitarian organisation UNICEF ranked the happiness and wellbeing of children across 21 countries in the developed world. UNICEF gathered and compared data on multiple dimensions of children's lives and experiences, such as how likely they were to suffer poverty and deprivation in the UK, the quality of their relationships with parents, and their exposure to risks such as alcohol, drugs and unsafe sex. Using this data, UNICEF placed the United Kingdom at the bottom of its ranks, along with the United States (UNICEF, 2007). Britain was 'officially' one of the worst places in the developed world to be a child.

The UNICEF report echoed concerns already raised by the UN Committee on the Rights of the Child (UNCRC), a collection of independent experts responsible for monitoring the implementation of the United Nations Convention on the Rights of the Child since 1991. In 2003, the UNCRC reported its concerns about child welfare and quality of life to the Joint Committee on Human Rights (House of Lords and House of Commons). In their responses to the concerns raised by the UNCRC, the Joint Committee noted that British law and direction of policy was not child-centred (Joint Committee on Human Rights, 2003).

In 2004, the post of Children's Commissioner was created in the UK, with a remit to understand what children and young people think about the issues that affect them and to represent their needs to policy makers. The Children's Commissioner role was established under the Children Act 2004, which sought to repeal and amend a number of existing statutes and, most significantly, to better coordinate government welfare and education services, following high-profile failures in child protection and, most notably, the tragic death of Victoria Climbié.[1]

Safeguarding and protection would become central motifs in the legislative developments that emerged from the Children Act 2004 and the office of the Children's Commissioner, with an emphasis on identifying children 'at risk' and intervening to protect and shield them from negative influences and stressors – particularly if those 'risks' were deemed to be their own parents and families. Val Gillies (2011) notes that despite its intentions to promote 'children's rights and needs', the UK response to the concerns raised by the UNCRC resulted in a preoccupation with 'wellbeing', at the expense of broader structural concerns around material and economic inequalities between families. Urgent issues, including high rates of child poverty, family homelessness and record numbers of children in custody, were supplanted by individualistic and mechanistic ideas of 'family competence', and a renewed appetite to target and govern intimate family life.

Across discussion and consultation documents, such as the flagship Green Paper *Supporting Families* (Home Office, 1998), and think-tank publications such as *Early Intervention: Good parents, great kids, better citizens* (Allen and Duncan Smith, 2008), the 'crisis' was named in moral terms of deficiency, using the language of debt, dependency, addiction and family breakdown. The discourses circulating around the 'dysfunctional base' of British society reproduced a history of concerns with the 'underclass', named variously as social problem families or the social residuum, and explained through cycle of deprivation theories (Welshman, 2013) and considered impervious to the interventions and best efforts of social work (Macnicol, 1987). As Ruth Levitas (2005) notes, the return to such cycle of deprivation theories, as popularised by Keith Joseph and implemented into policy by Thatcher, chimed with New Labour's discursive shifts in political action, away from addressing structural inequalities, towards piecemeal attempts to relieving (but not solving) poverty and addressing 'social exclusion'. This discourse of social exclusion relied on behavioural models of inheritance, which place culture, rather than structure, at the heart of inequality and consider inequality to be caused by individual defects which are transmitted from one generation to the next (Levitas, 2005).

The contestations surrounding these social exclusion debates are inflammatory and deeply moralised. Parent-blame, as we will see, forms a political battleground conducted through the vocabulary of feelings – bad parents designated as such by professionals, through their failure to provide adequate emotional care, to regulate their own feelings or to generate emotional resilience and skills in their children. This chapter attends to the psychological vocabularies that have manifested as the central pillar of neoliberal parenting moralism, and at the expense of sociological vocabularies of class, inequality and structures of disadvantage. It examines the collusion between such individualising and psychologising languages and the reproduction of fantasy 'tough love' parents, who are able to exert the correct (and elusive) combination of attentive nurture and confident discipline.

An 'army of Supernannies'

Government policies that propose to intervene in family life have often resulted in accusations that government is acting like a 'nanny state'. This shorthand has been used to great effect by politicians of all parties, as well as commentators and journalists, to stoke fears around the spectre of paternalism, the curbing of personal freedom and the micro-managing of private life. The idea of private life and autonomy, which should be left outside the 'remit' of state policy, has been been a central pillar in ideas of 'the family' throughout the 20th century (Gillies, 2011) and, indeed, is at the heart of liberal democracy. The idea of 'the birth family', in particular, was seen as having a 'sanctity' (Broadhurst et al, 2010) that should not be interrupted or disturbed.

Jan MacVarish (2014) tracks the aggressive de-validation of 'family privacy' across key New Labour policy documents. Discussion papers on parenting were initially cautious. The introduction to *Supporting Parents* (discussed in the previous chapter), for example, began with a reassurance that 'no-one wants to be preached at – particularly by politicians' (Home Office, 1998), and Home Secretary Jack Straw spoke of his 'great trepidation' at raising the issue of parenting at all (quoted in MacVarish, 2014: 96).

This early hesitancy soon evaporated, as private family life became reconstructed as *in itself* an object of concern and a site for intervention. The civil re-education project of New Labour, at first described as 'supporting' parents, always had a punitive undercurrent, which would become more apparent after the successes (and ostensible public appeal) of parenting television like *Supernanny*. In 2006, it was announced that a national grid of early parental intervention would be rolled out across specified areas identified as 'disadvantaged', as part of the Prime Minister's Respect Task Force. This grid of intervention would take the form of parenting experts – widely described across subsequent media coverage as an 'army of Supernannies' – drafted to 77 'regional hotspots' of anti-social behaviour. Prime Minister Tony Blair made the announcement in the *Sun* newspaper, pre-empting (and swiftly dismissing) 'nanny state' accusations, stating:

> The 'nanny state' argument applied to this is just rubbish. No one's talking about interfering with *normal family life*. But life isn't normal if you've got 12-year-olds out every night, drinking and creating a nuisance on the street, with their parents not knowing or even caring. In these circumstances, a bit of nannying, with sticks and carrots, is

what the local community needs, let alone the child. (Blair, 2006, emphasis added)

The Supernanny army, imagined as a national squad of parenting practitioners and experts, was earmarked with £4 million of funding – though later calculations would put the final cost at £34 million (see Parkinson, 2009) – and delivered by local authorities as part of the Home Office's Respect Task Force. The Respect Task Force was a cross-government strategy group, set up to tackle anti-social behaviour, by focusing on its alleged 'root causes' – poor parenting and 'problem families'. This Task Force, and the statecraft that emerged from it, would more intimately connect welfare and justice systems through a number of tools, including parenting programmes, parenting contracts and Parenting Orders, as well as Family Intervention Projects and Anti-Social Behaviour Orders (ASBOs).

Much of the rhetoric that underpinned this new punitive direction was not new. The first appearance of the catch-all term 'anti-social behaviour' appeared in the Public Order Act 1986 (see Burney, 2006), and the implementation of the fledgling 'ASBO industry' in Britain was facilitated by massive public investment in CCTV surveillance throughout the 1990s and a wider preoccupation with how to criminalise nuisance and enforce it through the courts (see Squires, 2008). As criminologist Peter Squires remarks, this focus on 'anti-social behaviour' worked to re-order the priorities of local governance and spending, in ways that had little to do with calculable 'social harm' and everything to do with an expanding rationale of criminalisation: this focus on anti-social behaviour, he concludes, was explicitly ideological.

The confidence with which this existing project of civic renewal and moral responsibilisation was now connected to 'problem families' was, to some degree, a consequence of the successes of popular parent pedagogy across media and particularly television. Some substantive critiques of parenting culture and pedagogy have drawn attention to the resonances between media entertainment programmes, such as *Supernanny*, and the state interventions into family life (including social workers, health visitors, maternity nurses and housing officers) and lamented the intrusion and dismantling of the private family realm (Bristow, 2009; Lee et al, 2013).

Other scholars have commented on the distinct separation of state social work and 'commercial' or 'privatised' family support. Ouellette and Hay (2008), for example, describe the 'TV nanny' (and parenting advisers and life-coaches) as being a world away from state social workers. The TV nanny, they argue, governs within the private context of commercial television, her interventions thus 'tolerable' and 'in synch' with the rationalities of privatisation and choice that characterise neoliberal culture. They propose that reality television has 'reinvented social work', offering a science for social living that has recast and neoliberalised social work within the context of personal responsibility and traditional morality. The governmentalities diffused by reality television (and other media and cultural technologies) are 'post-welfare', in the sense that they 'do the work that the State no longer has to do' (Ouellette and Hay, 2008: 66).

Similarly, Ron Becker's (2005) reading of *Supernanny* and *Nanny 911* regards parenting media as 'privatised' rather than 'socialised', in that it loads social responsibility onto individual families and, in doing so, sidesteps the stigma of state intervention. Anita Biressi and Heather Nunn (2008) propose that while privatised parenting and family help – from counsellors, therapists, childcare experts – is highly sought, even prized, state intervention in the form of social workers remains undesirable, stigmatising, 'rendered unpalatable by its classed connotations' and significations of failure. Biressi and Nunn try to imagine a reality television programme called 'Supersocialworker'; they conclude it is 'literally inconceivable' (Biressi and Nunn, 2008: 8).

These media analyses could not have anticipated the ways that 'privatised' parenting media would come to overlap with family statecraft such as social work, family intervention projects and local authority parenting classes. But perhaps the two realms were not so distinct in the first place; as Amanda Holt (2008) has pointed out, the 'privatised' media sites and 'socialised' sites of parenting intervention were always blurred. In 2005, families taking part in a youth offending team-led parenting support and counselling programme agreed to feature in a BBC Two observational documentary, *Blame the Parents*. An even more tautological example was 'The Great Parenting Experiment', a research study funded by the Respect Task Force, which sought to explore the effectiveness of media-delivered parenting programmes, and which was itself eventually broadcast as *Driving Mum and Dad Mad* (ITV, 2006). Holt proposes that the distinctions between state intervention to regulate 'deviance' and media intervention to regulate 'everyday practice' (if ever there was one) are fast disappearing; consequently, all parents can be 'co-opted' into the hegemony of parenting discourse 'as mutual agents of scrutiny' (Holt, 2008: 212).

Perhaps even more significantly, the entertaining and spectacular television advice offered by parenting pedagogues contributed to a wider public consensus that there was an unseen and hidden population of parents, who were failing to raise their children effectively. Popular culture, as Stuart Hall (1998) reminds us, is a site where power is affirmed but also contested; an arena of consent and resistance, where meaning, feeling and sentiment are struggled over. As we saw in the previous chapter, parenting television was complexly consumed with pleasure and discomfort, its experts both venerated and scorned – but both in and through this complexity, such media helped to make solid a broader commonsense that perhaps the intimate domains of emotional life needed intervention. This sudden eruption of family dysfunction on reality television, breaking down and tearing up right in front of the camera, was ideologically powerful. They seemed to lend symbolic weight to the disenchanted visions of family life articulated by policy makers, who saw an 'underbelly of humanity ... behind net curtains' (Henricson, 2008: 153). As different families voluntarily submitted to a range of parent pedagogues week after week on British television screens, a consensus was shaping up about parenting and problem families.

In 2006, the Respect Task Force commissioned an opinion poll that found that 80% of people thought parents should be held responsible for their children's bad behaviour, and, more controversially, that 53% thought anti-social behaviour was caused by parental failure (quoted in Burney, 2005: 47). The Respect Task Force would approvingly feed these opinion polls into research reports and use them in its promotional material and websites. An ideological loop had formed, whereby mediations of family dysfunction would inform public opinion, which would in turn be used to legitimate a more punitive direction in policy making.

When the Home Office's Anti-Social Behaviour Unit was renamed the Respect Task Force, and the ASB Unit's Director, Louise Casey, was appointed the Head of the Respect Task Force, this was favourably presented in press coverage and media interviews using the same Mary Poppins symbolism that was so resonant in *Supernanny* (and discussed in the previous chapter). One fawning profile in *The Guardian* described her 'reputation for frankness', approvingly quoted from colleagues who described her as 'courageous', 'uninhibited' and an 'iconoclast' (Bowcott, 2005). The resonances with the Supernanny Jo Frost, whose appeal was precisely around her willingness to deliver 'hard truths', however upsetting, could not be clearer. Casey was even described as the 'State Supernanny' in a profile interview in *The Telegraph*, which began;

> She takes a spoonful of sugar to council estates, she expects the rich to keep their toys tidy and she wants the middle

classes to know where their children are at 10pm. The 'respect tsar' believes that children can only have fun if they know their boundaries. Liberals have attacked her for being too strident and the Right have attacked her for not waving her umbrella enough. Tony Blair, however, thinks she is practically perfect in every way. (Sylvester and Thomson, 2007)

The *Respect Action Plan* (Home Office, 2006) continued with this shift of focus towards families as the principal site for establishing a 'culture of respect'. While funding and resources were promised to deprived neighbourhoods, in the form of youth activities and sport and arts opportunities, the prevailing tone was condemnatory and an escalating system of penalties and sanctions were emphasised (Burney, 2005). The language was of 'crackdown', 'getting tough' and punishment. Elizabeth Burney has described the use of civil and administrative orders, which carry a sanction for refusal or breach, as 'compliance by threat' and noted that the increasing trends towards such instruments have created a blending of welfare and punishment, and resulted in new forms of governance and state penetration in family life.

The extension of these 'compliance by threat' tools – which might, for example, threaten the removal of housing benefit unless a parent attends and completes a state-mandated parenting class or some other engagement with a named 'helping agency' – signals a new direction in the government of parents. Popular parent pedagogy in this moment drew on a deeply individualist sense of 'the family', which appeared to offer new cultural models for intimacy that would be transformative, emancipatory and egalitarian. But these cultural models would also, more problematically, come to entail the rationalisation of emotional conduct in the family. They would popularise and multiply new forms of emotional work and labour (unequally shared), and seek to transform messy emotional bonds and relationships into 'neutral' and 'cognitive' objects that can be 'emptied of their particularity and ... evaluated according to abstract criteria' (Illouz, 2007: 36).

Intimacy expertise: the political is personal

In 2007, Channel 4 broadcast *Bringing Up Baby*, a four-part documentary series, which invited six participating families to implement one of three different baby care philosophies with their newborns. Guided by a 'mentor' who represented one of the childcare approaches, these first-time parents were assigned to either the 'Truby King method' (advocating strict routine and forbidding unneccessary contact), the 'Benjamin Spock method' (emphasising parental instinct and flexibility) or the 'Continuum Concept method' (which promotes constant skin contact between parent and child and co-sleeping for the first year). *Bringing up Baby* dramatised the polyvocality and the range of contemporary parent pedagogy, and parenting advice is presented as a booming industry ('more parenting books are sold each year than babies born'), populated by multiple opinions and streams of discourse, different kinds of advice, techniques and philosophies, and differently qualified experts.

The programme captured, to some degree, the cyclical recycling of moral positions around discipline, regulation, theories of childhood and domestic management, though it presented these cycles as emerging from, and belonging to, discrete historical decades. This was signalled to viewers by the interchangeable references to 'method' and 'decade' – Truby King/1950s, Benjamin Spock/1960s, Continuum/1970s – and through the changing aesthetics of the opening animation.

The voiceover narrates the range of childcare approaches as a site of uncertainty and decision ('every new parent is terrified of getting it wrong') and asks that viewers suspend their own experiences in the quest to discover which approach is 'correct' or 'best'. As the opening voiceover declares:

> Every parent wants the best for their child. But what is the best way of bringing up baby? Every decade since the war has had its own advice when it comes to childcare. The chances are, *you* were a product of one of these theories. But which is *right*? (Bringing Up Baby, Channel 4, 2007; original emphasis)

The programme is described by the voiceover and in promotional material as an 'experiment', which will objectively compare each method in order to determine which is best, using surveillance cameras to document everyday life. The series uses fascinating footage from the archives of 'parenting science' and invites its viewers into a position of detached evaluation, 'weighing up' the moral, pedagogical and ethical worth of this approach over that one. *Bringing Up Baby* in this sense aims to illustrate and educate viewers about a proliferating cultural industry of parent advice, and in doing so to 'empower' them as consumers, who must navigate a busy, and perhaps bewildering, marketplace. The programme dramatises some of the social histories of parenting explored in Chapter Two, which posit that parents can choose to 'buy the book' rather than feeling compelled to go 'by-the-book' (Hulbert, 2003), or that they might 'dip into' childrearing philosophies, adapt philosophies or techniques, and discard what is not useful or does not work for them (Apple, 2006).

The programme also, however, sought to generate media currency and attention from audiences, by amplifying moments of conflict and drama through segments of heated discussion and disagreement between the three mentors. However appealing the idea of an objective parenting 'experiment' might be, in practice we see how moralising and polarising parenting culture is. The programme makers had either underestimated these antagonisms or had played to them perfectly – and *Bringing Up Baby* generated intense public debate on parenting discussion forums like Mumsnet, across media commentary and a number of health organisations and charities, concerning the content and worth of the three featured babycare philosophies, as well as the expert standing of each parenting mentor.

Bringing Up Baby's executive producer, Daisy Goodwin, remarked on the unexpected anger that had been provoked by the programme, including disturbing reports that some participating parents had been verbally abused and spat at, while shopping in their local supermarket.[2] The UK's media regulator Ofcom received over 700 viewer complaints about the programme, and the Foundation for the Study of Infant Deaths released a public statement expressing concern over the inclusion of the 'Truby King Method' in the programme, since it advocated parenting methods that increase the risk of Sudden Infant Death Syndrome (SIDS, also known as 'cot death'). Babycare writer Gina Ford penned a public letter regarding *Bringing Up Baby* to the children's charity NSPCC, in which she described the Truby King Method as a form of 'child cruelty' and urged the organisation to take action against the programme.[3] The chief executive of the Family and Parenting Institute, Mary MacLeod, co-wrote a public letter to television production companies (with six other childcare professionals), which was published in *The Daily Telegraph*, describing *Bringing Up Baby* as an 'exploitative parenting series', and advising that the techniques featured were outmoded and 'at best irresponsible and at worst dangerous' (see Adams and Womack, 2007). The public debate generated a specific controversy around Claire Verity, who featured as the programme 'mentor' for the Truby King 'mentor', and who claimed to hold maternity nurse qualifications from organisations that denied granting them (see Foster, 2007).

Bringing Up Baby was a fascinating exemplar of how the dominant modes of expression, which anchor politicised debates about parenting in the public sphere, have shifted considerably – from authoritarian modes of discourse (which presume that sources of authority are natural and unquestionable) to more populist and democratic modes. The appeal of such programming exemplifies a wider turn to intimate forms of address in public and political life. As Ros Gill (2015) notes, the changing nature of public space, and the redrawing of boundaries between private and public, has generated new forms of public intimacy across media texts. In this 'feminised public sphere', matters which would have been considered to belong to the private realm and unthinkable for television discussion, such as sexual dysfunction, child abuse and domestic violence, have been brought into public view through confessional and subjective media genres such as television talk-shows and reality media. The explosion of parenting media, including *Supernanny* and *Bringing Up Baby*, have transformed our greatest uncertainties, anxieties and failures – toddler tantrums, raging children, distressed and unsettled babies – into mainstream media fodder.

Yet, in making the problems of living visible, these publicly intimate forms of address also do a great deal of ideological work. They contain and depoliticise 'problems of living'; they become a matter of individual management, choice and transformation. Rather than illuminating the social context and causes of these intimate struggles and problems, such parenting media work to popularise individual solutions, where the struggling subject must contain and manage their dissatisfactions, rather than taking political steps to transform their causes.

Elayne Rapping notes the crucial connections in the United States between feminist consciousness-raising and the self-help movement; especially how the latter borrows from the vocabularies and sensibilities of the former (Rapping, 1996). As Rapping argues, feminism 'made visible' a diverse litany of problems, some of which we see made spectacular on parenting television – undervalued, miserable mothers trapped by domesticity, out-of-control children who 'rule the roost', fathers who are emotionally or literally absent, geographically distant extended family, demanding or long hours of paid employment, exhaustion, and so on. Self-help culture similarly makes such problems 'talkable'. The intimate 'experts of recovery' encourage us to 'talk out' our bad feelings, but in a way that Rapping sees as 'reactionary and repressive' (Rapping, 1996: 7), by monitoring, advising, disciplining and bringing our 'selves' into recovery. As Gill (2015) notes, it is precisely the *apolitical* nature of such recovery discourse that makes it so powerfully political. Self-help media has, in Gill's words, 'turned on its head' the feminist principle that the 'personal is political', presented instead a personalisation of the political, 'reframing every issue in individualistic terms and erasing any sense of the social or political' (Gill, 2007: 176). Potentially oppositional discourse, for example the frustrations of intensive motherhood, can thus be absorbed and depoliticised as private failure or individual family dysfunction, 'contained through personalisation' (Peck, 1995, cited in Gill, 2007: 75) and made amenable via therapeutic intervention.

The controversies exemplified in parenting media such as *Bringing Up Baby* must also be contextualised within the impossible demands made on mothers to be exhaustively attuned to the needs of their children. It is important to note that, of the three childcare approaches featured, it was the 'Truby King method', with its emphasis on discipline, boundaries and routine, which was criticised as being 'outmoded', old-fashioned, from another time and out of step with what 'we now know' about children. The remaining approaches – both Dr Spock, with his emphasis on parental instincts, playfulness and the importance of listening and responsiveness, and the Continuum method, which advocates continuous attention and contact – generated discussion, but none of the same controversy, disgust or anger. Both 'Spock' and 'Continuum' parenting methods segue much more easily with the tenets of the dominant ideology of 'intensive mothering' that underpins contemporary parenting culture.

Sharon Hays mapped this ideology in *The Cultural Contradictions of Motherhood* (1996), detailing how a diverse group of Californian women, from different socioeconomic backgrounds and employment arrangements, commit themselves to a labour-intensive and emotionally absorbing model of raising children. The ideology of intensive mothering requires that mothers offer choices to children, refrain from demanding obedience to rules and instead explain and negotiate with them, and be consciously attentive to children's wishes. How, then, was this fantasy figure of sensitive mothering institutionalised in parenting culture?

What *kind* of parent? 'Pure relationships' and the sensitive mother

The regimes of knowledge that are put into operation by parent pedagogy require that parents submit to categories of normality and govern themselves and their children in reference to normative developmental scales that mark what is desirable, age-appropriate and, therefore, 'good'. Through selecting a childrearing philosophy from the 'marketplace', through submitting to the authority of a chosen parenting expert, and through working on oneself – applying exercises, adopting parenting strategies and experimenting with parenting techniques – parents become liberal subjects and family life becomes a project to be worked on. Liberal parent pedagogy invites parents to first *reflect*; to keep a diary, to consult a checklist, to identify their problems and to evaluate themselves, their children and their orientations towards their family and children. It asks them to step out of their social and political worlds, turn their gaze inwards and ask: what kind of parent are you? What kind of parent do you want to be? Two of the bestselling books that emerged out of the parenting television industry begin in precisely this way:

> Take a step back. Imagine going to the theatre and sitting in the front row of the stalls. Your family – right now, right here – is the play. What do you see? How does it make you feel? What makes you cringe with embarrassment? What makes you burst with pride? What makes you laugh? What makes you cry? (Frost, 2006: 14)

> For the families [taking part in the programme] it was like having a mirror held up to themselves, where they could see how their own behaviour and reactions to their children were part of the problem. ... For many, watching a tape of themselves was a moment of truth. (Byron, 2006: 8)

Parent pedagogy and self-help media deploy a psychological ethic and orientation; one in which the material world and its inequalities recede, and the unitary subject takes centre stage. In these invitations to reflect on what 'kind' of parent to be, parent pedagogy requires parents to think of themselves as self-possessed entrepreneurs, confident and competent in weighing up different kinds of knowledges and cleanly applying techniques to their lives. Parenting culture thus assumes a particular kind of liberal parental self, one who is reflexively oriented towards their parenting, is autonomous, rational and able to act with agency. Parenting is conceptualised less as a relationship and more as a set of skills and capacities, which we can all learn and become technically proficient in. This psychologised, self-help approach to parenting rehearses and reproduces a specific orientation towards oneself, whereby parents are to assume a mode of professionalism in order to maximise the potential futurity of their child(ren).

In this sense, parent pedagogy powerfully echoes and reproduces the influential sociological theories that provided the theoretical underpinnings for the civilising project of New Labour discussed in the previous chapter (Skeggs, 2004; Gillies, 2005). In particular, the work of Anthony Giddens is crucial to understanding the family ideology promoted by New Labour and taken up by subsequent governments. Across his vast corpus of work, Giddens has argued optimistically that late modernity is characterised by a move away from the bonds and expectations of tradition, custom and ritual. He argues that technological advances – for example contraception, political movements such as feminism and gay rights, and the mainstreaming of psychoanalysis – have contributed to a democratisation of the private sphere, whereby we must individually negotiate or work out with one another the questions of 'how to live'. He holds that we are released from the old certainties and shorn of institutional obligations.

In *The Transformation of Intimacy*, Giddens (1992) posits that these conditions have enabled people to create 'pure relationships', which he describes as elective, negotiated and plural. Such relationships are sustained through ethical reflection, accounting for choices, revising priorities and commitments. Therapy and self-help culture are integral resources in these projects of the self; and the lifestyle choices we must constantly make, filtered through expert knowledge, enable us to create a 'reflexive narrative of self' (Giddens, 1992: 75). For Giddens, these shifts document a more profound equality in intimate relationships and families, and mark the potential for radical and positive social change. In his words, 'the possibility of intimacy means the promise of democracy' (Giddens, 1992: 188). This new malleability of intimate life echoes a wider preoccupation in mainstream sociology and popular culture with choice and individualism, celebratory of the 'end of class' and the replacement of 'old structures' with new, individualised risks and opportunities (see Giddens, 1991; Beck, 1992; Beck and Beck-Gernsheim, 2002).

The multiplication of parenting experts, vocabularies, evaluations, techniques and ethics thus appears to offer choice to parents. Among the many kinds of parent that it is possible to be, what kind do you want to be? But this 'choice' is always framed as 'intrinsically' psychological and, as Bev Skeggs notes, 'we have no choice but to choose' (Skeggs, 2004: 56).

The work to be done, the changes to be made, in order to address unhappiness and to overcome problems, is instructed at the level of the self and through better, more effective, expert-guided self-management. Parent pedagogy is one crucial site where we can see the advance of the cultural imaginary of psychology, and how individualised solutions have colonised debates about what were once considered to be collective social problems. Reality television was particularly well suited to the vocabularies of self-help culture, providing a medium through which spectacular effects of self-transformation could be narrated and presented. There is little sense of the wider social world in such media; its preoccupations mark: 'a revolution of sentiment; a revolution for the therapy age, where subjectivity is our only certainty and sorrow our greatest claim to heroism' (Gerard, quoted in Dovey, 2000).

As Les Back (2007) notes, the panels of experts who appear on reality programmes routinely include psychologists, nutritionists and life coaches, but have yet to include a sociologist. Others have noted how the broader ascendence of 'the self' across the cultural imagination has incubated a therapeutic, rather than sociological, ethos. We can see the employment of such psychological vocabularies in order to both diagnose and treat parenting malaise and struggles, whereby family struggle and 'bad behaviour' (which is visible and disturbing – tantrums, shouting, violence) is continually positioned as emanating from within the parental subject, through inadequacies that they possess and embody. The problematic parental subject is visualised on parenting television through the apparatus of the surveillant camera. Other parenting culture platforms, such as self-help books and websites, similarly make sensible the deficit parent subject through pseudo-therapeutic narratives, sprinkled with eclectic combinations of pop psychology and cognitive behavioural techniques.

The concept of the 'pure relationship' and the reflexive, communicative self has been hugely influential on how we configure and understand 'good' and 'bad' parenting. Good parents are those who are able and willing to absorb psychological knowledge, recognise their inadequacies, and transform and manage their 'selves'. This is framed as no less than an ethical duty. However, there is little space to consider the profound inequalities that shape who is, and who is not, able to perform as the hallowed reflexive self and experiment with and conceive of their life (and their parenting) as a project. The material and socioeconomic dimensions of everyday lives are simply absent from parenting advice culture, which presumes that all selves have equal access to resources.

Feminist scholars have drawn attention to how the pure relationship resonates with middle-class experience, and how the sociology underpinning these concepts authorises such experience and perspectives as universal. Bev Skeggs (2004) argues that the work of Giddens (and his contemporaries) relies on everybody enjoying even access to the same resources by which the self can be known, assessed and narrated. As she shows, 'the self' in fact works as a metaphoric space in which to store and display resources that are themselves unequally distributed along the lines of social class, race and gender. Barbara Cruikshank (1996) similarly notes that there is little consideration in these cultures of citizenship of how capitalism, racism and inequality govern the order of the self and its governance.

In her powerful critique of Giddens' concept of 'pure relationships', Lynne Jamieson (1999) notes how selective the psychological theory underpinning Giddens' work is. She draws on an extensive body of empirical research to demonstrate how everyday lives remain shaped and constrained by structured inequality and gendered struggle. Moreover, the power of popular discourse about 'pure relationships' and their desirability means that people may spend considerably more time creatively accounting for inequality, in order to sustain a fiction of democratic intimacy. Jamieson warns that the rhetoric of the 'pure relationship' – appealing as it is – ends up pointing people in the wrong direction personally and politically by feeding on, and into, a therapeutic, rather than a sociological, explanation for problems of practical love and care.

The call to 'parent' from a position of an assumed 'pure relationship' thus embodies very specific values, which emanate from cultural spaces and lifestyles that are resoundingly middle class (Gillies, 2005), even as they are constructed as being universal or 'normal'. Some mothers are better placed than others to accommodate the financial, emotional and time requirements of parenting intensively: but, as feminist sociological research has documented over several decades, the pressures and expectations of this ideology can generate a miserable, monotonous everyday life for all mothers, including those who are relatively advantaged. Ann Oakley's research with housewives (Oakley, 1974) was one of the first studies to listen seriously to the experiences of isolation and the monotony of being a full-time mother, and Lynne Segal (1994) mapped the 'silent sorrow' of mothers who felt trapped at home by their young children.

These experiences are not universal. Black feminist theorists have troubled the centring of white middle-class women's experiences, challenging parenting researchers to complicate their analysis of motherhood (and other issues) and attend to racism, poverty, welfare and work. Reflecting on the conceptual limitations of white feminism, bell hooks remarked that: 'we still do not have the language paradigms for white women to be able to express … privilege' (Childers and hooks, 1990: 63).

In order to understand the construction of the 'sensitive' or 'intensive' mother, our analysis must be broader than 'patriarchy'. It must attend to the ways that power and oppression are – at once – racialised, classed and gendered. Bridget Byrne's (2006) outstanding research with white South London mothers is an important response to this challenge. She tracks how the mothering practices of the mothers she interviewed, their interactions with schools and the construction of their friendship groups and collectives work to re-inscribe and reiterate classed and raced subject positions. The 'sensitive' mother, as Byrne reminds us, 'repeats and recites gendered, classed and raced norms' (Byrne, 2006: 106). If we celebrate the proliferation of (allegedly) polyvocal (multi-voiced) parenting advice without carefully questioning discourse of the 'pure relationship' in which such debates are cast, then we reproduce the fallacy that choice, reflexivity and autonomy are universally experienced by all families. Such theories of the pure relationship – between parents and between generations (parents and children) – work within a wider scaffold of individualisation, and disguise the messier picture provided by empirical research.

As we will see in the next section, and in subsequent chapters, the credence given to personal and 'inner' transformation in discourses of popular psychology works to sideline sociological concerns of justice and equality. In particular, the prominence given to the apparatus of confession and judgement is crucial to understanding the ways in which healthy selfhood is constructed.

Parental subjects

> We go about telling, with the greatest precision, whatever it is most difficult to tell … Western man has become a confessing animal (Foucault, 1978: 59).

Michel Foucault described the great paradox of liberalism in terms of how it obliges individuals to demonstrate their freedom and agency by controlling themselves, or by exercising freedom 'correctly'. Foucault offered a radically new conceptualisation of power, stating that, far from being prohibitive and repressive, power is a productive force. It is through social practices such as confession that power operates and turns us into individuals. In confessing our crimes, sins, thoughts and desires, illness and troubles, Foucault demonstrated that power operates through regimes of knowledge that produce meaning, create categories and form us into subjects. Across his corpus of work, Foucault tracked the production of 'dividing practices' (1982) that classified individuals as normal or deviant across a range of institutions – for example, the clinic developed practices that could divide the mad from the sane; the courts divided the criminal from the law-abiding citizen. When we are being most encouraged to be 'free', Foucault argues, we are most subjected to the machinery of power. Or, in Steph Lawler's words, 'power is at its most powerful when it is least apparent, when it is working through our desires' (2000: 21). Foucault's insight is that power in liberal democracy works *through* our desires, not in spite of them:

> There are two meanings of the word *subject:* subject to someone else by control and dependence, and tied to his own identity by a conscience of self-knowledge. Both meanings suggest a form of power which subjugates and makes subject to. (Foucault, 1982: 212)

Foucault described the process by which human beings become subjects as 'subjectification'; it is through this process that the circuits of power, which shape our social world, cleave subjects from one another, and cast each subject as an object of (scientific) knowledge. Subjectification is a process which 'folds' us into the relations of power. Although it might *feel like* autonomy and *feel like* freedom – the freedom to be/ become 'our true self' – they have regulation at their core. We do not feel ourselves being 'obedient' to power, but rather simply to be acting on our desire to be 'normal'. Under subjectification, we thus regulate ourselves in line with wider discourses and techniques of normalisation. In our desires to be 'good parents', and to be recognised as good parents by others, we are incited to scrutinise ourselves, monitor our behaviours and habits, and regulate our emotions. We become invested in particular forms of parenting that are culturally sanctioned and valued; parenting that is reflexive, intensive, expert-guided, thoughtful and self-scrutinising (Hays, 1996). We are subjected by the norms and rules of such parenting regimes and by their dividing practices; and in doing so, we become subjects.

In her inspired application of Foucault's principles to the discursive production of maternal and daughterly 'selves', Lawler (2000) demonstrates how the appeal of autonomy is at the heart of becoming a subject and of being subjectified. The question 'what kind of parent do you want to be' circulates and naturalises a particular vision of the parental subject, in the form of what Ouellette and Hay (2008) have termed 'idealised citizen subjectivities'. 'Good parents' therefore become objects of scientific knowledge, that can be known, surveyed, evaluated and assessed – and measured and classified in accordance with how far they match up with, or deviate from, agreed ranges of 'normality'. As Foucault argues, we are required (indeed, obliged) to relate to ourselves *as if* we are coherent, unified and whole. We are obliged to do this, even as we experience fragmentation, contradiction and struggle.

'Parenting' has thus come to refer less to specific methods, techniques and habits, and more to a set of orientations with being or becoming a particular kind of self, in accordance with the emergent culture of moral citizenship. Nikolas Rose calls this governance through the 'soul of the citizen' – integral to advanced liberal society, where freedom is 'the unceasing reflexive gaze of our own psychologically educated self-scrutiny' (Rose, 1990: 208). For Rose, becoming a subject is not an ideological crushing, but a discursive production, which draws on the vocabularies and techniques of psychology – counselling and therapy, mental hygiene, group relations and psychodynamics. The 'soul of the citizen' is the focus of a collection of concerned and humanistic experts, through which we are 'subjectified, educated and solicited into a loose and flexible alliance' (Rose, 1996: 79). One of the 'truth effects' of this 'regime of the self' is that the difficulties and struggles of living, and by extension all social problems, become thinkable *only* in psychological terms. Rose refers to the matrix of knowledges that produce these truths about the self as the 'psy' sciences (short for psychological), and argues that they have narrowed down the ways that we might understand ourselves to a 'psy' complex (Rose, 1990, 1996). In *Governing the Soul* (1990), Rose highlights how foundational the 'psy' sciences are in technologies of government, which produce citizen subjectivities. As he states: 'it has become impossible to conceive of personhood ... or to govern oneself, without "psy"' (Rose, 1996: 139).

The psychologising of parenting – and the 'dividing practices' that construct good and bad parents as objects and create prescriptions of 'normality' – represents a crucial set of sites, through which we can discern the cultural logic of neoliberalism and its reach into our intimate lives. Neoliberal sensibilities come to govern us, by requiring that we become particular kinds of subjects – through pressures, constraints and requirements, cultural scripts and (often) contradictory discourses. Rose argues that psy has become foundational to the technologies of government that produce these citizen subjectivities. Practices of the self (such as self-scrutiny, inspection, control of the body, speech and movement, the evoking of conscience and the provoking of reflection) all contribute, Rose argues, to a kind of moral subjectivity, through which 'individuals were to be subjected not by an alien gaze but through a reflexive hermeneutics' (Rose, 1997: 77). We should recall the importance of such self-surveillance in the recycled myths of 'perfect parenting' outlined by Christine Hardyment (1995) and her remarks that mothers today are caught up 'watching themselves' be mothers. These fantasies of perfect mothers and 'normal families' require that we think of all families as accessing and enjoying autonomy. Under the 'psy' complex, the fiction of autonomy regulates and governs subjects into acting *as if* they are autonomous.

Supernanny, and other products of the parent-blame industries, spectacularly dramatised the contradictions that are reproduced by powerful myths of the 'perfect mother'. This fantasy figure is unattainable – for who could possibly embody these endless and exhaustive requirements to be available, patient, reflexive, self-sacrificing, determined, rational, sensitive and energised? Who can step outside the unequal dynamics of power in their household, or the wounds and disappointments of their biographies and histories?

Parents continually fail, and resolve to do better. Similarly, these theories of governmentality recognise that processes of subjectification are not simple of straightforward, and that regulatory normalising discourses do not need to be unified. Indeed, it is precisely in their individualising effects – the dividing practices that delineate delinquent, difficult, troubled and 'normal' children, or competent and deficient parents – that the expert knowledges of parenting can colonise family life, and do so with a veneer of 'scientific objectivity'.

Reinventing 'tough love'

The construction of a parenting crisis, narrated through figures of parental failure, serves to reproduce ideologies of parenting that require parents (principally mothers) to become expert-led in all aspects of childrearing, child-centred, able to predict and avoid risk, and oriented towards optimising their child's development in line with discourses and markers of normality.

These cultures of contemporary parenting, which require complete devotion and emotional absorption in one's children, have been given many names. Douglas and Michaels (2004) examined what they called the 'new momism'; an unrealistic sacralisation (making sacred) of motherhood propagated by US media (and that has resonances in the UK media), which generates antagonisms between 'working' and 'stay-at-home' mothers, and serves to create intense feelings of failure for all mothers. Sharon Hays (1996) documented the powerful hold of 'intensive parenting' on the mothers of her research, whereby the contradictions between paid work and childrearing must be contained and resolved by mothers; principally by expending a great deal of emotional labour and financial resources on maximising the wellbeing of their children. Joan Wolf (2007) uses the term 'total motherhood' to capture how the 'needs' of children are put into productive antagonism with the 'wants' of mothers. Wolf refers to total motherhood as a 'moral code' that positions these antagonisms as a trade-off that mothers must bear, whatever the cost to them. Such parenting cultures, however labelled, share the requirement for parents to be subjected by and to powerful illusions of liberated, reflexive choice and intimate equality via the concept of the 'pure relationship'.

But at the same time, the kind of parenting that was made 'commonsense' in the populist parenting culture in the early 2000s also speaks back to the impossibilities of intensive parenting and pure relationships, by foregrounding parental authority and a welcome 'return' to discipline and boundaries. Media theorists Laurie Ouellette and James Hay (2008) point to how the advice on *Supernanny* can be interpreted as a reprieve from the 'lenient' or 'permissive' parenting popularised in earlier waves of parenting advice.

Indeed, the expansion of parenting policy at this time centred on the urgent need for parents to take back control from difficult and unruly children. One of the clearest messages in family policy documents was that deficient parenting could take many forms, *including* lenient or permissive approaches. A much wider sense of 'parenting neglect' was operationalised, encompassing not only extreme (and rare) cases of abuse but also failures to 'attach' or 'attune' to children or to display appropriate levels of 'sensitivity' or 'positive parenting'.

The *Every Child Matters* report (Department for Education, 2003) was crucial in extending the scope of state policy to infiltrate and surveil family life, and in creating new grounds on which to intervene if parents were deemed to be failing by parenting professionals working in collaboration with child protection, health services, the police, schools or family support services. Parton (2006) notes that the *Every Child Matters* framework marked an intensive policy emphasis on 'prevention' and in intervening at increasingly earlier stages for problems that would (allegedly) become apparent later in life, such as educational attainment, crime and even unemployment. McVarish (2014) notes that, after the *Every Child Matters* framework, experiences and events that would previously have been considered within the normal range of family life (such as children becoming overweight or parents becoming angry) could now potentially fall into the categories of 'abuse' and 'neglect'.

Connected to these more expansive notions of 'parent deficit', we can also see stronger policy claims about the power of 'good parenting' to mediate against disadvantage and even prevent 'social exclusion'. Indeed, the vocabularies of social inequality and class structure appear to have disappeared from some policy documents altogether. In 2010, Frank Field MP penned a report on *The Foundation Years: Preventing poor children becoming poor adults*, which claimed that the circumstances of birth now need not hold any major significance in children's life chances, stating (contrary to evidence) that:

> A healthy pregnancy, positive but authoritative parenting, high quality childcare, a positive approach to learning at home and an improvement in parents' qualifications, together, can transform children's life chances, and trump class background and parental income. (Field, 2010: 126)

Notwithstanding the complex ways in which the items on Field's 'list' are *themselves* shaped by, and reflective of, class background and parental income, we see here an interesting reference to the crucial empty signifier of UK family policy in this moment: 'authoritative parenting'. Across developmental psychology, it is the sensitive mother who is held up as the ideal. Through endless labour, creative work and invention, the sensitive mother must disguise her generational authority over the child and sustain an illusion of democracy, through offering choices and reasoning, in order to protect and foster children's self-esteem and a sense of autonomy. She must disguise the 'spectre of authoritarianism' (Walkerdine and Lucey, 1989). 'Authoritarian parenting', which demands obedience from children, is anathema to liberal parenting and it is pathologised in developmental psychology and silently coded as working class. But 'authoritative parenting' is the prized object of parenting science and culture, and it begins to develop a complex life in the moralised and mythologised versions of 'good parenting' that inform policy documents and political discussion, and eventually, parenting initiatives.

Tough Love as parenting style

One example where we can track the production of 'authoritative parenting' can be seen in the report *Building Character* (Lexmond and Reeves, 2009), from the think-tank Demos – a literature and policy review that drew on a dataset from the Millennium Cohort Study. The Millennium Cohort Study, a large-scale, longitudinal study carried out by the Centre for Longitudinal Studies, Institute of Education, examined the development of children born in the same week of April 2001 in three data sweeps (at eleven months, three years and five years).

Building Character defined 'character' as specific attributes and skills (empathy, application and self-control), and sought to connect child outcome scores for these attributes to the type of parenting practised in the families of those children. 'Character' is thus narrowly defined as skills that facilitate success, and widening opportunity initiatives are cast as a matter of inculcating the 'right' personality. The report proposes four distinct parenting styles – 'tough-love', 'laissez-faire', 'authoritarian' and 'disengaged' – according to two axes of conduct (warm/hostile and permissive/controlling). Thus, 'tough-love' parenting is warm and controlling; responsive, assertive without being aggressive or restrictive, and deploying reasoning rather than punitive disciplinary methods. 'Laissez-faire' parenting is warm and permissive; highly responsive, non-confrontational and non-traditional, running lenient and democratic households. 'Authoritarian parenting' is hostile and controlling; rule-based, valuing obedience and structure, and using firm discipline with little regard for the feelings of children. 'Disengaged' parenting is hostile and permissive; 'hands-off', low in warmth and discipline and, at the extreme ends of the quadrant, neglectful.

Having defined four parenting styles, Lexmond and Reeves analyse the 'child outcomes' of children whose parents exhibited a clear preference for one particular parenting style, paying particular attention to the traits of application, self-regulation and empathy. They report that children of 'tough love' parents are two-and-a-half times more likely than those with 'disengaged' parents to score within the top fifth for these child outcomes. Concurrently, the children of 'disengaged' parents were found by this analysis to be three times more likely than children with 'tough love' parents to score within the bottom fifth for the Strength and Difficulties Questionnaire (SDQ) used in this research to measure child outcomes. They further report that children with 'laissez-faire' parents fare better in child outcome scores than those whose parents were 'authoritarian', and conclude that 'parenting style' is, in its own right, the *most* significant factor in terms of building character, practically neutralising other background factors: 'parents on a low income, but who are confident and able, are as effective at generating character capabilities in their children as parents on a high income. It is not income itself that causes the different outcomes but other factors' (Lexmond and Reeves, 2009: 36).

There are three points to be raised briefly in response to the discourse of 'tough love' as it has been operationalised in the *Building Character* report and elsewhere (for a fuller discussion, see Jensen, 2010).

First, the evidence base detailed in the report has been colonised by developmental specialists, whose 'objective' psychometric tools disguise narrow normative assumptions (Holt, 2008). The focus on 'self-control', for example, as a desirable character trait simply reproduces the idea of restraint as a virtue that symbolically reproduces and explains middle-class success (Skeggs, 2004). Yet other attributes, which we might include under a broader sense of 'character' – self-acceptance or interdependence, for example – and which fit within other classed frameworks of value, are here unrecognised and unacknowledged (Gillies, 2007). The 'soft skills' that are seen to identify good character are thus already tied to specific classed frameworks of success, mobility and aspiration that assume and normalise a reflexive, middle-class subject (Savage, 2000). Notions of 'best practice' parenting are thus already inscribed, from the moment of definition, within classed systems of meaning and value.

Second, the analysis of the Millennium Cohort Study data in *Building Character* is distorted by a large residual category; 59% of parents had to be discounted from the analysis, because they did not clearly or consistently follow any of the four 'parenting styles'. This 'residual' category, larger than all the other categories put together, exposes the failures of this taxonomy to illuminate the data. The ways in which we divide up and classify people create 'data' – these are invented categories that people can conveniently fall into and thus be 'ordered' in the world. This significant residual makes the reported findings far less impressive, yet this was barely explored by enthusiastic press discussion and dissemination, which over-emphasised the findings and used distortive graphs and figures to order parenting style into clear hierarchies (see, for example, Shields, 2009).

Third, Lexmond and Reeves (2009) argue that there is no necessary correlation between socioeconomic class and child outcomes – that 'tough love' parenting can be found across different income brackets, and that wherever 'tough love' is practised, child outcomes are more likely to be higher. Yet the report also declares that there *is* a classed pattern to the findings. 'Tough love' parenting was more likely to be reported in wealthier households, and 'disengaged' parenting was more likely to be reported in poorer households. The failure to interrogate this classed pattern reveals the substantive problems with using self-report questionnaire methods to research usefully vague concepts such as 'character'. Such methods capture parents' *perceptions* of their parenting and their children's personal traits. However, perceptions of one's competence, confidence in one's ability, and self-esteem around 'parenting' are rooted in classed cultures of value, marked deeply by biography, history and memory, internalisations of popular and media representations of who is to be valued as a parent. Middle-class parents are more likely than their working-class counterparts to describe themselves as competent and confident, and to creatively account for challenging aspects of their children's behaviour (Walkerdine and Lucey, 1989; Reay, 1998; Gillies, 2007).

Tough love, authority and class

The wider 'evidence base' of family biopolitics is similarly haunted by fantasies of objectivity. 'Authoritative' or 'tough love' parenting is an important ideological tool in the arsenal of parenting intervention. We can project our own meanings regarding the appropriate balance between warmth and discipline, the mysterious alchemy that might facilitate 'good child outcomes', social mobility and aspiration. Its positivity and emptiness makes it a powerful signifier. It crops up in many different places, in intimate and political spheres and in the intimate public (Berlant, 1997; Plummer, 2003). But more than that, 'tough love' has become part of the 'emotional regime' (Reddy, 2001) of neoliberalism, framing our collective expectations about what should constitute appropriate or normal emotional behaviour.

Importantly, 'tough love' rhetoric is counterposed not only against permissiveness or leniency, but also against the parenting styles of the past, which are narrated as obliging unthinking obedience, blind authority and generational hierarchy. 'Tough love' is not simply a return to authoritarian parenting, which is understood as equally damaging; it is envisioned to be more complex than simply what our parents and grandparents did. Such authoritarian parenting, with its emphasis on discipline, obedience and authority, is also imagined as thoroughly classed and pathologised on that basis. In *Democracy in the Kitchen*, Valerie Walkerdine and Helen Lucey (1989) painstakingly show how working-class women's interactions with their daughters are interpreted by developmental psychology through a classist framework that routinely patronises their lives. Reflecting on the ideology of 'intensive mothering', Sharon Hays notes that 'providing choices and engaging in negotiation are luxuries' (Hays, 1996: 93). Val Gillies (2007) documents the classed resonances around children and their behaviour, and argues that who gets attributed as a 'bad child' (and by extension, a 'bad parent') is already shaped by how their social class is read. As Gillies remarks, a middle-class child 'acting out' will likely be interpreted as bored or expressing themselves. Walkerdine and Lucey note that children's behaviour is always interpreted through social class: 'If working-class children were quiet in the waiting room of a doctor's surgery, they were repressed. If they were noisy they were hooligans. If middle-class children were noisy and ran around they were "independent and autonomous"' (Walkerdine and Lucey, 1989: 41).

The reinvention of 'tough love' in contemporary parenting culture is part of a wider declassificatory popularising and myth-making of 'meritocracy' (see Littler, 2017), which holds that the successes of middle-class children in institutional settings (such as schooling) must be an effect of the competent – and authoritative – parenting they have received. 'Tough love' has become part of a vocabulary used in policy initiatives and reports that name character education, resilience and 'grit' as qualities that children and young people have instilled within them at home and at school (see Allen, 2016).

As Kim Allen and Anna Bull (forthcoming) have brilliantly shown in their recent research, the emergence of an alleged 'commonsense' around the merits of 'character education' has been manufactured by a relatively small number of think-tanks, philanthropic organisations and some academics. They cogently argue that far from being a 'grassroots' consensus, this fetish for 'character' represents 'astroturfing' by powerful and well-resourced lobbying networks. These networks seek to invisibilise structural conditions and prioritise 'responsible' subjects of neoliberalism. The usefully vague terminology of 'character' can be deployed to evade discussion of the profound social divisions and injustices that shape the opportunities (or lack thereof) and the resources open to differently positioned families. 'Character' education, for example, has been used to 'explain' why privately educated pupils tend to do better in examinations and to be awarded places at elite universities – with private school headteachers patronising other schools with offers to train them in the provision of such character education (but not, importantly, offering to share their vast material resources more equitably, or foregoing their tax exemptions, or making any meaningful action to address the chronic underfunding of state education). Allen and Bull show how influential networks (including representatives from private schools and elite universities) have sought to 'naturalise, legitimate and institutionalise character education as a policy solution' (Allen and Bull, forthcoming: 3)

The significant resources, class privileges and structural advantages that are at work here are able to disappear under a familiar narrative and policy agenda that names behavioural and moral deficiencies as the guarantee of good child outcomes (see Reay, 1998; Gillies, 2007). Social justice, recast as simply engineering 'better character' in the lives of those at the bottom, becomes an individualistic policy intervention in the intimate lives of the socially excluded themselves (Haylett, 2000). As Sharon Gewirtz (2001) asks with mock exasperation, 'why can't working-class parents behave more like middle-class ones?'.

Tough love reproduces the ideal of the 'democratic family' as a microcosm of liberal democratic society. The fashioning of the good family – as one in which relationships are managed democratically and produced through communication and emotional management – is illustrated in the power of notions such as the 'pure relationship' (Giddens, 1992), which foregrounds reflexive self-knowledge over familial domination and automatic generational power.

The tenacity of these distinctly therapeutic notions and the mainstreaming of the ordinary neuroticisms of the middle-class family have been considered by Eva Illouz (2007) to constitute an emotional micro-public sphere. As Illouz argues, the relentless communication of emotions and feelings – as no less than a marker of emotional health and self-competence – contributes to the decontextualising, objectifying and intellectualising of emotional life. These therapeutic languages – like the 'warmth' of parenting style, which promises to free children of any social or economic disadvantage – are *both* neutral and subjectivist. They name complex and ambivalent emotions that we feel deep within us, promise to make them knowable through language and offer to train us culturally in their proper expression. This, for Illouz, is emotional capitalism, and it has effected an entire army of professionals who have institutionalised themselves and made themselves indispensable. Parenting is one of the intimate realms into which emotional capitalism is stretching.

The language of tough love has spread from television media to parent pedagogy formats to policy initiative. It is used to govern the intimate conduct of families, to monitor and advise families on the right combination and enactment of toughness and warmth, and ultimately to discipline those families marked as failing. The biopolitical dimensions of tough love can be seen in the ways that it would come in the first decade of the 21st century to direct statecraft and family intervention policy agendas.

Tough love in the supernanny state

The magnifying loop of 'problem family' rhetoric worked to legitimate the extension and intensification of family interventions by the state that sought to target families marked as 'dysfunctional'. The discourse of 'tough love' and 'getting tough' as a necessary and legitimate action for families asking TV nannies for help was extended and used by politicians and policy makers seeking to 'get tough' on their failed citizen-subjects.

Stephen Crossley (2016) tracks the increasingly assertive and even 'muscular' language used by David Cameron, after the English riots of 2011 and his announcement of a 'Troubled Families' initiative which, like the Respect Task Force that had preceded it, would 'sort out' and 'intervene' in the lives of workless or troubled families. 'Troubled families', defined as those involved with crime or anti-social behaviour, whose children had poor school attendance or school exclusions and where an adult was claiming out-of-work benefits, were portrayed by Cameron as 'victims of state failures' that sought to 'rescue' them but ended up 'making excuses' for them (Cameron, 2011, quoted in Crossley, 2016). As Crossley notes, this muscular language was used to legitimate family interventions like the Troubled Families scheme and reflected a wider remasculinisation of the state under neoliberalism (Wacquant, 2010), whereby governments seek to control, dictate, monitor and punish those citizens who are deemed to have failed in their social obligations.

The Troubled Families programme was a nationwide policy initiative premised on identifying, labelling and targeting interventions on a small subset of parents who had been labelled as 'troubled' by their local council and 'referred' to the programme. It represented an intensification in the supernanny state that was in embryonic development via the latticework of state-funded parenting classes, Parenting Orders, anti-social behaviour policy initiatives and numerous family intervention projects that had been established to enable state penetration into the everyday lives of 'challenging' and 'problem' families. The Troubled Families programme would offer 'payment by results' to local authorities, who were tasked with identifying a national 'problem population' of 120,000 'troubled families', assigning a dedicated key worker, 'getting in the front door' and 'getting to grips with' the everyday struggles and challenges they were facing, which might include routine, hygiene, cleanliness, truancy and behaviour. Crossley (2017) critiques the infantilising language of the Troubled Families programme, which assumes that family troubles are caused by maternal weakness, failings or incompetence.

Ruth Levitas (2012) usefully tracks the invention of the 120,000 figure and shows that this data came from a 2007 research study titled *Families At Risk*, which calculated how many families *had* troubles (including overcrowded housing, mental health problems, illness or disability and/or were living in poverty). This research was later distorted and misrepresented as having calculated how many families were *causing* trouble (addiction, criminality, violence). By the time the Troubled Families programme was launched, politicians were speaking confidently of the 'families from hell':

> If you live near one you know very well who they are. ... police, health and schools know who they are, because they spend a disproportionate amount of time and money dealing with them. These families are both troubled and causing trouble ... truanting, antisocial behaviour and cost to public services. (Eric Pickles, Secretary of State for Communities and Local Government, quoted in Levitas, 2012: 5)

Any sympathy for disadvantaged and vulnerable families was then replaced wholesale with a language of stigma and scapegoating. Louise Casey, the state supernanny who headed the Respect Task Force, was later appointed Head of the Troubled Families programme. She described it as an opportunity to shake up social work and radically transform family intervention – and, most importantly, to 'toughen up' on families who have been left to decline under 'compassionate cruelty' (Cameron, 2011, quoted in Crossley, 2016). Crossley catalogues Casey's descriptions of social work as 'cuddly' and failing to instil a sense of responsibility in its 'clients'. In multiple public speeches and interviews, Casey describes social work programmes as 'wrapping everybody in cotton wool', over-assessing families, but failing to take decisive action. As Crossley comments, this punitive, sanctions-based language works to complement and legitimate broader policy shifts that seek to understand poverty and 'trouble' as being largely inherited, behavioural and moral.

While press coverage and political discussion of this new direction in this 'supernanny state' tended to frame *all* families as potentially needing support and intervention, such intervention programmes tended to be directed towards the moral regulation, surveillance and sanctioning of the most marginalised families, and the effects of this policy direction were far from even for all families. Amanda Holt (2008) analysed the 7,000 Parenting Orders that were issued to parents between June 2000 and December 2006, and found that they were disproportionately issued to lone mothers, black Caribbean parents and parents who were refugees and asylum seekers. Holt details one instance where a Parenting Order was issued to a mother in place of an unaffordable court-ordered fine, a decision clearly 'at odds' with the rhetoric of 'parenting support'. Val Gillies (2005) catalogues instances where the mothers taking part in her research were inappropriately referred to counselling, advice and therapy, when what they really needed was safe and permanent housing and protection from violent and abusive ex-partners.

Under an initial rhetoric of 'engaging' and 'supporting' parents, a supernanny state has flourished, which identifies and marks 'problem' families through new, secretive forms of bureaucracy. Crossley (2017) counts 55 pieces of information that local authorities are required to collect and compile in order to identify suitably troubled families, and rightly raises concerns about how this data is organised, shared and managed, particularly in the expanded phase of the programme. The state capture and storage of personal information is rarely transparent, and families may not even know that the 'parenting support' they are being offered or coerced to take up is part of the Troubled Families programme. These developments highlight the ways that family statecraft has moved into a more authoritarian, algorithmic and surveillant direction.

In her examination of the emotional politics that drove the acceleration of the perceived 'crisis' in social work and child protection systems, Joanne Warner (2015) notes how conjunctions of media power and popular protest become animated in national imaginings of disgust and anger. Warner highlights how dramatic forms of moral indignation are produced in relation to specific problem groups. We can see the importance of moral indignation as animated in parenting media such as *Supernanny*, which dramatises and makes spectacular the ordinary failures of families to neutralise ordinary instances of familial conflict. What is interesting is how this moral indignation can then be captured, ballooned and directed in the public and policy imagination to construct marginalised groups as polluting, threatening and contaminating. This kind of language saturates policy and discussion reports, which reference 'problem families' as 'a creeping expansion' (Allen and Duncan Smith, 2008: 9) of families who are ungovernable and a threat to the moral order.

In the next chapter, we will examine how these ideas of ungovernable families were put to ideological work in a new era of austere policymaking. The discourses of 'tough love' that were initially deployed in reference to misbehaving children, were expanded and applied to 'troublemaking families' who were constructed across popular culture and public debate as undisciplined and morally lax.

The rhetoric of the supernanny state ('getting tough') would forthwith be used to legitimate the dismantling of welfare provision itself.

Notes

[1] Victoria Climbié was a girl, born in the Ivory Coast, who moved to France and then to the UK under an informal fostering arrangement with her great-aunt, Marie-Thérèse Kouao. Over her 15 months under Kouao's guardianship (who was joined by her boyfriend and accomplice Carl Manning), Victoria Climbié was neglected, tortured and eventually murdered by them. The pathologist who examined her body described it as the worst case of child abuse she had ever seen. Kouao and Manning were found guilty of child cruelty and murder and sentenced to life imprisonment. Following a public inquiry, the social services teams of Haringey and Brent Council in north London were described as seriously defective. Child protection services had been allowed to deteriorate and had been virtually paralysed by a major restructure and chronic underfunding. The public inquiry exposed a catalogue of individual and systemic failures, and made 108 recommendations to reform child protection procedure.

[2] Director Daisy Goodwin discussed these events at a roundtable discussion, '*Bringing Up Baby*: Parenting, expertise and the media', held in Cambridge on 14 December 2007.

[3] Ford's own parenting philosophy has itself been the subject of intense debate; her baby care manual *The Contented Little Baby Book* advocates the use of very strict routines with newborn babies and has been the focus of many polarising discussions. Most notably, in 2006 Ford threatened parenting website Mumsnet with legal action after a number of discussion posts that Ford described as 'gross personal attacks'. She accused the site of waging a 'defamatory campaign' against her. Mumsnet took the unusual step of banning members from posting any more discussion related to Ford or her baby care philosophy. This extraordinary turn of events, whereby a bestselling parenting manual cannot be discussed on the UK's most populated parenting discussion website for fear of legal action, reveals much about the provocations of contemporary parent pedagogy.

FIVE

Parenting in austere times: warmth and wealth

In January 2010, the then leader of the Conservative party David Cameron was invited to speak at the launch of *The Character Inquiry* (Lexmond and Grist, 2011). Published by the think-tank Demos, this report proposed that in order to achieve greater levels of wellbeing, policy needs to look beyond material wealth and instead consider how to build and shape the character of its citizens. Cameron would become Prime Minister four months later and he used this keynote speech, titled 'Building the Responsible Society' (Cameron, 2010a), to set out his new agenda for character education, which would place strong families, marriage and parenting (especially parenting in the early years of childhood) as the crucial bedrock for social renewal.

The content of this speech is fascinating. It illuminates how Cameron, and the Coalition government he would lead until 2016, would draw on – and extend – the individualised and moralised tenor of the parenting discourse that preceded him through the Blair and Brown years of the New Labour government. The speech also shows how concerns about rising *material* inequalities between families, and the consequences these inequalities have been shown to have on children's outcomes, would be further sidelined in policy making. This speech precedes a period of intense welfare reform that would further impoverish the most marginalised and vulnerable families in Britain.

In order to understand how these reforms were made 'commonsense', we must unpick the 'bad parent' explanatory threads that made them seem, and feel, sensible. The sensibilities that Cameron draws on in this speech are by now familiar to us. 'Parenting' becomes a verb, something that parents *do*, rather than something they *are* (Williams, 2004); parenting is a set of skills, capacities and abilities, which we can all learn and acquire; anybody can be a good parent or a bad parent, no matter what their circumstance are. Cameron acknowledges these inequalities, only to dismiss them: 'Of course there is a link between material poverty and poor life chances, but the full picture is that that link also runs through the style of parenting that children in poor households receive. Research shows that, while responsible parenting is more likely to occur in wealthier households, children in poor households who are raised with that style of parenting do just as well. What matters most to a child's life chances is *not the wealth of their upbringing but the warmth of their parenting*' (Cameron, 2010a, emphasis added).

In speaking with this vocabulary of parental 'doing', Cameron is drawing on the models of 'tough love' outlined in the previous chapter, and popularised by cultural texts such as *Supernanny* (see Chapter Three), which locate the causes of broader social problems within the intimate conduct of family life. We can interpret his comments as part of a deep-rooted evasion of privilege and a denial of social class from politicians and public figures: a refusal to name, engage with and take seriously the injuries of class (Sennett and Cobb, 1973). We might equally interpret these comments as a distortion of moral sentiments that too often leave oppressed classes in the double-bind of being pathologised or patronised (Sayer, 2002). Cameron's dismissal of how significantly material resources impact on the conditions of parenting – and the classed cultures that celebrate some parents and pathologise others – recycles the same kind of commonsense meritocracy that has legitimated decades of deepening class inequality (Littler, 2017).

This chapter examines the historical shift at work as the New Labour government (1997–2010) was replaced by a Conservative/Liberal Democrat Coalition (2010) and then by a Conservative government (2015 onwards). In particular, this shift was characterised by a focus on 'runaway' and 'uncontrollable' public spending and by repeated messaging that the national deficit had become unmanageable. On his ascent to the premiership, Cameron often described his politics as being driven by 'social responsibility' (Cameron, 2006), a usefully vague term that could be used in reference to national budgets, seeking economic efficiencies and cutting waste, as well as in reference to household and domestic management, in a language of, and directed towards, individually 'responsible families'.

An 'ordinary' family

Indeed, throughout his premiership, Cameron sought to acknowledge – but ultimately to downplay – the significance of wealth in his own trajectory of success. His narration of his upbringing emphasises what his parents did, how they 'parented' him in an abstract and replicable sense, rather than the wealth they commanded, the social resources they were able to mobilise, the networks and connections at their disposal.[1] In their biography of Cameron, Ashcroft and Oakeshott (2016) report an alleged self-deprecating quip made by Cameron that he was born with 'two silver spoons in his mouth'.

Like Tony Blair, who he most clearly emulated,[2] Cameron presented himself as an ordinary, dutiful family man and an engaged, hands-on father. Discourses of 'family' and 'marriage' would be central pillars in Cameron's project to modernise and detoxify the Conservative brand and to realign it with the values of social liberalism (Hayton, 2010), particularly in his endorsement of civil partnerships. Robert Busby (2009) tracks the importance of ideas of 'family' in the Camerons' marketing of themselves as 'ordinary'. He outlines how, beginning with the Conservative leadership election in 2005, the Camerons began to minimise their connections to wealth, evade reference to his elite education and aristocratic connections, downplay their vast personal and family fortune, and instead emphasise the mundane details of their family life. For example, in a profile interview with *Harper's Bazaar* in 2007, Samantha Cameron conveyed an image of herself as constrained by domestic and financial pressures, saying: 'I'm a working mum. We have to pay for childcare. I don't have huge amounts of cash to spend on designer clothing ... you feel poorer than you've ever been' (quoted in Busby, 2009: 181). At a public meeting in Manchester in 2010, Cameron defended cuts to public services aimed at poorer families and infamously described himself and his wife as 'part of the sharp-elbowed middle-classes' (Groves, 2010). His most awkward interview moments were where his carefully cultivated image of himself as 'ordinary' were punctured. In a 2009 interview with *The Times*, he hesitated on the matter of how many houses he owned, and became anxious that he would be made to 'sound like a prat'. His decision to speak at a launch for Demos – a think-tank most often associated with Tony Blair – should be seen as part of his attempts to 'decontaminate' his party's brand and associations with privilege and to extend open hands to organisations that were also trying to position themselves in a post-Blairite, media-friendly policy consensus.[3]

Yet the accusations of leading a privileged 'Eton mafia' into Westminster would dog Cameron throughout his premiership. The dynastic wealth of the Camerons is indisputable. His father was estimated to be 'worth' £10 million, inherited through a long line of financiers and increased through his lucrative career as an adviser on tax avoidance. Cameron sought to distance himself from the family business, recognising that any association with offshore funds and tax irregularities would muddy his self-presentation as 'tax transparent' and his stated aim to 'crack down' on aggressive tax avoidance. However, he was hit by fresh scandal in 2016, when the publication of the 'Panama Papers' revealed a direct link to his father's tax-avoiding fund.[4] When Cameron married his wife Samantha, their combined wealth made them multimillionaires. Samantha Cameron's family wealth includes a property portfolio worth £20 million, her father's baronetcy and shares and stakes in several family businesses. The income, wealth and property portfolio of the Camerons are, like all dynasties in the 'superrich', elusive; but biographers agree that they command a combined fortune somewhere in the region of £30 million (Ashcroft and Oakeshott, 2016; Seldon and Snowdon, 2016).

Cameron's claims to being 'middle-class' in light of his extensive wealth and privilege are as outrageous as they are instructive. His preference for discourses of 'warmth' over 'wealth', in explaining why some children 'fail' and some 'succeed', needs to be excavated in the context of deep lineages of dynastic wealth that have accumulated in his own family over generations. The great chasm of inequality which separated Cameron – and indeed much of his Cabinet – from the majority of the British population (whom they ostensibly represent) becomes evaded and euphemised in political discourse that positions the importance of 'warmth' over 'wealth'. The launch of *The Character Inquiry* (Lexmond and Grist, 2011), where Cameron begins his speech with a perfunctory acknowledgement of the links between family poverty and poor life chances, mirrors his perfunctory acknowledgement of being born with 'two silver spoons' – neither remarks lead to larger and broader engagement with the structures of privilege that reproduce social advantage. The huge familial wealth of the Camerons matters – and the concentration and consolidation of wealth in the richest UK families over the past thirty years matters. The rich have indeed made an extraordinary comeback (Sayer, 2014). The production of fantasies that 'family responsibility' can work as a panacea for such social inequality and poverty – and the participation in those fantasies by an immensely privileged politician such as Cameron – is indeed a cruel irony.

This preference for explanations of 'warmth' over 'wealth' form part of a much larger policy rewriting of the very terms of social security, entitlement and welfare, and a reinvigoration of the dichotomy of 'deserving' and 'undeserving' in relation to parental behaviour and morality. 'Poor parents' are recast as agents of blame; neither victims of structural inequality nor personifications of the effects of injustice, but as 'failures in self-governance, unable or unwilling to appropriately capitalise on their lives' (Gillies, 2005: 837). We can imagine how and why good parenting narratives that emphasised 'warmth over wealth' have a great appeal to parents across the socioeconomic spectrum – whether as convenient alibi or hopeful mantra. But, crucially, these narratives were also crucial for generating popular consent for a raft of policies that would intensify the project of unravelling the welfare state in the name of 'austerity'. Indeed, the idea of becoming 'austere' – of trimming the fat, tightening the belt, finding ways to go on with less – would come to serve as a powerful romance in this next phase of 'responsibilising families'.

'Broken Britain': public spending as waste

The 'credit crunch' of 2007 would become a full financial crisis in 2008-09 and lead to the most prolonged period of recession, in Britain and elsewhere, since the Great Depression of the 1930s. The financial crisis of 2008-09 was caused by the collapse of the speculative housing market, global inflation resulting from emerging commodity markets, the over- inflation of asset prices and other high-risk lending practices in the banking industry. In response to the recession, and incredibly in an attempt to promote growth, a latticework of economic measures were implemented on national and international levels in an attempt to encourage recovery, most taking the form of fiscal 'austerity', or reducing public spending. Economists warned that this recession was part of the cyclical boom-and-bust nature of late capitalism, pointing to how capitalism itself is a never-ending series of crisis and recovery (Krugman, 2012). They cautioned that the idea of 'expansionary austerity' – that cutting spending leads to higher output – was 'about as plausible as a unicorn with a bag of magic salt' (Blyth, 2013: x).

'Austerity', the quality or state of being austere and the condition of enforced economy, was named Word of the Year in 2010 by the Merriam-Webster dictionary, and has since been attached to a raft of neoliberal economic policies that have been concerned with deficit reduction, reduced public spending and diminishing/disappearing welfare benefits and payments. 'Austerity' is also the central agenda under which the responsibilities of the state towards its citizens are being reconfigured, for example in new, tighter conditions being imposed on those receiving financial aid and assistance.

In the UK, the General Election of 2010 delivered a hung Parliament with no party achieving an overall majority. After a series of negotiations over five days, the Conservative and Liberal Democrat parties were able to form a Coalition government, which surprisingly would go on to last the full five-year government term (see Laws, 2010; Adonis, 2013). The short tenure of outgoing Prime Minister Gordon Brown (2007–10) had been blighted by the global recession. Despite receiving wide praise for taking early decisive action to make government funding available to British banks and thus ameliorate a potential banking collapse, Brown's broader fiscal policies of extending state support to families with children would subsequently be framed as a 'poisonous legacy', which attempted to 'make as many people as possible dependent on the state' (Porter, 2012).

David Cameron had spent the year before the election building the groundwork for an 'age of austerity', characterised by restraint, thrift and transparency in public spending, and positioned as a necessary response to the alleged profligacy of the previous Labour government. In one speech to the Conservative spring forum on 26 April 2009, which typified the tenor of his election campaign, Cameron stated that 'the days of easy money are over', referred to the Labour government as 'spendaholics', 'irresponsible' and 'a party of extravagant waste', and described the debt crisis as a result of public overspending and lack of fiscal restraint. Across key speeches that year, he would go on to repeat these distinctions between the out-of-control indebtedness of the past and the 'necessary' lean fitness of the future:

> Why is our economy broken? ... Because government got too big, spent too much and doubled the national debt. Why is our society broken? Because government got too big, did too much and undermined responsibility. Why are our politics broken? Because government got too big, promised too much and pretended it had all the answers. Do you know the worst thing about their big government? ... It is the steady erosion of responsibility. (David Cameron, 2009 Conservative party conference, quoted in Slater, 2014)

These distinctions were mediated through a range of metaphors, specifically around the 'solvent family', the hardworking family and, above all, the *responsible* family, which lives within its means and saves in order to spend, rather than borrowing in order to spend. These metaphors are further illustrated in the following remarks from George Osborne, Chancellor of the Exchequer, in which the promises to embrace austerity as a government are linked explicitly to the economic realities of the responsible family:

> We are going to ensure, like every solvent household in the country, that what we buy, we can afford; that the bills we incur, we have the income to meet; and that we do not saddle our children with the interest on the interest on the interest of the debts we were not ourselves prepared to pay. (Osborne, 2010)

Osborne is not the first politician to explicitly link national economic policy to the balanced household budget. During her time as Prime Minister, Margaret Thatcher famously claimed that her knowledge of how to balance a household budget qualified her to take decisions about the British economy, drawing on powerful tropes of the prudent housewife and her own mythologised past as a grocer's daughter (Campbell, 2001). Now, as then, national 'solvency' is aligned with the responsibility, thrift and temperance of the individual household. What is illuminating about Osborne's comments is how they reinvigorate older notions of a 'social crisis' (particularly a crisis of responsibility) and attach these to the financial crisis (via debt), thereby magnetising ideas of the need for an 'age of austerity'. The term 'social recession' has been a popular device across the political spectrum, including the progressive left, for some time, appearing even before actual economic recession began (see Rutherford and Shah, 2006).

To understand this stitching together of responsibility, debt and austerity, we have to go back to ideas of 'social recession' and specifically its populist expression through the discourse of 'Broken Britain'. 'Broken Britain' welded together anxieties about a responsibility deficit (people making immoral 'lifestyle choices'), welfare dependency and social reproduction. It pathologises conditions of dependency in order to reanimate those familiar moral categories of deserving/undeserving poor, holding the undeserving as responsible not only for their own predicament but also for that of the 'bloated' welfare state.

These narratives of individual deficiency and moral decline would scaffold political debate around the UK in local by-elections (Mooney, 2009), as well as directing the tenor of national debate. One of the most grotesque narratives that emerged from the financial crisis was that the extraordinary levels of public deficit accumulated after the 2008-09 recession were not a consequence of the failure of high-risk speculative capitalism, but rather of the 'wasted populations' (Bauman, 2003) who subsist upon the public purse. This narrative was deployed to legitimate fiscal discipline as the 'solution' to the current crisis of capitalism, responding to the precarious future by shrinking the state, compacting and condensing public spending, becoming lean, pursuing 'efficiency' and eliminating 'waste'.

These repetitions of 'Broken Britain' notions of fiscal discipline in turn revived notions of the 'underclass' – popularised in the UK by the embrace of Charles Murray, whose US-based research (1990) conceived of poverty as a set of social pathologies, including illegitimacy, crime and unemployment. In his later work, Murray elaborated on the significance of the family (and its collapse) in the alleged generational transmission of these pathologies. Murray's notion of the 'underclass' has been repeatedly discredited by social scientists, who found his statistical analysis to be highly selective, his sociological methods unsound and his evidence of a 'dependency culture' among the poor and unemployed lacking (for the detailed critique, see Gallie, 1994; Oppenheim and Harker, 1996; Kempson, 1996; for an overview of this work, see Lister, 1996).

Despite the robust critique of Murray's work, the concept of the 'underclass' keeps returning to political debate. Indeed, sociologists have described it as a 'zombie concept' (MacDonald et al, 2014) in various guises, incorporated by successive UK governments, replacing 'underprivileged' – the preferred term of the 1970s – and in turn subsumed in the later 1990s by the term 'socially excluded' (Levitas, 2005). These (mis)understanding of poverty revive late-Victorian moral categories of pauperism, and popularise disgust about poverty, framing it in the language of disease, contamination and moral hygiene (Lister, 2006), which in turn distinguish between the 'deserving' and 'undeserving' poor. Murray himself commented on the 'ugliness' of the concept of the underclass, yet it remains a potent political tool and offers a neat synergy with the explanations of public spending as wasteful. Underclass discourse forms a key pillar in the substitution of class politics with the culturalisation of poverty (Levitas, 2005; Haylett, 2001) and the attendant vocabularies of inequality, which recycle and circulate fantasies of meritocracy.

The flexibility of these moral discourses of poverty mean that a shifting constellation of moral 'failings' can be diagnosed as its symptoms – indeed, we can see an ever-expanding palimpsest of categories that construct the alleged familial roots of the underclass. Where Gordon Brown spoke of 'chaotic' or 'dysfunctional' families in his 2009 Labour Party Conference speech, David Cameron preferred the term 'problem families'.

Murray's work was politically reinvigorated and enthusiastically embraced by the Centre for Social Justice, a highly influential think-tank led by Conservative MP and Secretary of State for Work and Pensions Iain Duncan Smith. The Centre for Social Justice bequeathed specific and prolonged attention to 'family breakdown' as one of the principal causes of poverty, and positioned marriage as the cure. The Centre for Social Justice produced numerous publications that repeated this rhetoric around chaotic, dysfunctional, broken families. These publications are based on negligible sociological evidence – as Tom Slater (2014) notes, not a single social scientist was invited to contribute to the Centre's 'landmark' study of the causes of poverty, the multi-volume *Breakdown Britain* (2006). Yet despite this absence of sociological expertise, the Centre's message of a moral crisis in the family was institutionally amplified across parliamentary discussion and fed into public debate. The moral annotations that sutured familial 'irresponsibility' to a bloated welfare state were crucial in legitimating the 'age of austerity'. Slater contends that the production of 'Broken Britain' myths by the Centre for Social Justice illuminates the processes of 'agnotology': the wilful, conscious, institutional production of ignorance. This 'strategic ignorance' works to deny and evade robust evidence, replacing it with opinion polls and repetitions of easily digestible soundbites, consequently diverting attention away from the structural failures that lead to poverty.

Politicians were quick to exploit high-profile events and disturbances as 'evidence' of this 'slow-motion moral collapse' (Cameron, 2011b). Chapter One of this book began with a discussion of the English riots of August 2011 – three days of social unrest and looting that were 'sparked' by the killing of Mark Duggan and the failure of the Metropolitan Police to mediate with his grieving family and community – and these events were themselves immediately sutured to the 'Broken Britain' mythology. David Cameron used his Troubled Families speech in December following the riots to assert confidently how they demonstrated that the institution of 'the family' was 'going wrong' and thus perpetuating 'a culture of disruption and irresponsibility that cascades through generations' (Cameron, 2011c). Enterprising politicians were quick to blame the riots on individual families, who were failing to keep their children at home (May, 2011) or who had become afraid to discipline their children (Lammy, 2011). Media scholars tracked the discourses deployed by politicians and commentators immediately after the riots. They identified a number of salient themes: a repeated emphasis placed on 'troubled families'; gang activity; ideas of 'feral' children; and families and other figures of failed and improper citizenship (de Benedictis, 2012; Allen and Taylor, 2012, Casey, 2013; Tyler, 2013).

Commonsense 'explanations' quickly gained traction[5] and explicitly connected the 'failings' of the welfare state to the 'criminality' of the rioters and serve to speak to the broader ideological project to 'fix' 'Broken Britain'. Cameron's expedient use of the riots to justify his austerity project of welfare reform is extraordinary:

> One of the biggest parts of this social fight-back is fixing the welfare system. For years we've had a system that encourages the worst in people – that incites laziness, that excuses bad behaviour, that erodes self-discipline, that discourages hard

work and above all that drains responsibility away from people. (Cameron, 2011b)

In rekindling this discourse of dependency, and specifically of an 'epidemic of the diseased will' (Berlant, 2013), a sickness for which the cure is austerity and the removal of the weakening succour of welfare, a powerful set of attendant fantasies around the austere family was also mobilised. The austere family – a mirror image to the troubled, chaotic or dysfunctional family that depends on the welfare state and is unable to manage the extensive public money lavished on them – convenes around the ideals of thrift, responsibility and restraint. The political and cultural myths assembled under the banner of 'Broken Britain' work to construct a fantasy family of the past; reproductively responsible through marriage (and held in place through the useful stigma of 'wedlock'), financially responsible and self-denying ('doing without'), inventive, resilient, grateful and morally upstanding. The mythologies of 'Broken Britain' assembled a cultural politics of wanting, which pathologised poor families as irresponsible and feckless overconsumers – wanting the wrong things, unable to budget and constantly mismanaging the resources that were funnelled to them by the responsible taxpayer. Cameron spoke directly to the cultural politics of wanting in an address published in *The Sun*, which called forth an imaginary workless/workshy 'other':

> When you work hard and still sometimes have to go without the things you want because times are tough, it's maddening to know there are some people who could work but just don't want to. You know the people I mean. You walk down the road on your way to work and you see the curtains drawn in their house. You know they could work, but they choose not to. And just as maddening is the fact that they seem to get away with it. (Cameron, 2010b)

Here, Cameron directly addresses those who are feeling squeezed by the global impacts of neoliberal policy, regional de-industrialisation, global migrations of capital, tax evasion and consolidation of wealth by a new class of super-elites, the wilful destruction of organised labour, and new topographies of work, which normalise insecurity. He addresses them in order to direct their attention *away* from these structural failures, and towards the stigmatised populations who are figured as social waste (Tyler, 2013). Such comments amplify and solidify latent desires to punish those positioned as 'dependent', via discourses of the good citizen who is already 'doing their bit' for the nation by 'going without' in an age of austerity. These popularising myths of the feckless and irresponsible underclass work in part by interpellating the good citizen of austerity, who is enduring 'tough times'; they are both 'underclass-blaming' and 'nation-building'.

'Broken Britain' rhetoric is thus a powerful mythologising tool that evades discussion of the intensified precarity of *all* labour – the rise of short-term contracts or 'zero hours' work, underemployment, low wages, the threat of outsourcing, diminishing returns on maternity pay and sickness pay, the failure to recognise caring responsibilities, 'flexploitation', the shift of education and training costs and risks to the individual, and so on (Ross, 2009; Weeks, 2011; Standing, 2011). 'Dependency discourse' is transformative of austerity; through a kind of 'magical alchemy' (Clarke and Newman, 2012), austerity becomes a necessary intervention into a munificent welfare system, which is said to have 'gone soft', as well as an invitation to the good citizen to 'toughen up' and embrace these precarious times with dignity and invention. This cultural politics of wanting works to animate and validate desired and desirable austere selves. In the case of the austere subject, these animations operate through transformations such as becoming financially lean, embracing restraint, doing more with less and perhaps opting out of some kinds of consumption altogether.

Blitz spirit and ration romances

The magical transformation of austerity, from an ideological assault on the welfare state into a positive opportunity for good citizens to embrace a leaner and more sustainable form of living, was 'made sensible' after the 2008–09 recession through a proliferation of austerity romances. Speaking on the flagship current affairs programme *Question Time*, Conservative MP Caroline Spelman demonstrated the hold of these austerity romances, when she stated that austerity 'works' as an economic policy at both a household and national level, and proposing that we rename austerity as 'thrift'. She stated: 'Let's call it thrift then because thrift is a virtue and thrift needs to be part of the solution to our nation's problems … thrift is living within your means' (Spelman on *Question Time*, 10 April 2012). Drawing on positive discourses of solvency, efficiency and financial competence, Spelman's remarks responded to an audience member – whose question pertinently challenged how public services were being dismantled in the name of austerity – and recast this as a set of virtuous household fiscal habits.

These discourses of the *virtues* of thrift were spectacularly realised in one of television's surprise hits of that year, *Superscrimpers* (Channel 4, 2011, 2012), which produced a kind of 'austerity chic', interspersing talking-head clips of 'commonsense' wisdom from its 'army of thrifters', with pedagogic segments, in which groups of volunteers learn a 'lost' domestic skill from an expert. Hosted by 'Miss Moneypenny' (Heather McGregor), *Superscrimpers* berates British consumers for spending beyond their means, getting into debt, failing to save and put by, wanting too much and being wasteful. Each episode centres on a staged intervention by McGregor, forcing a 'spendaholic' to acknowledge the annual cost of their runaway extravagance (ranging from clothes to beauty products and magazines), effecting their shame and subsequent resolve to become restrained and virtuous.

Superscrimpers explicitly draws on fantasies of post-war resilience and restraint, in order to narrate the British citizen/consumer of today as unable to control themselves, chaotically spending and saddled with unsustainable debts. It mobilises a nostalgia for the 'Blitz spirit' of the Second World War and the resolve to endure the post-war years of rationing. The opening minutes of the programme use footage (from the Pathé archives) of housewives queuing outside shops, hunting for bargains, or trying an outlandish innovation that sought to address the constant limitations and shortages of essentials created by the rationing system. The voiceover presents these activities as evidence of pleasurable ingenuity, in which we must become reskilled:

> 'For postwar Brits, bagging bargains was a matter of *national pride* ... now in 2012 we're *rediscovering the thrill* of being thrifty, finding clever ways of having the lifestyle we want without paying as much for it. Leading the way is Mrs Moneypenny, and her army of superscrimpers. Between them, they will help us all waste not, want not.'
> (*Superscrimpers* opening voiceover, emphasis added)

Superscrimpers works as a text of austerity romance, positioning thrift as not simply a matter of economic survival, but rather as transformative of the relationship between the self and consumer culture. This is thrift aestheticised – saturated with retro-kitsch appeal, and threaded through with anxieties around overconsumption, waste and indebtedness. 'Thrift' is here offered as a moral reorientation, which will cure us of the condition of dependence. It animates a consoling and constructed national nostalgia, and (re)circulates pathologies about the 'wrong' kind of consumption.

UK lifestyle television was quick to generate a psychologised vocabulary of recession, developing an instructional genre of 'austerity pedagogy' television that promised to show viewers how to engage in 'smart spending', how to be competent consumers and how to be 'savvy'. As well as *Superscrimpers*, other examples like *Economy Gastronomy* (BBC Two, 2009) and *The Ultimate Guide to Penny-Pinching* (Channel 4, 2011) framed the constraints of a tightened budget as a source of pleasure, and set participants the challenge of doing more with less and creating luxury with little.

Heather Nunn (2011) describes this genre as 'retreat TV' and notes that it prioritises home as a space of emotional comfort, 'affording its subjects (primarily middle-class) the privileges of self-reflexivity with, and often without, expert advice' (Nunn, 2011: 175). 'Retreat TV' emphasises being 'smart', and offers philosophies for resisting and opting out of consumption, including downshifting, upcycling and repurposing. Nunn rightly situates the strand of television within a broader post-recession disillusionment with white-collar work and disenchantment with consumerism, and points out that the strategies to address such disenchantment in fact (paradoxically) require money, mobility and competence. In other words, even pedagogies of penny-pinching are classed and classing. As Nunn argues, retreat TV is 'retrogressive', in the sense that it reproduces dominant models of 'lifestyle' self-improvement, which ostensibly it is trying to escape (Nunn, 2011: 176).

Concurrently, the field of self-help literature was also capitalising on the pedagogical opportunities of recession and austerity, generating an intense period of publishing that sought to instruct readers in the moral dimensions of frugality and restraint. *Be Thrifty* (Catton and Suntree, 2009) promised to show readers 'how to live better with less'; *Ausperity* (Tobin, 2013) promised to show 'how to live the life you want for less'; and *Live More, Want Less* (Calomagno, 2011) instructed readers on how to 'find order in your life'. The messages across this genre are complex, speaking both to the desire for luxury, style and satisfaction ('the good life') alongside the pathologising of certain forms of wanting or overconsumption. These recessionary cultural texts seek to resolve contradictions and ambivalence about (over)consumption, by emphasising an ethos of surveillant self-transformation. The forensic charting of spending, debt and consumption, and of identifying opportunities for financial efficiencies – the process of becoming thrifty – is signalled as joyful, pleasurable, and a productive rediscovery of the ingenuities of past generations.

These romanticisations of austerity connect the current production of 'responsibility crisis' with eulogies of very specific past periods of austerity, in Britain most clearly fetishising the post-war rationing period.[6] The principles of rationing have been enthusiastically adopted on multiple thrift and frugal living weblogs, which crystallise lay attitudes around austerity as a positive opportunity to remake habits and everyday practices. The weblog *Rationing Revisited*[7] documents the challenges of its author to feed her family of five on wartime rations. Its author claims that a return to rationing is not only viable for the modern family, but is also a way to save money, get healthy and (along with other 'drastic downsizing') be happy. *The 1940s Experiment*[8] is a blog that documents the experience of surviving on wartime rations for a year in order to lose weight. These weblogs are scattered with vintage wartime propaganda posters, which extol the virtues of the kitchen garden, the allotment, vegetables, 'making do and mending', keeping calm and carrying on, and so on: the combination of vintage imagery and rationing chronicles working to eulogise frugal shopping and cooking.

Of course, being thrifty and 'pinching the pennies' has *always* been a crucial and necessary component of survival for those at the sharpest ends of poverty. This hidden labour of living on the breadline – creatively using up food leftovers, foraging for food, growing vegetables, quick-fix insulation to reduce heating bills, shopping strategically and 'shopping around', buying from secondhand and charity shops – and the experiences of poverty that make such labour necessary has so often been shaming, stigmatising and unspoken. On the fringes of austerity Britain, we have also seen the rise of survival strategies that are more ambivalently read with unease, embarrassment and even disgust, such as skip-diving for food.

We should also note how thrifty living has formed an important countercultural mainstay of anti-consumerist movements, ecological and environmental activism throughout the 20th century. These movements have promoted inventive ways to endure and thrive with few resources, and have built a significant critique of consumption, 'disposable culture' and the waste of late capitalism. It is not surprising to see thrift guidance proliferate in a time of austerity – but the shape and texture of contemporary thrift and the affects it mobilises are interesting. Far from being a means to survival, or a politicised rejection of capitalism and consumerism, the mainstreaming of these austerity romances promotes and circulates thrifty living as a lifestyle; pleasurable, deliberately chosen, a source of cultural value and a site of classed distinction. The contemporary *cultural* expression of pleasurable 'new thrift' (Jensen, 2012) and austerity-romance, in the period following recession and the implementation of austerity, were largely disconnected from necessity, and instead became anchored to fantasies of pleasurable retreat. Under 'new thrift', under the romances of austerity, such practices can be transformed into aesthetic pleasures and artforms.

Austerity romances, in these cultural arenas, become an opportunity for social distinction: to showcase consumer competence and thus cultural value. Austerity activities – which once were money-saving and now have 'retro' appeal – such as knitting, crocheting and crafting, can now be fairly costly when comparing the prices of materials versus the inexpensive finished products of global capitalism. Complexly, these distinctions work to pathologise classed 'others', who become constructed as insufficiently austere; who do not reuse, recycle, upcycle, who are wasteful, who pay full price for the new consumer goods they want but do not 'need', who participate unthinkingly in the proliferation of consumer 'stuff', and so on. The cultural politics of austerity romances at this moment are centrally (and contradictorily) about taste and taste cultures, and the *desire for austerity* is resonant with 'Broken Britain' rhetoric, remaking moral value, by countering the habits of the 'spendthrift' and the incompetent consumer.

Lauren Berlant (1997) has described these transformations as a production of the 'intimate public', whereby citizenship becomes reconfigured as the sum of the private acts. This 'intimate public' is, for Berlant, traditionalist, nostalgic and directed towards the family sphere, a downsized version of citizenship, in which 'the family' is implicated ever more intensely within the blueprint of the nation.

It is fascinating to track how rapidly ideas of 'austerity' were taken up as a cultural annotation through the intimate public, in the longer-term politicisation of parenting examined throughout this book. Austerity is not simply a set of economic policies, but also something that takes hold through the affective dimensions of citizenship, nation and belonging. Austerity romances made an appeal to return to another time, when families were allegedly 'fitter', able to endure hardship and limitation. These romances invite good citizens to rediscover the pleasures of respectable, responsible restraint, working in part through attaching moral worth to austere lives and pathologising others who have failed to adopt practices of austerity: thrift as not simply a matter of survival, but as a matter of transforming the relationship of the self to itself. Austerity romances animate a new cultural politics of wanting, whereby to want and to desire is marked as vulgar, irresponsible and a sign of excessive attachments to the material world. Thrift culture repeatedly states that these orientations to the material world – its acquisition and possession – and the desire for the 'good life' have weakened our moral resilience and our ability to defer our pleasures until we can pay for them. Austerity is presented not only as fashionable and fun, but also as a source of personal self-esteem and thus of national transformation. The self-help end of austerity culture exploded after the 2008-09 recession and, like other avenues of transformation pedagogies, worked to individualise social problems as a result of the everyday practices and habits of flawed, damaged or incompetent subjects and the 'bad' cultural choices they were making.

Austerity is good for you! The happy housewife

Several major analyses of the effects of austerity policies have pointed to the multiple ways that these policies disproportionately impact on women. Women are more likely to be recipients of welfare and social security, since they tend to be in caregiving relationships with children, young people and people with disabilities and chronic health conditions. They are more likely to be the primary caregivers of children in the event of parental separation, divorce and relationship breakdown. They are more likely to be in low-paid or precarious work that can lead to them moving in and out of the labour market. They are more likely to be in part-time paid employment and have their incomes supplemented with welfare benefits. They are more likely to be employed by public institutions like the NHS, or by state agencies (for example as housing officers or welfare advisers), that are facing cutbacks and funding reductions as part of austerity. They are more likely to use local services as part of their everyday lives.

Calculations of the 'austerity burden' have estimated that 75–80% of public spending cuts and welfare retrenchment are falling onto the shoulders of women. This has been described as an 'historic transfer of wealth from the purse to the wallet'.[9] (For a fuller picture of the gendered impacts of austerity, see Women's Budget Group, 2012; The Fawcett Society, 2012; Gingerbread, 2013; Unison, 2014.)

The shape and texture of austerity policy have been experienced unevenly by different women. The impacts of austerity measures for ethnic minority women have been catastrophically and disproportionately worse (Bassel and Emujulu, 2017). Single-parent families (overwhelmingly headed by women), who were already twice as likely to be living in relative poverty before the age of austerity, have been disproportionately affected; more likely to fall into debt traps and having recourse to a shrinking safety net (Rabindrakumar, 2013).

Commitments to gender equality have never seemed so precarious. The Coalition government neglected to carry out a rudimentary gender audit, before pledging an age of austerity. Public spending, and its gender redistributive effects, were deemed unaffordable and unsustainable.

It is not surprising that in this context of gendered austerity, the proliferation of austerity romances and thrift guidance should make specific interpellations to women. In particular, we see the symbolic repetition and circulation of one crucial figure of austerity – the frugal and thrifty mother, who is not only able to find creative solutions to family (over)spending, but who is also courted as the saviour of the problems of broader consumer waste and national fiscal incontinence. In her examination of the cultural politics of austerity, Rebecca Bramall (2013) tracks the fantasy figure of the 'austerity housewife', in which visions of post-war domesticity were recycled as an exemplar for our austere times. Bramall untangles the multidirectional strands of austerity discourse and the political struggles over how to define and legitimate austerity. She offers a clarifying map of the competing contestations around austerity, tracking the political uses to which austerity culture has been put – from the 'green' (ecological) and 'red' (anti-cuts) factions of the disparate political Left, to feminist and anti-capitalist/ anti-consumerist protest movements, to retrogressive and conservative formations around domestic retreat, community spirit and the 'home front'. As Bramall shows, the 'austerity housewife' is signified, resisted and celebrated in complex and contradictory ways. She is both heralded as a palatable and practical feminist subject position, which seeks sustainable alternatives to capitalism, and also dismissed as a regressive and anti-feminist subject, which fetishises domesticity at exactly the moment when feminist gains in the workplace, civic institutions and public and economic life were stalling and under intense threat.

The repetition and accumulation of affective power that is produced in this ambivalent figure of the austerity housewife can be seen across austerity texts that construct austerity as an opportunity, for mothers in particular, to become happy. The promise of happiness is stitched through austerity culture. Self-help literature documents the gendered instructions for happiness – the 'happiness scripts' of austerity. These scripts are, in the main, written by women for women, and thus interpellate a post-feminist, autonomous, feminine subject, whose pleasure comes in her ability to spend *wisely* and to reduce her overall spending.

In scripting happiness in these ways, the figure of the austerity housewife cues us into the gender politics of 'being happy'. The concern with 'happiness' as a goal of policy making and the rise of 'happiness science' described a new kind of orientation to happiness, which peaked in the boom years of New Labour (see, for example, Layard, 2005). It understood unhappiness as emanating from individuals, who needed to learn how to govern their emotions. Critics of 'happiness science' pointed to how the injunction to 'be happy' has tyrannical effects that supplant demands for social and political change with emotional self-transformation (Ehrenreich, 2010; Ahmed, 2010; Cromby, 2011).

'Happiness science' was particularly preoccupied with mothers, and with what forms of living could secure their happiness. Some research reported that working mothers are happier than their 'stay-at-home' counterparts (Mendes et al, 2012), other research that 'stay-at-home' mothers are happier, provided that their husbands are 'emotionally engaged' (Wilcox and Nock, 2006). It is impossible to state whether it is 'really' staying at home or working that makes mothers happy; these experiences are so complexly shaped by additional factors such as income, quality of paid work, security, and so on. What is interesting is how happiness is constructed as being incommensurate with demands for social change. As Sara Ahmed (2010) argues, unhappiness is constructed as a consequence of feminism and demands for gender equality: 'it is feminism that gives women the desires that have made them unhappy' (Ahmed, 2010: 53). Feminist scholars have rightly critiqued the 'reinvigorated romanticisation of the housewife' (Littler, 2013: 232) and the retreatist fantasies that promise women they will come back 'to themselves' when they 'come home' (Negra, 2009).

The costs of motherhood are well documented. Correll and Barnard (2007) tracked the impacts of what they called 'the motherhood penalty', a series of disadvantages that women experience in the workplace after each child – including a wage penalty and being evaluated as less competent, less dependable, less authoritative – which leads to subtle discriminations in hiring, promotion and salary decisions. Fathers experience none of these when they become parents, and some research suggests that they may experience a 'fatherhood bonus' when they become parents (Budig, 2014). Gatrell's (2005) research with high-earning women finds that, even with their relative privilege, career trajectories are powerfully inscribed with the impacts of parenting, and their 'work–life balance' involves hard labour, balancing expensive or inadequate childcare, and managing incompatibilities between unpaid care and paid labour. In 2016, the Equality and Human Rights Commission reported on the scale and type of pregnancy and maternity-related discrimination and disadvantage in the workplace. Based on its large-scale research, it estimated that three in every four mothers had negative, discriminatory experiences during pregnancy, maternity leave or on their return from maternity leave, including harassment, being discouraged from attending medical appointments, being dismissed, made compulsorily redundant or feeling so poorly treated that they left their job (Equality and Human Rights Commission, 2016).

Motherhood creates both glass ceilings and sticky floors in places of employment. Yet in the paradigm of happiness science, it is not these social, economic and material costs which create the unhappiness of mothers, but rather the demands and expectations incubated within feminism itself that women 'have it all'. Feminism is allegedly 'at fault' for obligating women to be 'more than' mothers. These narratives also resonate with cultural tropes that describe feminists as 'selfish' (Tyler, 2007) and other anti-feminist forms of backlash (Faludi, 1991).

The unhappy housewife, suffering a 'problem with no name', is a figure that has haunted feminist theory (Friedan, 1963), and the housewife and the feminist are often positioned as pursuing antithetical and incommensurable projects. The emergent articulations of the austerity housewife script a future promise of happiness, in part through exposing the *unhappiness* of the political present. Austerity romances seek to 'explain' the unhappiness of mothers, by highlighting the misdirection of their energies towards material accumulation. Pursuing the 'good life' via the labour market and a dual family income is no longer possible or desirable. Indeed, these pursuits will incur further costs, as the valuable (and unrecognised) labour of the stay-at-home mother must now be outsourced (for example through prohibitive childcare costs, premiums on prepared food and clothing, and housework outsourced to paid cleaners and domestic workers). The working mother's principal scarcity is *time*. In an austerity landscape – and having 'done the math' (Hayes, 2010) – her time cannot be adequately compensated through the stagnating wages offered under neoliberalism. Perhaps she would be 'better off' (and made happier) by retreating from the labour market and embracing the invisible, unrecognised, unpaid (but oh so satisfying) tasks of social reproduction in the domestic sphere.

These happiness scripts are powerful mythologising tropes that have animated the austerity themes of downsizing, retreating and the joy of less. The happy housewife puts flesh on the bones of austere ideology – she fixes austerity to happiness and, in so doing, transforms the exposed workings of social inequity into a manifesto for utopia. This is illuminated particularly well on a US website Miserly Moms, subsequently published as a book (McCoy, 2009). The website hosted a user-generated forum, titled 'Coming Home', on which mothers are invited to contribute stories of retreating from (unhappy) working lives and becoming (happy) housewives. The details of these 'Coming Home' stories vary enormously, but what is striking is the impossibility of surviving and thriving in an increasingly brittle social landscape and a retracting safety net. Women recount tales of hostile employers, who refuse to accommodate requests for flexible work, unexpected financial emergencies that push family budgets into crisis, escalating mortgage and loan repayments, endless guilt, inadequate and expensive childcare provision, and non-existent leisure and 'family time'. 'Jenny' posts:

> I believe staying at home has made me a much better person and has been the greatest thing I've done with my life. However, it has been stressful on us financially, causing tension in our marriage ... I have great pride in what we are doing ... I just think it's annoying (and a little pathetic) when I hear people say, 'We just can't afford to have a parent at home.' It's not a matter of affording it, but about changing one's priorities and lifestyle, and about being brave. Children need us – it is so apparent in our youth today.

Jenny's quote is typical of the diversification of affects which are attached to the process of becoming a 'happy housewife' – pride, frustration, annoyance – and which 'give her a more complex affective life' (Ahmed, 2010: 51). This post documents the painful fantasies of happiness that are scripted and inhabited via austerity culture, and the cruelty of optimism that reattaches us to worlds, practices and institutions that, as Lauren Berlant details, diminish us and deliver negligible returns (Berlant, 2011).

What is remarkable through the repetition and circulation of these 'Coming Home' stories is the paralysing responsibility that their narrators pronounce for the fraying of their fantasies for 'the good life'. These are 'fantasies of upward mobility, job security, political and social equality and lively, durable intimacy' (Berlant, 2011: 3). The *Miserly Moms* contributors exchange stories of present contingency and precarity as a necessary trade-off for future happiness: enduring less now in exchange for the promise of a future free of debt; retreating from employment (which they often talk of enjoying), in order to save on wasteful extravagances (such as childcare); foregoing consumer pleasures; and withstanding hardship with creativity and dignity.

The figure of the happy child saturates the 'Coming Home' stories. The happy child is intimately bound to the happy housewife. The child's happiness can only emerge through the presence, energy and time of mothers, and not through the consumer goods or discretionary luxuries that her salary might afford her. This returns us to the rhetoric of warmth over wealth that was discussed at the opening of this chapter. Such exchanges about the happy child rehearse moral anxieties about late capitalist consumption, whereby meaningful social relationships are alleged to have been replaced with competitive acquisition. Moral panics around childhood consumption are both described and critiqued in academic, policy and popular publications. These document: an intensified anxiety around the 'problem' of the child consumer (Schor, 2004; Linn, 2004; Mayo and Nairn, 2009); the 'toxicity' of childhood consumption (Palmer, 2006); or, more recently, the 'problem' of screen-time, networked cultures and the digital spaces of childhood (Livingstone and Sefton-Green, 2016).

Such panics circulate a vision of children as defenceless against the appeals of consumerism, and of family life as rapidly eroding in a time vacuum, itself driven by increasingly frenzied workloads as parents attempt to keep financial pace with the demands to 'live well'. Parents are cast as overcompensatory consumers, driven by spiralling guilt, who must learn how to reinstate authentic living and scale back on all fronts. In his account of the aftermath of this panic, David Buckingham (2011) highlights how a powerful nostalgia for the 'happy childhoods' of the past starts to circulate, which tends to narrate subsequent moral decline through accumulation. Buckingham draws attention to the classing effects of narratives of 'toxic childhoods', which attach toxicity to 'dysfunctional' working-class children and produce powerful moralising effects around class and restraint.

Miserly Moms – and the catalogue of cultural sites where austerity romance is made sensible through the figure of the happy housewife – works as a site where the economically crunched can produce new forms of solidarity around their conspicuous *non*-consumption. Miserly, austere and frugal mothers situate their retreat from worker and consumer subjectivities as a counterpoint to being 'families in crisis', who lack fiscal discipline, are chaotic, impulsive and unable to defer gratification or to be disciplined and restrained, their family lives measured in money and objects rather than in time and warmth.

Within the constellation of austerity texts, there is a complex (and commendable) challenge to the systems of worth that are implicit within contemporary regimes of capitalist accumulation, as well as (often) a strong sense of environmental and sustainability activism.

This is excellently captured in a book by US writer Shannon Hayes, whose *Radical Homemaking: Reclaiming Domesticity from Consumer Culture* (2010) encapsulates the 'unsustainable' demands of labour and domestic equality. Hayes positions her 'radical homemaking' as a 'sensible' response to an employment economy which would require that she spend much of her wage on buying food she could grow, paying for a commute she could avoid and childcare she could do herself. Having 'done the math', Hayes outlines her rationale for reclaiming homemaking as an educated, feminist woman, stating that 'the key to success isn't in how much money you make, but how much money you don't have to spend' (2010: 11). She proposes that having less income can be liberating if you have less to outsource, and that mothers will be happier and stretched less thinly if they embrace domestic retreat.

Hayes' book is a fascinating portrait of how aspirations for a better life and world become defined, managed and deferred through the family. The generational and intergenerational strivings and failings that result in classed formations and systems of privilege are bypassed in the somewhat romantic portrait she offers of a reconfigured future, which secures happy childhood, 'authentic' living and the health of the planet. The retreat from the 'extractive economy' that Hayes and her husband successfully manoeuvre for themselves, is absolutely reliant on the family farm of her parents. The emerging 'new thrift' publishing market she is able to exploit in her writing career is dependent on their college educations and the accumulation of knowledge and resources which (despite the claims to frugality) put them in the third highest quintile of US incomes. Hayes' manifesto for radicalism requires a great deal of unexamined privilege.

Austerity romances thus take us back to the crucial problematic of care and who is going to do the labour of care. As Sarah Hall (2016) documents in her ethnographic research of everyday austerities, the languages of 'getting by' and 'coping' are partial and problematic ways of describing a profoundly gendered set of expectations and moral responsibilities around caring and sharing, which are themselves being transformed under the privations of austerity. The social infrastructures of care-work have been eroded and have had their funding cut in the austerity fallout – and it is still women who are expected to do this work, now in a context of quiet retreat. Austerity romances rest on the fallacy that it is *overconsumption* that creates debt, unhappiness and the estrangement of parents from their children. This is a misattribution: for economically crunched families, the issue is not overconsumption, but stagnating wages, insecure and precarious underemployment, rising basic costs of living, inflated housing and rental costs, and classed divisions. How much trimming of the household budget 'fat' is there really left to do? The political rhetoric around 'tough choices' and the austerity agenda exacerbates the sense of bankruptcy caused by public welfare support, and provides the social cues which legitimate a substitution of social altruism with amoral familism[10] (Rodger, 2003) via the enterprising and thrifty family. The powerful fantasies around thrift might be theorised as an extension of the gendered tyrannies of the family, willingly retreated into as the remnants of collective solidarity and care infrastructure (in the form of the welfare state and related systems) are being dismantled, outsourced and undermined.

Following Bramall (2013), we need to ask why the 'symbolic resources' of austerity culture always go back to a particular period of history for the same forms of nostalgia – the ubiquitous Keep Calm and Carry On poster, the Dig for Victory paraphernalia, the same semiotic cues of utilitarian enamel buckets, linen, bunting, wicker baskets, wooden tools and gingham fabric. The desire *for* austerity, as articulated by this nostalgic production of cultural memory from specific historical periods (post-war Britain and pioneer America), is a vital component in the machinery of 'public spending' commonsense in the neoliberal political present. They require that we reimagine those historical periods as times of virtuous restraint and joyful, resilient invention. The daily humiliations of post-war rationing – the drudgery of visiting multiple shops every day for basic goods that were not available, the repetitive and often poor-quality ingredients, the petty oppressions of shopkeepers and bureaucrats – are entirely ignored in new thrift texts, which rewrite rationing as an entirely beneficial solution to contemporary overconsumption, irresponsibility and wastefulness. Historian David Kynaston documents the quiet desperation and relentless hunger of the rationing era in his often-heartbreaking *Austerity Britain* (Kynaston, 2007), which draws on Mass Observation diaries and interviews to paint a vivid account of dirt, damp, weariness, scarcity and avarice. This powerful book offers a sobering counterpoint to the rationing fetish of 'new thrift' culture. It also illuminates the new class discourses of contemporary Britain, whereby conspicuous *non-consumption* is emerging as a new marker of cultural value. The working-class witnesses of Kynaston's austerity Britain – their misery and their survival strategies – are caricatured by thrift and rewritten into lessons of hardy resilience.

The aesthestics of 'new thrift' culture are therefore distinctly classed and gendered, via the fragrant respectability of the restrained and happy housewife. These aesthetics also symbolically hark back to a vision of domestic fortitude and resilience, through the conscious consumption of particular 'happy objects' (Ahmed, 2010) of thrift, as detailed across these cultural analyses of contemporary white, middle-class, affluent consumption (Jensen, 2012; Bramall, 2013; Biressi and Nunn, 2013). Diane Negra and Yvonne Tasker (2014) have termed these richly semiotic cues of a particular fantasy period of self-reliance and resilience as 'recessionary culture'. Negra and Tasker see this as a series of mutually reinforcing media texts and pedagogies, promoting the transformative potential of individual enterprise under duress, and preventing a meaningful critique of the consumptive and exploitative capitalist logic that underlies financial crisis.

Yet 'new thrift' culture, like all popular culture, is a site of deep contestation and struggle. As the after-effects of the global recession continue to reverberate, and the consequences of the austerity regime and the post-welfare retrenchment that it has ushered in continue to bite, recessionary culture has started to fracture. Different economies of 'new thrift' are becoming more apparent. What kinds of thrift are desirable and hold potential value? And in what settings? Some aestheticised versions of new thrift can be more directly capitalised on, such as the 'farmer's market' in gentrifying neighbourhoods or the launch of retro-austerity product ranges in luxury home stores. Other forms of 'penny-pinching' are less easily converted into symbolic capital and remain suspect − for example, the ubiquity of high street 'pound stores' or fast fashion chainstores continues to be constructed as problematic. While some forms of 'penny-pinching' can therefore be transformed into cultural capital and are to be celebrated and encouraged, others are positioned as 'merely' cheap consumption − the 'wrong kind of wanting' (Jensen, 2013) − and as contributing to a crisis of capitalism.

Permanent austerity

By focusing on 'austerity' as a cultural and discursive site of contestation, rather than as something fixed or essential, we can better see its mobility and the unexpected and unpredictable work it is put to in policy formation, representations, identity, cultural memory, and the constitution and reconstitution of history. By holding onto the multiple social and cultural meanings of austerity − the commodity histories, the ethical and political subjectivities, the cultural imaginaries − we can better understand how it gets inside us. In surveying the complex objects of austerity, Rebecca Bramall (2013) shows that the 'anti-feminist' cupcake, the 'nationalist' street party, the 'reactionary' bunting are not overdetermined in meaning, but rather they work to animate layers of meaning in austerity culture.

In the 'tough' economic climate, the social advances around gender equality as they pertain to parenting (and specifically motherhood) have been among the first to come under political attack. We can already see how they are being eroded in, for example, the reduction of tax credits for working parents, including elements that contribute to childcare, such as a shortening of the time for which lone parents will receive an income that recognises their childcare responsibilities and the removal of universal child benefits for higher earners. Emerging evidence also suggests that maternal discrimination in the workplace is increasing as a result of the recession (see Maternity Action, 2013), with some media commentators stating that halting maternity benefits would boost economic growth, reduce unemployment and increase flexibility (Phibbs, 2011). We can see the shifting principles of solidarity that are emerging in the socially brittle terrain of austere neoliberalism, and how different groups of mothers are pitted against one another in an emergent cultural imaginary. This imaginary posits that hard-won equality and diversity entitlements – for example those that make maternity discrimination illegal or that guarantee access to specific welfare benefits for parents – are constructed as an unaffordable extravagance that can no longer be collectively funded and organised.

Austerity has been constructed as a permanent necessity and as a nation-saving salve against 'unsustainable' levels of public investment and 'unaffordable' commitments to redistribute and take meaningful action on inequality. This has required that other political periods be made monstrous and serve as a warning. In their analysis of these repetitive returns, Anita Biressi and Heather Nunn (2013) stage a fascinating reading of two periods of historical resource that have been used by contemporary austerity architects: the 'dystopian' late 1970s and the 'utopian' late 1940s. Biressi and Nunn argue that both periods must be conscripted to formulate a compelling narrative for responsible citizens to embrace austerity, however painful.

As Biressi and Nunn show, the first period – the late 1970s – has been used to symbolise industrial strife and division, and to warn of the peril of returning to an 'outmoded and dangerous form of class politics' (2013: 171). They argue that the mythologies of this period, dominated by 'greedy unions, unruly protestors and selfish strikers' (2013: 173) have formed a useful backdrop to current debates around entitlement and responsibility. They show how a rapid deployment of selective references to this period of industrial militancy, during the first years of the current austerity programme, helped to generate and sustain the spectre of a too-powerful labour force that refuses to 'tighten the belt'. The second period – the 'austerity years' of 1945-51 – has served political and popular debate with an equally important historical resource, which has been exploited as a rallying call to citizens feeling the pinch today and exhorting them to both keep calm, and indeed, to carry on. The commendable citizenship of today is performed via restraint, resolve and resilience; sacrifice in the short term in order to secure the future. As Biressi and Nunn highlight, the divergent staging of the two historical periods most plundered in the current austerity regime is distinctly gendered and classed:

> If the 1970s was painted as an essentially brutish era of masculine working-class power in the context of a divided society, then these mid-century austerity years connote a more middle-class feminine ideal in the context of a nation unified by adversity. (Biressi and Nunn, 2013: 171)

Austerity is thus deployed and made hegemonic, not only in the fantasy return it stages to post-war restraint, but also as a necessary corrective that will inoculate Britain from returning to the dangerous militancy of the 1970s.

On a related note, Gargi Bhattacharyya (2015) theorises austerity as a manufactured crisis-response, which has accelerated – and will continue to accelerate – a permanent state of diminished expectations, in which some of us will now always settle for less. Rebecca Bramall (2013) was somewhat reluctant to interpret the cultural romances of austerity as an attack on 'hard-won entitlements' – as she says, there are complex meanings to austerity – but Bhattacharyya is more willing to make this claim. She tracks the powerful political effects of austerity culture, and how it 'gets inside us', not only as a desirous or fetishised series of objects, but also as an unravelling of social bonds and the destruction of mutuality.

The notion that 'austerity is good for us' helped to reconstruct the post-war years. This period was a distinctly pro-welfarist and future-oriented period, offering a vision of equality through redistribution, social security and collective risk-sharing. Despite this, the hegemonic version of austerity, its 'commonsense', was put to distinctly *anti-welfarist* ends. As Bhattacharyya argues, justification for austerity presents welfare reform of the most punitive kind as a necessary corrective to habits of waste. The political present plunders a pro-welfarist historical period to generate consent for and to 'make sensible' anti-welfare ideological policy making. The desire for austerity, for others to receive less and for what they receive to be scrutinised and made conditional, has undermined the temporary settlements of security that were gained through collective endeavour and mutuality. Bhattacharyya's crucial argument is that, in some ways, this desire for austerity responds to institutional failures. Forty years of neoliberalism have ensured that the political energy and action of the 1970s have not translated into equality in Britain. Yet something is lost; in the embrace of austerity, social life has become more atomised and more mean-spirited.

Bhattacharyya invites us to think critically and reflexively about austerity and our investment in it. If austerity is a point of cultural formation and a political discourse that fractures our connections to one another, what work do we need to do to heal those fractures and develop an alternative vocabulary around wanting and entitlement? In what ways are we complicit with the romances of austerity culture? How might we foster attachments and desires for 'other' kinds of austerity – degrowth, anti-consumerism, ecological sustainability – and desires to to break and remake the hegemonic common sense of austerity culture?

In the next chapter, I examine how these contested cultural austerity romances were mobilised to create high levels of public consent for 'austere' policy making. In particular, I examine how the classed romances of retreat and virtuous thrift came to feed the fire of moral indignation around the perceived excesses of the welfare state.

Notes

[1] The significance of Cameron's family connections can be seen in unattributed reports, allegedly from the Conservative Central Office, that in 1988 on the morning when David Cameron was due to attend an interview with the Conservative Research Department, they received a telephone call from 'an unnamed male at Buckingham Palace', who told them: 'you are about to meet a truly remarkable young man'.

[2] Cameron's immediate predecessor, Gordon Brown, maintained a far greater privacy around his family, which was so at odds with the broader personalisation of politics (Corner and Pels, 2003) and the 'celebrification' of Prime Ministers (Drake and Higgins, 2006) that many journalists expressed surprise when he exited 10 Downing Street with his wife and two small boys. See Angela Smith (2008) for a further discussion of Brown's fatherhood.

[3] Demos was established in 1993 with the aim of building research and policy consensus (as had the Thatcherite think-tanks of the previous decade), but it has been criticised for a lack of intellectual clarity, lightweight research and for being driven by media-friendly soundbite appeal rather than bedrock political issues. Journalist John Harris catalogues some of this criticism and suggests that Demos's rise and influence illustrate a replacement of 'hardened politics' with trivia and outlandish headline-chasing (Harris, 2006).

⁴ The 'Panama Papers' refers to the disclosure of more than 11 million files from the world's fourth biggest offshore law firm, Mossack Fonseca. An anonymous source leaked the files to a German newspaper, which then shared them with the International Consortium of Investigative Journalists, in turn leading to a global exposure of the rogue offshore financing industry. The 'Panama Papers' investigation revealed how 143 politicians around the globe, including 12 national leaders (one of whom was David Cameron), their families and close associates, were using secretive offshore intermediaries to hide their wealth and avoid paying tax. Cameron's father, Ian Cameron, was found to have used complicated financial instruments in the management of his company, Blairmore Holdings Inc., which meant that it had not paid a penny of UK tax in 30 years.

⁵ Subsequent social research on the riots significantly challenged these commonsense explanations (Roberts et al, 2012; Riots Communities and Victims Panel, 2012) and found little evidence that either poor parenting or gang activity had had any bearing on rioter profiles. Contrary to London Mayor Boris Johnson's statement that we need 'less sociological analysis', this research has shown that we in fact need more – if we want to avoid repeating (inaccurate) myths.

⁶ There is a parallel set of austerity romances in the US, but these tend to hark back to a different period of frugal living, notably the pioneer homesteaders of the mid- to late 19th century.

⁷ https://rationingrevisiteddotcom.wordpress.com

⁸ https://the1940sexperiment.com

⁹ This phrase is a reversal of the phrase 'transfer from the wallet to the purse', used by Barbara Castle MP in 1975, then Secretary of State for Health and Social Services, as the Child Benefit Bill was passed. This Bill replaced the preceding Family Allowance, and importantly would be paid (on Castle's insistence) to *mothers*, not fathers.

¹⁰ Amoral familism is a term used to describe an ethos which privileges the interests of the isolated nuclear family over and above the shared common interests of the neighbourhood or wider society.

SIX

Weaponising parent-blame in post-welfare Britain

Tracey Jensen, with Imogen Tyler[1]

'The benefit system has created a benefit culture. It doesn't just allow people to act irresponsibly, but often actively encourages them to do so.' (David Cameron, Conservative Prime Minister, 2011)

'We are not the party of people on benefits. We don't want to be seen [as], and we're not, the party to represent those who are out of work.' (Rachel Reeves, Labour Shadow Minister for Work and Pensions, quoted in Gentleman, 2015)

As we saw in the previous chapter, the political turn to explanations of parental warmth over parental wealth as a way of understanding the profound inequalities in outcomes for children was accompanied by a proliferation of romances about austerity: that doing 'more' with 'less' can be a joyful and even liberating experience. It is no coincidence that these explanations and romances co-exist – indeed, they are mutually reinforcing components of the neoliberal biopolitics that underpin contemporary parenting culture. Such biopolitics insists that success and failure can be understood as a consequence of the individual behaviour of the nuclear family, from the choices that families make. This biopolitics is underpinned by a presumption of equal footing and a refusal to name the structural inequalities that shape opportunity and access to resources.

The symbolic commitment to meritocracy across British culture and politics – to the idea that success is entirely down to individual hard work, merit and talent (see Littler, 2017) – persists as a powerful structuring myth, in spite of decades of social and economic research that documents otherwise. Indeed, such is the importance of meritocracy to national fantasies, that the welfare state – a national undertaking designed to prevent destitution and to make some intervention into

143

structures of inequality – has itself been willingly dismantled in the name of 'toughening up' citizens, who are cast as pathologically dependent upon its succour. Across the political spectrum (with few exceptions), politicians on the left and the right have committed themselves to the retrenchment of the welfare state and to welfare reforms that will reduce citizen entitlements to state support.

To understand the enthusiastic public embrace of welfare retrenchment, we need to attend to the reimagining of the welfare state: how welfare has been rewritten as a blockage to meritocracy and how welfare claimants have been designated as objects of disgust. The welfare state was imagined by its original architects as a 'cradle to grave' safety net for citizens: a 'welfare commons' of 'shared risks', which would function to ameliorate economic and social hardships, injustices and inequalities (see Timmins, 2001; Lowe, 2005; Glennerster, 2007). The landmark publication of the Beveridge Report in 1942 saw people queuing outside government offices in their desire to get their hands on a copy of this blueprint for a new welfare state (Page, 2007: 11) and the report sold over 100,000 copies within a month of its publication. This public excitement communicated a deep and broad political and public desire for a new kind of social contract between citizens and state.

As Pat Starkey notes, this idealised welfarist imaginary portrayed 'a unanimity of aspiration across class boundaries for the reconstruction of British society, with its best features intact and its recent economic difficulties and unemployment absent' (Starkey, 2000: 547). However, Starkey also reminds us that the welfare state was always a moral and disciplinary project, conditional upon certain kinds of ideal citizens and behaviours, and grounded in classificatory distinctions between the 'deserving' and the 'undeserving'. As Fiona Williams has extensively detailed, unequal social relations, not only of class but also of gender, 'race', disability, age and sexuality, have always underpinned 'welfare regimes, their outcomes, the organisation of labour ... the delivery of services, political pressures and ideologies and patterns of consumption' (Williams, 1994: 50). Indeed, what remains of the post-war welfare state today was indelibly shaped by struggles against disciplinary welfare regimes and against the forms of patriarchy and state-racism it reproduced.

Nevertheless, writing today in a context where democratic futurist welfare dreams have been consigned to history, when many forms of welfare provision are being cut, and where those who claim benefits and entitlements have become deeply stigmatised, it is important to recall the powerful ideological commitment to welfare that transformed post-war British society. The transition to a post-Keynesian welfare regime in the late 1970s has been well documented in critical social policy studies (see, for example, Burrows and Loader, 1994; Jones and Novak, 1999; Ferguson et al, 2002). Many note that the Thatcherite assault on the welfare state, and the subsequent embrace of neoliberal policies by New Labour, led to 'deepening inequalities of income, health and life chances ... on a scale not seen since before the Second World War' (Hall et al, 2014: 9).

One of the major characteristics of welfare reform from the 1970s onwards was the emergence of a consensus (across the political spectrum) that the welfare state was in 'a permanent crisis' (Langan, 1994: xi). Through this 'crisis lens', the welfare state was reimagined as fostering toxic forms of 'welfare dependency' among citizens, itself considered to have a stagnating effect on economic growth and national prosperity. In a stunning reversal of the 1940s welfare imaginary, 'welfare' came to be understood across a wide range of political, social and cultural milieus as a cause of poverty and social problems, including 'intergenerational worklessness', drug dependence, anti-social behaviour, 'troubled families', teenage parenthood, crime and other 'social ills'. The idea that a 'bloated' welfare state is responsible for the persistence of entrenched social problems is central to the generation of anti-welfare sentiments today. These sentiments are spectacularly realised in key cultural figures, who circulate through political discourse, popular culture and public debate and come to serve as 'evidence' that the welfare state *causes*, rather than solves, poverty.

The focus of analysis in this chapter is one of the key figures of anti-welfare commonsense: the 'benefit brood' family. The co-production of 'benefit broods' across cultural and political sites of mediation in 2013 became intensively focused on particular kinds of families within the news media and popular culture, and coincided with the implementation of the Welfare Reform Act 2012. 'Benefit broods', as this chapter will demonstrate, came to function as a 'technology of consent' for a deeper political programme of welfare reform. In particular, the case of Mick Philpott – found guilty in 2013 of the manslaughter of six of his children – activated 'mechanisms of consent' around ideas of acceptable family forms and welfare reform. In April 2013, the then Chancellor George Osborne directly linked the Philpott case to excessively generous child benefit and welfare payments. Figures such as 'benefit broods' are culturally and politically crafted to play a central role in neoliberal policy formation, operating both as technologies of control (through which to manage precariat populations), but also as technologies of consent through which an anti-welfare commonsense is effected.

Crafting commonsense: the Philpott case

On 2 April 2013, a jury at Nottingham Crown Court found Michael Philpott guilty of manslaughter by setting a blaze at his home in Derby which took the lives of six of his children; thirteen-year-old Duwayne, ten-year-old Jade, nine-year-old John, eight-year-old Jack, six-year-old Jesse and five-year-old Jayden.

Philpott had led a plot, along with his wife Mairead Philpott and friend Paul Mosley, to frame his ex-girlfriend Lisa Willis for arson. Philpott's objective appeared to be acquiring custody over their children. In sentencing Philpott, the judge, Mrs Justice Thirlwall, described his actions as 'callous stupidity' (*R v Philpott, Philpott and Mosley*, 2013: 5). She described Philpott as a controlling misogynist and a 'disturbingly dangerous man', who used violence and psychological abuse to dominate and control the women in his life. The legal judgment was very clear about the misogynistic abuse that Michael Philpott had subjected his girlfriends and wife to, noting that Willis had fled to a women's refuge with her children and that Mairead was in 'a form of enslavement' (*R v Philpott, Philpott and Mosley*, 2013: 5). Polly Neate, the chief executive of Women's Aid, described Philpott as a serial perpetrator of domestic violence and stated that the case 'lifted the lid' on domestic abuse (see Neate, 2013).

However, the dimensions of gender-based violence that underpinned this case were erased in the media narration of this tragic case. The day after the verdict, it was not the 'domestic abuse' that took centre stage, but rather the 'welfare abuse' apparently enacted by the entire Philpott family. The *Daily Mail*, for example, led with the headline 'Vile Product of Welfare UK' (3 April 2013) and a family photograph of Philpott posing with his six dead children taking up the entire front page. In the *Daily Mail* account, Philpott was motivated purely by economic greed, and his plot was described as an attempt to secure a bigger council house and restore the 'thousand pounds a month of benefits' that his children 'brought in', stating that he treated his children as 'cash cows' (see Dolan and Bentley, 2013).

This narrative quickly gained media traction and, on 4 April 2013, *The Sun* ran an editorial titled 'In the Gutter', reflecting that:

> It's hard to imagine a more repulsive creature than Mick Philpott, the lowlife benefits scrounger convicted of killing six of his children in a fire. And who paid for his disgusting lifestyle? We did. Philpott may be the dregs of humanity. But the welfare system helped him every step of the way.

> Thousands a month in handouts *flowed into* the council home ... The more children he produced, the richer the State *made* him. He fathered 17 while dodging work and *sponging off* partners. He *grasped* every benefit going while *demanding* bigger council houses *for his tribe*. Was such feckless greed what the founding fathers of the welfare state intended to promote? (*The Sun Says*, 2013, emphasis added)

This *Sun* editorial advises the reader (and 'those who oppose welfare reform') of the 'lessons' of the case: 'when benefits are so generous, easily obtainable and dished out indiscriminately, they can debase humanity' (*The Sun Says*, 2013). In its leader on 3 April, *The Sun* made even more powerful implicatory comments about the alleged causal relationship between social security, child benefit levels and the Philpott case, concluding: 'let's hope this is the last time the state unwittingly subsidises the manslaughter of children'. This final line was edited in later editions of the newspaper to read 'unwittingly subsidises a monster like Philpott'.

The positing of a causal relationship between excessive benefit levels and the manslaughter of the Philpott children was not restricted to reports in the tabloid press. On 3 April 2013 the broadsheet newspaper the *Daily Telegraph* led with an article by Allison Pearson titled 'Mick Philpott, a good reason to cut benefits' and subtitled 'something has gone awry when skivers like Mick Philpott feel all-powerful and society cannot summon the moral will to say "No. Enough"' (Pearson, 2013). Pearson described the Philpott household as a 'child benefit farm' and concluded by asking: 'if child benefit was stopped after the third baby, would so many have been born to suffer and die?' On 4 April 2013, in an editorial titled 'Family Value', *The Times* described Philpott as a 'violent fool', who was 'milking the system' and whose 'reckless choices' were 'subsidised by the rest of the nation' (*The Times*, 2013). The *Times* leader concluded that it is time to 'look again' at proposals to limit or cap child benefit payments to the first two children only, echoing calls made in the House of Commons as the Welfare Reform Bill 2012 was making its way through the parliamentary system.

A news media consensus was solidifying, in which the Philpotts had been adding children to their family, and had hatched an arson plot, in order to extract the maximum amount of welfare benefits from the state and to acquire a larger council house. A corresponding consensus was also consolidating, namely that the Philpott household was indicative of broader corruptions of the benefits system, which was failing to inculcate individual responsibility in its citizens and was instead encouraging particular kinds of large families to adopt a 'welfare lifestyle'.

This consensus was amplified, and transformed into political capital, on 4 April 2013, with public remarks made by George Osborne, then Chancellor of the Exchequer and a key architect of the Welfare Reform Act 2012. Osborne, who was on a tour of the Royal Crown Derby porcelain works, stated that:

> Philpott is responsible for these absolutely horrendous crimes and these are crimes that have shocked the nation; the courts are responsible for sentencing him. But I think there is a question for government and for society about the welfare state – and the taxpayers who pay for the welfare state – *subsidising lifestyles like that*, and I think that debate needs to be had. (Osborne, cited in Tapsfield, 2013, emphasis added)

Prime Minister David Cameron later defended Osborne's comments, insisting that 'we should ask some wider questions about our welfare system, how much it costs and the signals it sends', adding that 'welfare is only there to help people who work hard and should not be used as a "life choice"' (in Mason and Dominiczak, 2013). The expedient use of the Philpott case by politicians and policy makers, to legitimate and extend their commitment to welfare retrenchment, demonstrates a longer history of neoliberal experimentation, policy making and thinking, whereby the underlying problem to be solved in post-industrial states is the 'condition of "welfare dependency," rather than poverty per se' (Peck and Theodore, 2010: 196). These comments highlight the cultural and political formation of anti-welfare commonsense, via the production and proliferation of a particular figure of disgust: the 'benefit brood' family.

Weaponising policy: the politics of disgust

According to his biographer Janan Ganesh, George Osborne believes that it is important to 'weaponise policy', so it can be deployed for political ends (Ganesh, 2012). Writing in the *Daily Telegraph* in 2014, the journalist Isabel Hardman discussed 'the Chancellor's desire to "weaponise" welfare policy' (Hardman, 2014) in particular. We can see how the Philpott case became 'weaponised' as part of an ideological arsenal in anti-welfare commonsense. Media commentators and politicians (including Osborne) congregated around the Philpott case and positioned it as emblematic of a wider social problem of 'benefit broods' who had become dependent on excessively generous welfare benefits.

The amount of money coming into the Philpott household was repeatedly and forensically charted in the days and weeks following the conviction – and often wildly distorted. Pearson (2013), writing in *The Telegraph*, declared that the Philpotts received 'two thousand pounds plus a month in child benefit thanks to his extensive brood', inflating the true figure by three times. Other estimates were less precise: an editorial in *The Sun* echoed a vision of easy money, when stating that 'thousands of pounds a month in handouts flowed into the council house' (*The Sun Says*, 2013); while the *Daily Mail* used a crude taxation calculation to claim that Philpott 'claimed the equivalent of a £100,000 salary in benefits' (Duell and Tomlinson, 2013). The overcrowding of the Philpotts' three-bedroom, semi-detached house (home to eight children and three adults) was ignored in favour of a focus on the material possessions within it, such as the family snooker table, which were cast as symbols of opulence.

In becoming 'weaponised' in this way, the actual material and financial circumstances of the Philpott household income recede as the family's figuration as objects of 'welfare disgust' are made solid. Philpott himself did not actually claim *any* benefits, but this inconvenient truth does not prevent him from being described as the head of a 'child benefit farm'. The production of this narrative of Philpott forms part of a broader cultural political economy of 'welfare disgust' that would subsequently explode into media coverage of other alleged 'benefit brood' families. The Philpott case, where the actions of a domineering misogynist became rewritten as emblematic of a broken welfare system, would initiate a process of orchestration, whereby informal ideologies around deficient parenting, welfare dependency and abject fertility are managed. The production and repetition of 'revolting subjects' such as 'benefit broods' are a central mechanism through which anti-welfare commonsense is crafted (see Tyler, 2013; Jensen, 2014). The receipt of state welfare, hitherto marked as disgusting, and now linked repeatedly to the manslaughter of six children, became powerfully weaponised and, in turn, shapes public perceptions around state welfare in general. Through broader citations of large families as a 'welfare problem', disgust reactions can be anchored to the figure of the 'benefit brood'.

'Benefit brood' is a cultural figuration of disgust aimed at families that are deemed to have become 'excessively' large as a result of overgenerous welfare entitlements; 'benefit brood' parents are regarded as almost pathologically fertile in their desire to secure greater amounts of welfare payments by having more and more children. In the comment sections, message boards and letters pages that accompany such 'benefit brood' mediations, we see the 'awakened lay attitudes' (Hall et al, 1978: 136) around welfare that are procured and crystallised through these representations. While a swell of revolted public opinion appears spontaneous, by approaching such figurations as 'structured in dominance' (Hall et al, 1978: 155), it is possible to discern the social and political formation of consent. The 'benefit brood' family provides what Hall et al term the 'lynch-pin of legitimation' (1978: 137), referring to those orchestrations of public opinion that provide tacit support for an already circulating commonsense ideology about the welfare state and welfare dependency.

'Benefit broods', along with the unemployed, irregular migrants and asylum seekers, come to function in this neoliberal order as 'national abjects' (Tyler, 2013), stigmatised figures who serve as 'ideological conductors mobilised to do the dirty work of neoliberal governmentality' (Tyler, 2013: 9). These national abjects, constituted in a range of media, cultural, social and political sites, come to accumulate meaning through repetition and movement across these sites. They become overdetermined and caricatured. National abjects come to shape perceptual realities, at multiple levels of social interchange. In this shaping, they work to organise public opinion; in this case, to incite consent for welfare retrenchment.

Such orchestrations should, we argue, be seen as a cultural political economy of disgust, which operationalises disgust as part of anti-welfare architecture. Such architecture, or commonsense, not only procures consent for welfare reforms, but also in the process transforms abject populations, such as 'benefit brood' families, into lucrative and electorally potent political capital. The public comments made by Osborne, and supported by Cameron, are a powerful example of the weaponisation of welfare reform policy by political elites. By fuelling public hostilities towards populations imagined to be a parasitical drain on resources, these weaponised cases are employed to sway voters and are so affectively powerful that they disable oppositional attempts to produce alternative political narratives (see Ganesh, 2012).

Televising the 'benefit brood'

The Philpotts are just one spectacular example of an abjectified large family, but the cultural economy of disgust – within which this example is anchored – is expansive, capacious and multi-sited. The speed with which the Philpott conviction was re-narrated, mediated and circulated within public culture reveals a broader pre-existing architecture of mediations and lay attitudes around the figure of the 'benefit brood' that were awakened by this case.

'Benefit brood' narratives form a staple of disgust across news media, lifestyle and 'real life' magazines, and pseudo-documentary (reality) television. Tracking the movement of 'benefit brood' families across these different media sites, we see that the same families are constantly circulating through a cultural economy of disgust; from magazine exposé, to newspaper article, to television production, and back again. (See, for example, the recycling of the same 'benefit brood' families in Andrews, 2010; Chapman, 2010; Peev, 2010; Platell, 2010; Sims, 2010; Jorsh, 2012; Chorley, 2014). The Philpott family themselves had previously been part of this 'benefit brood' pseudo-celebrity circuit, having featured on television talk show *Jeremy Kyle* and *Ann Widdecombe Versus the Benefits Culture* (both ITV, 2007).

Post-Philpott, these same vocabularies of disgust and techniques of abjection have been deployed in the production of 'welfare disgust' narratives across a new genre of reality television. Focusing on the lives of benefit claimants and known popularly as 'poverty porn', this genre has produced repetitive mediations of 'benefit brood' families and other figures of welfare disgust, which have extended into public consciousness (see Allen et al, 2014; Jensen, 2014; MacDonald et al, 2014).

'Poverty porn' exploded in 2013, and while there are some important examples of welfare documentary prior to this, it is important to note that the multiplication of the genre coincides specifically with the implementation of the Welfare Reform Act 2012 and the sentencing of Philpott in 2013. In July 2013, as part of its *The Cost of Living* season, the BBC broadcast *We Pay Your Benefits* (BBC One, 2013), a programme which invited four 'taxpayers' to analyse the spending habits of four 'welfare claimants', in order to assess whether the current rates of unemployment support are too high. In August 2013, Channel 4 broadcast *Benefits Britain 1949*, setting benefit claimants the challenge of living by the benefit rules of 1949, the first year of the welfare state. In October 2013, Channel 5 broadcast *On Benefits and Proud* (part of a series that also included *Shoplifters and Proud* and *Pickpockets and Proud*), where the 'and proud' of the title works as an ideological hook, suggesting that the only 'correct' feeling towards benefit receipt should be shame.[2] In November 2013, the BBC broadcast *Britain on the Fiddle*, a series exploring what the programme makers termed 'the runaway problem of benefit fraud'.

In a relatively short time, the genre of 'poverty porn' has acquired record viewing figures and demonstrated its potential to generate lucrative attention currency and thus multiple revenue streams for different media industries. *Benefits Street* delivered Channel 4 with its highest viewing figures in 2014, creating advertising space valued at around £1 million (Collier, 2014). 'Poverty porn' would also go on to contribute to enhanced valuations for the production companies behind them: Love Productions, for example, would report an increase of 25% in its annual profits following the production of *Benefits Street*. Directors and commissioners claim that such programming fulfils the public mandate to 'inform, educate and entertain' and thus to address a public concern around welfare (De Benedictis et al, 2017). However, this swathe of programming directs existing curiosity about poverty away from a critique of its causes and indignities and towards a moral anthropology anchored in the pleasures of scrutiny, dissection and assessment. This is television that transforms poverty from a profound social injustice – one with structural explanations that take us to the heart of neoliberal inequality – into a challenge, an experiment or an opportunity for voyeuristic tourism, to scrutinise the habits of the poor and to assess how 'deserving' they really are.

Bev Skeggs and Helen Wood argue that it is crucial to theorise and understand television's interventions in class formation, 'particularly at a time when political rhetoric is diverting the blame for structural inequality onto personal, individualised failure' (Skeggs and Wood, 2011: 2). The genre of 'poverty porn' reinvented politically useful mythologies of 'the underclass' for the purposes of a highly orchestrated debate about welfare reforms, which were *at that very moment* immiserating the most marginalised and precarious families and communities of Britain. The moral economies of judgement and evaluation that were occasioned by this genre reflect an assembly of incendiary and retributive ideas about classed others more broadly across media culture, at a time when the language and vocabularies of social injustices are being denied, obscured and euphemised.

'Poverty porn' has generated such lucrative currency for media producers by staging a moral theatre of poverty as personal failure; and by staging personal failure to television cameras, delivered to the viewing screen of the nation, as something to be peered at, dissected, judged and assessed. The 'characters' that are 'cast' in poverty porn are presented as undisciplined, lazy and shameless, neither legitimate citizen nor consumer, exiled from the routine of the working day and forever trying to grasp yet more from the very benefits system that has created their condition of dependence. As Steph Lawler notes, in her reading of classed disgust, reality television has been a crucial site, where classed others have been made 'both horrifically near and intriguingly distant' (Lawler, 2005: 442). In constructing the 'others' on the screen as dysfunctional in their choices and behaviour, the welfare state also becomes framed as dysfunctional in permitting, enabling, even rewarding such behaviour. In such a framework, the 'poverty porn' viewer is compelled to understand social insecurity as a problem of self-discipline and individual responsibility, rather than as a consequence of the extensions and excesses of neoliberalism.

Underclass media mythologising has been ambivalent, even occasionally celebratory of the entrepreneurial zeal and inventive survival strategies of the most socially marginalised in Britain's 'post-working class' (see Biressi and Nunn, 2010). *Benefits Street*, for example, presented momentary glimpses of resourcefulness, such as the character of Smoggy 'the 50p man', who is shown going door to door, selling household items to his neighbours. The introductory voiceover to *Benefits Street* states that the programme will show how residents come together in mutual support through hard times, as benefit cuts become implemented. In spite of these more complex and contradictory moments and storylines, the overall effect of this genre is to generate 'national abjects' (Tyler, 2013), which transform precarity and poverty into a moral failure, worklessness into laziness, and social immobility and disconnection into an individual deficit of aspiration.

Crafting anti-welfare sentiment

We now turn to one specific example of 'poverty porn' television, which demonstrates how such programming, far from 'lifting the lid' on poverty, is in fact essential to embedding public consent for the rollback of welfare entitlement. This example also highlights how central the figure of the 'benefit brood' family is in mediations of welfare dependency and in the animation of social disgust about benefit claimants.

Life on the Dole was a six-part series broadcast on Channel 5 in 2014, which promised to 'get up close and personal with the people behind the headlines as it explores the lives of those living on benefits'. Episodes were loosely themed around specific places, one focusing on seaside towns ('Benefit Brits by the Sea'), another in communities in South Yorkshire ('Benefits, Babies and Jail'). Illustrating the importance of repetition and recycling in 'poverty porn', the series finale is described as 'revisiting' families in the series – but is in fact simply a rebroadcast of the previous year's *On Benefits and Proud* with a new voiceover.

The third episode in this series, 'Benefits House: Me and my 22 kids', focuses on three families, who are repeatedly described by the voiceover as 'supersize families'. In the first few minutes, a twin mythology becomes cemented: first, that these children are being produced to maximise welfare entitlements; and second, that the welfare state is creaking under the weight of such families and welfare reform is essential to dissuade such 'benefit-dependent' families from forming in the first place. The opening voiceover states that 'big benefits families need big homes – that's one of the largest benefits bills'. It goes on to detail how one of these featured families has 'raked in half a million quid', while another 'knows that a big family can be a benefit goldmine' and that 'now the family is definitely quids in'. A vocabulary of easy money flowing into overfertile families – almost identical to that used in the media narration of the Philpott manslaughter case – is used in this television episode to position large families as grasping and greedy, and as evidence of an insatiable and bloated welfare state. The 'benefit brood' child is presented in such media texts as a tragic figure, neglected, in constant competition with siblings for attention and resources, produced only to maximise welfare entitlements, in contrast to the cherished child of the small, lean family.

Crucially for the construction of an anti-welfare sentiment, the requirements of each of the featured families must be made illegitimate or suspect. Thus, we see the recasting of their struggles to secure their entitlements as evidence that they are trying to extract yet more from the welfare state. For example, all of the families live in housing that is inadequate for the needs of their families. One family is living in overcrowded conditions: four children sleeping in each bedroom, one mother sharing her double bed with a baby and two children, a father sleeping on the sofa. Another family has a disabled son, whose physical requirements cannot be met in their current home. Their repeated attempts to secure a tenancy in a larger home – to which they are legally entitled – are described scornfully by the voiceover as 'demands'. When they are told that their home will finally be extended through to the neighbouring house, the voiceover sarcastically states: 'they'll get double the space but it won't cost them a penny'. When this same family comments on the domestic upheaval they are experiencing as disruptive extension work is carried out – having to cook on a camping stove in the living room, for example – the voiceover states with a sigh that, 'for *some* people, it's never enough'. This is particularly cowardly television, which carefully edits camera footage to elicit judgement, alongside a sneering voiceover that the participants cannot know and to which they cannot respond.

One of the standout features of 'poverty porn' television is its failure to reflect on the part it plays in the theatre of media cruelty for welfare claimants. All three of the 'supersize families' featured in *Life on the Dole* have been the subjects of scathing and stigmatising newspaper coverage and speak on camera about these experiences. Peter shows coverage in the local newspaper of his 'scandalous' housing request and asks why this should attract greater anger than the neighbouring story in the same newspaper, which details the grotesque pay rise of a local politician. Marie comments that the stigma faced by her and her children as a result of a newspaper exposé of her family is worse than would be experienced by a convicted murderer. Tim and Mandy, meanwhile, show a printout of 'firebomb' threats made towards their family home through social media and resort to installing CCTV surveillance in order to feel safe.

Such moments, where participants detail the damaging and frightening consequences of having been 'exposed' as 'supersize', are not meaningfully interrogated within the programme. There is no reflection on how 'poverty porn' television will in all likelihood renew such incitements of hatred. Stigmatising media coverage of the 'supersize' families is presented as unavoidable; the voiceover simply stating that: 'big families on benefits can often find themselves hitting the headlines. And with 26 kids it's not surprising.' There is little sense of how the processes of casting, filming and broadcasting material *produce* these narratives of pathology, deficiency and dependence, which 'poverty porn' participating families have to then contend with in their everyday lives. Nor is there any reflection by the programme makers of their ethical responsibilities as documentary makers in 'casting' families who have already been targeted and threatened with violence. The narrator describes such mediations as a simple reflection of local feeling, stating: 'it's a bit of nightmare. Some of the locals are far from happy.'

A disgust-consensus: from nanny state to daddy state

The orchestration of welfare disgust, circulating in fast media culture such as 'poverty porn', in everyday conversation and across informal sites of disquiet, also feeds back into political conversation and into the restless reform of 'fast policy' (Peck and Theodore, 2015). It is astonishing how quickly and efficiently the commonsense of 'poverty porn' was transformed into political capital in the House of Commons.

When Conservative MP Philip Davies raised a question around *Benefits Street* and *On Benefits and Proud* in the House of Commons, he exposed his inexperience of poverty (assuming that these programmes simply 'documented' poverty), his media illiteracy (unable to see the production of semiotic cues in such representations) and his lack of sociological imagination (unable to anchor individual narratives within wider social structures). Importantly, Davies also shows his ruthless ambition, in exploiting media content to demonstrate his political allegiance. In his reply, Iain Duncan Smith, the central architect of the Welfare Reform Act 2012, does not miss a beat and references 'the public', who – seeing the programme too – *of course* see it as exemplifying the urgent need for welfare reform.

Conservative MP Simon Hart remarked at a Prime Minister's Questions session that 'sadly there is a street like this [*Benefits Street*] in every constituency in the land', exposing a profound lack of curiosity and a willingness to trade in commonsense myths. Hart was not required to provide any evidence for such an outrageous claim: social research has since robustly debunked such myths that there are entire streets of workless communities or multiple generations of families that have never worked (MacDonald et al, 2014). In his reply, Prime Minister David Cameron simply agreed that welfare dependency was 'at the root' of unemployment.

This highly editorialised 'debate' between fast media and fast policy recycles and solidifies a disgust-consensus in a mutually constitutive feedback loop – and documents the revolving door between politician and 'social commentator', where new forms of welfare 'commonsense' start to congeal. Indeed, it is the *co-production* of such figures of disgust across media and policy concurrently that should trouble us most deeply. In her analysis of the politics of disgust produced around the figure of the 'welfare queen' in the US, Ange-Marie Hancock (2004) points to the importance of pre-existing, uncontested cultural frames that perpetuate emotions such as disgust even in public institutions that are ostensibly accountable and evidence-based. Hancock proposes that the easy exchange of 'disgust figures' like 'welfare queens' (or 'benefit broods') across and between media and political discourse illuminates a crisis of representational thinking and a fractured and damaged solidarity between policy makers and the groups they are supposed to serve.

The disgust-consensus procured through the figure of the 'benefit brood' family had similarly profound implications for the ease with which the Welfare Reform Act 2012 was implemented in 2013. Despite warnings from anti-poverty campaigning and advocacy groups and from policy experts who foresaw a looming crisis of poverty in the proposed measures of the Welfare Reform Act 2012, its proposed restrictions and conditionalities were implemented, with barely a whisper of concern from mainstream media and parliamentary debate, and indeed even referencing the tragic case of the Philpott children:

'It has been most encouraging to see how warmly the country has received our changes, particularly the £26,000 limit on families receiving benefits. The Philpott case was an eye-opener to many, highlighting that far too many people in this country are living a wholly immoral lifestyle on public finance, and we need to crack down on that.' (Gerald Howarth, House of Commons, 2 May 2013)[3]

These comments on 'immoral lifestyles' are not incidental: they are central to the disgust-consensus surrounding welfare claimants and attaching here specifically to the figure of the 'benefit brood'. They also speak to the ways that the financial crisis of 2008 was rewritten as a welfare crisis, allegedly caused by the Labour government 1997–2010 (explored in the previous chapter) by a reluctance to moralise about family life and a reluctance to place limits and boundaries on what family forms are acceptable (and thus entitled to the protections of the welfare state).

The epithet 'the nanny state' was gleefully attached to the New Labour government by its critics, referring to its alleged micromanagement, hectoring policy, bureaucracy and undermining of personal responsibility (see, for example, Huntingdon, 2004). Whereas the New Labour 'nanny state' was positioned as an abject maternal figure, inducing dependence and creating 'feminised' (that is, weak) workforces and a bloated and 'broken Britain' (see Hancock and Mooney, 2013), the Conservative and Liberal Democrat Coalition government framed its welfare reform project as one that would withdraw 'nanny state' succour and eradicate its associated pathologies. In austerity Britain, we are told, citizens need to 'relearn' the lessons of hardy resilience, independence, motivation and personal responsibility, in order for the nation to be able to compete again on a global scale.

On the eve of the British General Election in 2010, Stephen Brien of the think-tank the Centre for Social Justice detailed the 'lessons' of a welfare nanny state that would become central to effecting the Welfare Reform Act 2012. As he wrote:

Welfare dependency is one of the most pernicious problems facing modern Britain and its deprived communities. When William Beveridge was planning the welfare state, he spoke about the giant evil of idleness: not just a waste of economic potential, but of human potential too. The tragedy is that his welfare system has gone on to incubate the very problem it was designed to eradicate. It was intended to support those who were unable to work, or for whom there were no jobs. But the benefits system now actively discourages people from taking a job, or working more hours. For millions, welfare dependency is now a way of life. (Brien, 2010)

Loïc Wacquant argues that since the 1970s, liberal democracies of the global North have sought to transform from Keynesian 'Nanny States' to authoritarian 'Daddy States' (Wacquant, 2010). This shift, he argues, is characterised in policy by 'the new priority given to duties over rights, sanction over support [and] the stern rhetoric of the "obligations of citizenship"' (Wacquant, 2010: 201). The Coalition government explicitly positioned itself as the 'daddy state' inheritors and architects of tough welfare reform that the 'nanny state' New Labour government was unable to effect. This repositioning seems to have been successful, at least if we consult the hardening of public opinion towards welfare claimants after the Coalition government was formed in 2010 (see Taylor-Gooby, 2013; Hills, 2015) and following the election of the Conservative government in 2015.

One of the most enthusiastic embracers of the 'daddy state' rhetoric has been Iain Duncan Smith, the former Work and Pensions Secretary (2010–16) and the architect of a matrix of welfare reforms that he proudly described as 'aggressive' (Duncan Smith, 2013). Indeed, in overseeing the Welfare Reform Act 2012, Duncan Smith positioned himself as the saviour of the welfare state, claiming that the previous Labour government had 'spent thirteen years letting the rot set into the welfare state, and I am now busy putting things right' (Duncan Smith, 2013). One of the most salient examples of the tough welfare reform policy, which has particular relevance to the moralised significance of work/worklessness and the figure of the 'benefit brood', was the household benefit cap element of this Act.

The end of entitlement

As part of the Annual Spending Review in 2010, the Coalition government announced its intention to cap total household benefits at £350 per week for a single-person household and £500 per week for couples, with or without children, and single-parent households. Households are exempt from the cap if they move into paid employment. According to the impact assessment for the cap, the rationale for these calculations is to 'restrict the total amount of money a non-working household can receive to broadly the level of the average earned income of working households' (DWP, 2012: 5) – currently around £26,000 a year. This new welfare regime also requires that unemployed claimants sign a personalised 'claimant commitment', which sets out the requirements and conditionalities for receiving welfare benefits and the consequences of not meeting them (see DWP, 2013). Failure to comply with these commitments, decided upon by your 'work coach', results in sanctions (such as loss of benefits for a fixed period), in order to 'incentivise' claimants.

The household benefit cap has antecedents in previous welfare policies, for example in the 'wage stop' of the Social Security Act 1966, whereby supplementary benefits for unemployed claimants could be reduced if their receipt would result in the total benefit payments exceeding the claimant's 'likely wage'. However, unlike the 'wage stop', which was administered under discretion and regularly reviewed, the household benefit cap is comprehensive and inflexible. Most importantly, the 'wage stop' existed within a broader welfarist imaginary, whereas consent for the household benefit cap has been consciously procured through anti-welfare commonsense. The household benefit cap, in particular, has been consistently legitimated via 'the taxpayer in work' and as 'delivering fairness' to the taxpayer and to 'hardworking families'. In so doing, the proponents of these anti-welfare policies dramatise a new classificatory politics around work/ worklessness. Duncan Smith has been a keen and consistent advocate for this substitution, giving several high-profile media interviews, where he delineates between 'hardworking families' and 'benefit brood' families:

> The benefit cap has addressed the ludicrous situation we were in where people were receiving far more in benefits than the *ordinary hardworking family* earns. It is not right that before we introduced it some families could *rake in* more than double the amount that the average taxpayer takes home. (Duncan Smith, cited in Chorley, 2014; emphasis added)

One of the unusual aspects of the British welfare state (in the European context), is that it is funded primarily through individual taxation, 'rather than social insurance payments from employers, workers and government' (Taylor-Gooby, 2013: 3). These financial arrangements enable the ideological pitting of abstracted 'hardworking taxpayers' against 'benefits claimants'. As Winlow and Hall (2013) rightly point out, the resurgence of an abstracted 'taxpayer' in times of austerity redraws common economic interests between low-wage earners and an extravagantly paid elite (as 'hardworking taxpayers') rather than between low-wage earners and/or benefits claimants (as precarious citizens, who may move in and out of welfare and labour systems). Such newly drawn equivalences work to generate hard divisions between 'universal benefits' (such as the National Health Service, school-age education and pensions) and selective benefits (such as unemployment and disability benefits), and to divide people 'along a vampiric axis of blame for diminishing social resources' under 'conditions of heightened precarity across a large swath of the class spectrum' (Tyler, 2015: 506).

While one of the initial objectives for the household benefit cap was ostensibly to deliver fiscal savings, when the detail of such savings came under question, welfare reform architect Lord Freud appeared to change tack. He insisted that the message being sent by the cap 'is a behavioural one much more than a cost-based one' (House of Lords, 2011a). Indeed, the vast bulk of households – three quarters – that are impacted by the household benefit cap have lost less than £100 a week; small amounts in the grander welfare scheme, yet for each household this may mean hardship, eviction, and displacement from schools, social networks and family.

The Department for Work and Pensions (DWP) has resisted Freedom of Information requests about families who have been capped by higher amounts, although many of those cases will be disproportionately connected to higher housing costs in London and the South East. Such a behaviourist policy agenda is concerned with disciplining families, rather than 'fiscal restraint', and the household benefit cap is symptomatic of a wider 'behaviourist turn' in policy formation, accompanied by an intensive social, political and media focus on 'behaviourally recalcitrant' social groups (see Jones et al, 2011: 3). Indeed, as Lynne Friedli and Robert Stearn have documented, neoliberal governmentality increasingly involves 'the recruitment of psychology/psychologists into monitoring, modifying and/or punishing people who claim social security benefits' (Friedli and Stearn, 2013).

The household benefit cap unravels, and effectively marks the end of state welfare grounded in assessed need, a shift that was described in the House of Lords by Lord Kirkwood as 'a direct and dangerous attack on entitlement and the concept of entitlement' (House of Lords, 2011b). The cultural political economy of disgust serves to draw a veil over the dissolving of a rights–based understanding of state support for vulnerable populations, which was precisely the common, consensual basis of the creation of the welfare state in post-war Britain. Large families – so-called 'benefit broods' – constitute a tiny proportion of those who receive welfare benefits (the largest group of claimants is in fact pensioners, whose state pensions dwarf other components of the welfare bill), yet they are constantly presented, along with other figures of crisis such as unemployed people and immigrants, as major parasitical drains. Large families, rare in number yet hyper-visible through repetitive media coverage, fast became one of the main signifiers in a 'welfare war' waged by the Coalition government, as it sought to procure consent for the Welfare Reform Act.

There are many individual and intersecting policies – across social security benefit payments, housing, disability, health, education – which could be pointed to in order to illuminate the new normalised cruelty of the austerity welfare state. The £8 billion of cuts announced in June 2010 became a deep abyss in 2015, with the announcement of a further £12 billion pounds of cuts; all, incredibly, in the name of enhanced 'fairness' and reducing poverty (see DWP, 2015). The punitive nature of these cuts can be seen in, for example, ending the so-called 'spare room subsidy' (known as 'the bedroom tax') from housing benefit payments, whereby disabled people are now penalised for having 'spare bedrooms' to store equipment and non-resident parents are penalised for having 'spare bedrooms' for visiting children to sleep in. This penalty is enacted whether or not alternative housing can be found.

It is particularly significant that the household benefit cap has been the *single most popular policy* of the entire duration of the Coalition government. According to a YouGov poll conducted in January 2013, some 76% of respondents agreed with this component of welfare reform (YouGov, 2013). The household benefit cap has since been reduced to £20,000 per year (outside London) and, while still a minister, Duncan Smith spoke publicly of his desire to reduce the cap eventually to £18,000 a year (Stone, 2016). It is likely that he would have enjoyed popular support for these further reductions: the same YouGov survey found that 49% of those surveyed would support a cap of just £15,000 a year.

New and emergent bodies of painstaking research are mapping the devastations caused by this lattice of austerity policy, and the violent capacities of public (and increasingly, private) institutions, agencies, programmes and initiatives which have been drafted in to effect what Cooper and Whyte (2017) have described as the 'mundane and everyday' violence of austerity. As Cooper and Whyte outline, the welfare state was, from the outset, the scapegoat for the financial crisis, and it was through perpetuating myths that this crisis had been caused by 'reckless overspending' on social security and by the 'problem of dependency' that the ideological facade of austerity and 'being all in it together' was initialised. However, as Cooper and Whyte's collection shows, this deception of fiscal discipline, far from creating bonds of solidarity between belt-tightening citizens, has opened up divisions and great chasms of inequality between different groups; requiring claimants to compete with one another, comply with increasingly punitive welfare conditions, and continually 'prove' their disabilities and health conditions. These repeated cycles of mistrust, degradation, humiliation and stigmatisation are, as Cooper and Whyte's collection shows, creating physical and emotional pain – fatigue, stress, depression, exhaustion. These experiences are also forensically charted in several other volumes of work (see Stuckler and Basu, 2013; O'Hara, 2015; Patrick, 2017).

'Benefit brood' families were one of the early 'ideological conductors' (Tyler, 2013) that condensed a wide range of popular discontents with the welfare state, and they have been configured and mobilised as emblems of a larger crisis of 'welfare dependency'. The generation, weaponisation and mediation of these cultural figures of disgust – alongside the other figures of parental failure that this book has explored and tracked – marks a shift away from pro-welfare imaginaries of the 1940s towards the anti-welfare consensus of the political present tense. 'Benefit broods' form part of a wider cultural political economy of disgust, used to dramatise 'the giant evil of idleness' (Brien, 2010) and to provide an ideological apparatus to secure consent for punitive forms of welfare conditionality, which can then be extended and deepened. The Philpott case and its subsequent weaponisation by the architects of the Welfare Reform Act 2012, reveals the ways in which the crafting of 'revolting families' (see Tyler, 2013) – as opposed to small, fiscally autonomous, 'hardworking' families idealised under austerity (and explored in the previous chapter) – is a central component of anti-welfare policy formation. These abject families are part of a wider and deeper cultural political economy, which has reshaped public understandings of the welfare state and incited consent for policies of impoverishment.

Notes
[1] This chapter builds on joint research with Imogen Tyler, which was originally published as '"Benefit broods": The cultural and political crafting of anti-welfare commonsense', *Critical Social Policy*, vol 35, no 4, pp 470-91. Edited sections of that journal article are reproduced here with kind permission.

2   In 2014, 5Productions broadcast *Gypsies on Benefits and Proud*, signalling a new racialising direction in the politics of welfare disgust. The series, under a new name … *& Proud*, is now being produced by Elephant House Studios, who describe it as a 'provocative documentary series exploring the lives of the Britons who are proud to break society's rules'. Programmes in production or forthcoming include *Football Hooligan and Proud* and *Dangerous Dog Owner and Proud*. See www.elephanthousestudios.com/productions/and-proud/

3   Available online via *Hansard*.

SEVEN

Epilogue: 'Mummy Maybot': a new age of authoritarian neoliberalism

In June 2016, the UK voted by referendum to leave the European Union (EU). David Cameron almost immediately resigned as Prime Minister and after a brief leadership contest in which, one by one, her opponents stepped down from the competition, Theresa May was declared UK Prime Minister. A few months later, in November 2016, the United States elected multimillionaire business tycoon and reality television celebrity Donald Trump as their new President. After his inauguration, Trump quickly began to appoint his White House staff with a crew of far-right white nationalists, climate change deniers and his own children. The 'special relationship' between the UK and the US was under the custodianship of a Prime Minister who had won a leadership contest by default and a President who had never previously held any kind of political office.

May's unexpected premiership was initially greeted with excited enthusiasm from the mainstream media, particularly the right-wing tabloid press still flushed with Brexit, and May was widely described as the successor to Thatcher, nicknamed 'Iron Lady 2' and 'Maggie May'. Her first speech, at the door of Downing Street, seemed to promise a change of direction in the Conservative government and to acknowledge in particular the effects that precarity and uncertainty could have on families and children. May stared unflinchingly into the assembled news cameras and stated:

> 'If you're from an *ordinary working class family*, life is much harder than many people in Westminster realise. You have a job but you don't always have job security. You have your own home, but you worry about paying a mortgage. You can just about manage but you worry about the cost of living and getting your kids into a good school. If you're one of those families, if you're just managing, I want to address you directly.' (Theresa May, 13 July 2016)

These early commitments to 'just about managing' families (neatly acronymised as the 'JAMs') certainly had soundbite appeal. They are nebulous enough to speak to expanding constituencies of the working poor, as well as any family that has had to, or perceives itself as having had to, make belt-tightening sacrifices, feeling the squeeze of wage stagnation or benefit reduction: in other words, most families. Think-tank researchers had already tried to define more precisely the JAM terminology that May had adopted, and to quantify the JAMs that she now sought to address directly from outside Downing Street (see Frayne, 2015; Finch, 2016),[1] but in a sense the detail does not matter. JAM is a deliberately (and strategically) vague term. It seeks simply to cleave a politically expedient (and electorally profitable) sense of 'precarity' from the wider failures of neoliberalism, like yolk from an egg, and to suture those experiences of precarity with moral registers of 'being decent', working hard, doing the right thing. In doing so, it transformed resentment into political capital that would legitimate a new government and heal the crisis of national division so spectacularly realised in the EU referendum.

The cumulative effects of more than thirty years of neoliberalism, euphemised under New Labour, then magnified under the austerity agenda of the Coalition and subsequent Conservative government, carved a socially brittle landscape, which cracked in Brexit. May began her premiership by seeking to reassure 'just about managing' families that she, unlike others in Westminster, understood their struggles. She sought to contain resentments about austerity and the crushing material privations caused by the retrenchment of the welfare state.

In the following weeks and months, those resentments would be displaced onto some familiar figures – the workless, the 'feckless', the benefit-dependent – as well as some new ones. At the Conservative party conference in October 2016, May derided the 'left-wing, activist, human rights lawyers' and liberal politicians who 'find your patriotism distasteful, your concerns about immigration parochial, your views about crime illiberal' (May, 2016). Her speech emphasised the return of the nation-state, announced (in a barely coded message to any party 'Remainers' hoping to challenge the referendum result) that anyone believing they were 'a citizen of the world' was in fact 'a citizen of nowhere', who 'didn't understand the word citizenship' (May, 2016). There were several warnings around corporate 'misbehaviour'; to bosses mistreating workers or taking excessive pay, to energy firms exploiting consumers on high-price tariffs. Despite these centrist-sounding commitments to remake Britain as a 'Great Meritocracy', the policy detail was extremely thin. The party conference detail was, however, thicker and bolder in regard to the policing and disciplining of the nation-state's edges. Several consultation policies were announced that signalled new kinds of hostile borders on movement and migration, including a proposal that companies be required to publicly declare how many of their staff were foreigners, that new restrictions are introduced for overseas students, and that landlords face criminal prosecution for renting properties to illegal migrants. While the hard-right components of the Conservative party and the right-wing press were delighted with these directions, other policy commentators sensed with growing alarm a decidedly illiberal future. Even the free-market liberal magazine *The Economist* was scandalised by May's party conference speech, and its leader column warned that 'the sheer intellectual swagger of its authoritarianism sets Mrs May's speech apart' (Bagehot, 2016).

On 21 January 2017 in the US, an estimated half million people marched in the Women's March in Washington DC in response to the misogynist and offensive campaigning comments made by Trump and in support of broader reproductive, migrant, worker, LGBT and environmental rights, which were all felt to be under threat by the new administration. An estimated five million people took part in affiliated marches and protests around the US and globally. Just five days later, Theresa May became the first national leader to visit Donald Trump after his inauguration. She addressed the Republican Party's 'Congress of Tomorrow' event in Philadelphia, stating that the 'new Global Britain that emerges after Brexit' would be seeking a renewed 'special relationship' with the United States. Her speech was filled with lofty rhetoric, but the policy detail was again thin; the only specific commitments were around defence spending and the renewal of the nuclear deterrent Trident. While on her visit, May was photographed holding hands with Trump as they walked down a colonnade of the White House on their way to deliver a joint press conference. May later tried to brush off the hand-hold as 'a moment of assistance', but it was a media disaster and became the defining image of a new trans-Atlantic age of neoliberal authoritarianism.

The vicar's daughter

Like Thatcher, May sought to position her Conservatism, her political values and her personal competence within her own family history. Where Thatcher qualified her economic knowledge as a result of being a 'grocer's daughter', May was fond of referring to herself as a 'vicar's daughter'. She described the 'principles that my parents taught me in the vicarage of Southern England' as being at 'the heart' of her plan for England, going on to name 'nationhood, family, economic prudence, patriotism' (May, 2016).

But other, more contradictory, soubriquets have also been attached to her. Having called a surprise General Election in 2017, when party polling figures were high, the Conservatives launched the most presidential-style, personalised campaign in living memory, which was centred firmly on the figure and brand of Theresa May. The slogan 'Theresa May for Britain' and a personalised campaign entreated the British populace to strengthen May's hand at the coming EU negotiations (May herself declaring 'every vote will make me stronger'). But May's 'likeability' proved wanting as the campaign went on, and her reserved, aloof personality and stage-managed appearances with small groups of the party faithful contrasted unfavourably with other energising and ebullient campaigns, especially Labour party leader Jeremy Corbyn's increasingly large and spontaneous rallies for the Labour party. It was, in Margaret Scammell's memorable words, 'a personal brand in search of a personality' (Scammell, 2017). The phrase 'strong and stable' was repeated so often, and with so little policy detail, across an uninspired Conservative election campaign beset by uncertainty and U-turns, that May soon acquired the moniker 'the Maybot' and was 'represented as an unfeeling, unnatural, machine-like creature' (Thompson and Yates, 2017).

Shelley Thompson and Candida Yates (2017) situate the complex attachments to Theresa May within the gendered nature of contemporary politics, which they argue remains by default a masculinised sphere that judges women as cold and aggressive when they are assertive, and flaky and weak if they express emotion. The powerful 'loving and loathing' emotions that were attached to May across media and political discussion reflect and reinforce this wider emotional framing of women politicians. But perhaps the most complex (and chilling) soubriquet mobilised and attached to May came in the form of an (unnamed) Conservative activist's tweet, which declared 'here comes Mummy' and unintentionally confirmed the rumour that the party's secret preferred term of endearment for their leader was 'Mummy'. Thompson and Yates ponder the maternal anxieties and fears that this label connotes, and propose a psychoanalytic reading, whereby women holding positions of power are defensively idealised or denigrated as objects of love or loathing;[2] they offer examples of Hillary Clinton's pathologised ageing body and the profound 'misogynoir' (Bailey, 2013)[3] directed at Diane Abbott (see Yates, 2015; Gabriel, 2017).

These complex fantasies and fears are distilled in the following cartoon (Figure 7.1).

Figure 7.1: Cartoon published in the *Evening Standard*, dramatising the ambivalent regard towards Theresa May

Source: Adams© *Evening Standard*, 1 June 2017

But, as Thompson and Yates note, the private whisperings that designate May as 'Mummy' also animate other mediations, and illuminate May's complex relationship to feminism and femininity. Her voting record on political issues most associated with the lives of women – restrictive abortion laws, child tax credit cuts, welfare reform, the retrenchment of social security and cuts to public sector jobs – reveals a disavowal with the feminist politics of social justice, and an alignment instead with neoliberal feminism. Like Thatcher,[4] May's womanhood has been used to present Conservativism as 'progressive' – and also like Thatcher, May's actual politics have synergised with, and helped build on, a wider project of what Angela McRobbie has termed a 'popular neoliberal hegemony' (McRobbie, 2013).

This book has attempted to engage with the good parenting scripts, emerging from popular culture, policy discussion, public debate and across media, all of which foreground the normality of virulent competition between families and the extension of economic imperatives into intimate life and conduct. These good parenting scripts have championed affluent, ambitious and aspirational maternity in particular, and created and sustained a vocabulary of 'individual responsibility' and 'hardworking families'.

The arguments of this book have been inspired by the cultural studies approach developed by Stuart Hall (among many others), who insisted that popular consent was crucial in order for a neoliberal 'commonsense' to take hold, and specifically that the newly imagined middle class interpellated by Thatcher and her inheritors was central to the neoliberal project (Hall and O'Shea, 2003). More recently, Angela McRobbie has complicated Hall's arguments and proposed that we must also think through neoliberal politics with an eye on gender and maternity. As McRobbie (2013) argues, it is the professional, middle-class wife and mother who is so ubiquitous in, and central to, the cultural formations of contemporary neoliberalism. As *Parenting the Crisis* has endeavoured to show, these neoliberal formations endorse particular strands of liberal feminism, while discharging any sense of social obligation to those who are less privileged and more marginalised under liberalism.

The production of good parenting scripts, saturated in the language of meritocracy and sidelining issues of poverty and inequality, hold that social problems of dispossession, disenfranchisement, precarity and unemployment can be directly traced back to family failure to 'pack' children with enough of the individual resources ('character', 'resilience', 'grit', 'resolve') required to succeed in a competitive world. Good parenting scripts are veiled with a thin multiculturalism and a tokenistic nod to diverse family forms ('anyone can be a good parent'), yet continue to silently presume a two-parent family, with unwaged carework and reproductive labour still under the remit of mothers.

All this has unfolded in a wider context of deepening against and even disgust for parents claiming social security and welfare benefits. Nancy Fraser (2013) tracks how the nuanced second-wave feminist critique of sexist and stigmatising welfare state bureaucracy, which paternalistically intruded into women's lives, was taken up and skewed by the neoliberal architects of the Thatcher era and beyond. Far from reforming welfare so that it worked better for families who needed it, the project became one of retrenchment and dismantling; and so began a longer-term project of reducing payments, capping disbursements and excluding whole groups from entitlement. The drive to 'reform' welfare was, perversely, no longer concerned with reducing poverty, but rather with reducing the alleged 'dependency' of families on public aid. Fraser rightly critiques the complicity of liberal feminism with this process, and asks that feminist politics seeks to reactivate its emancipatory second-wave motivations and return to foundational issues of social justice, poverty and equality.

'Bringing the poor to heel': the future of social insecurity

A startlingly clear condensation of this neoliberal co-option of the liberal strands of feminism can be seen in a key piece of authoritarian policy making, which sought to punish families that did not conform to gender and family norms. The Conservative government announced in 2015 that it would be introducing a two-child cap on payments of Child Tax Credit, taking effect for all 'third children' born after 6 April 2017. This represented another brick in the wall of welfare restrictions, and spoke, in particular, to the manufactured crisis around 'benefit broods', as explored in the previous chapter.

Some exceptions were proposed to the two-child cap – including where third children were a result of multiple births, adoptions, and non-parental caring arrangements – and, most horrifyingly, an exception described in the amendment regulations as 'non-consensual conception'.[5] This amendment would become known as 'the rape clause'. It required women wishing to claim the exemption to provide either evidence of a conviction of rape, controlling or coercive behaviour, proof of a compensation award, or a corroborating statement from someone on a list of approved organisations. In short, mothers seeking to claim benefit payments for a third child conceived by sexual violence or in an abusive relationship would have to fill out an extensive eight-page document, detailing the circumstances. Far from challenging or halting this proposed clause, the Conservative party under the leadership of Theresa May persisted in bringing it to Parliament, describing it in a Prime Minister's Questions session in April 2017 as being driven by a 'principle of fairness'. The Equalities and Human Rights Commission (EHRC) described the amendment as 'regressive' and 'inhumane', and urged the employment minister Damien Hinds to rethink, stating that the Impact Assessment by the Department for Work and Pensions had been insufficiently detailed and that the policy could violate human rights law. As Rebecca Hilsenrath of the EHRC said in the letter:

> In our view the exception raises serious issues in relation to a child and mother's right to private life under Article 8 of the European Convention on Human Rights … the exception, which purports to prevent women from being penalised requires, in our view, invasive reporting requirements of intimate details … including the potentially traumatic process of having eligibility assessed and the risk of re-traumatisation upon survivors of rape. (Hilsenrath, 2017)

Other organisations swiftly moved to condemn the amendment. The British Medical Association stated that it would support doctors who refused to take part in the assessment process, describing the clause as 'ill-conceived' and 'fundamentally damaging for women', since it forced them to disclose rape and abuse 'at pain of financial penalty' (BMA, 2017), and could have devastating effects for children through the creation of a record. The authoritarian consensus that underpins this amendment cannot be overstated. Equally troubling is the imminent exit of Britain through Brexit from precisely the judicial apparatus that might be used to challenge such policy, in this case the European Court of Human Rights.

Mapping the feminisation and infantilisation of poverty, and the symbolic figures that ostensibly legitimate such trends, Loïc Wacquant (2009) tracks the deployment of behaviourist philosophy in deterring, surveilling, stigmatising and applying graduated sanctions to modify individual conduct. We can see the same remaking of the state at work in policy amendments such as the rape clause, which seek to transform the welfare state into a penal state, oriented towards what Wacquant calls 'bringing the poor to heel' (2009: 88) and being expansionist in its disciplinary and punitive instruments. As Wacquant argues, the calls for an authoritarian makeover began in the 1990s – under Clinton in the United States and Blair in the United Kingdom – and the construction of a 'war on welfare' on both sides of the Atlantic. Importantly, Wacquant sees this demand as driven by both right-wing politicians *and* liberal intellectuals, circulating a barely critiqued notion of 'personal responsibility'. The disentitlement strategies proposed then have moved from the fringes of political discourse to the central policy machinery of the welfare state. These include: denying public aid to unwed mothers under the age of 18; denying public aid to children born while parents are claiming welfare; denying public aid to mothers declining to identify the fathers of their children; and the reclassification of disabled people as being 'fit to work'. As Wacquant states: 'As the poor grew darker in the collective conscience, they were also cast in an increasingly unsympathetic and lurid light, as irresponsible, profligate and dissolute' (2009: 83).

These increasingly unsympathetic and lurid portrayals of poverty, and the rising resentments over social security that they animate, have been the central concerns of this book. As we have seen, different categories of parent are more and less easily designated as irresponsible, feckless and 'bad'. Wacquant proposes a range of racialised figures that populate the welfare reform debate landscape in the US of the 1990s – the 'welfare queen', the 'deadbeat dad', the 'black teen mother'. We have seen the symbolic proliferation of overlapping 'problem populations' in the UK, as welfare reform has been weaponised and deployed at the intersections of class, race, gender, nation and dis/ability; most notably, the 'troubled family' and 'the benefit brood'. We can detect even now the rapid deployment of new problem populations at the bottom of the socioracial order; witness, for example, the media hysteria generated by reports that European migrants working in Britain were able to claim child benefit for children living elsewhere in the EU. The strategic deployment of such racialised figures both feed and tap into rising resentments towards social security – and can then be used to bolster demand for new welfare restrictions. This is the machinery of authoritarian populism that this book has sought to unpick and to illuminate.

The recent lurches to the authoritarian right in both the UK and the US are parallel manifestations of connected neoliberal histories. Both the EU referendum result in the UK and the Trump election in the US have been favourably cast by populists as 'the people' speaking back to 'elites', and as a welcome supplanting of 'identity politics' with a renewed attention to growing forms of class inequality. Indeed, 'identity politics' has become a euphemistic bogeyman for critiques of sexism, racism, homophobia, transphobia, disablism. To be accused of 'playing identity politics' is to be accused of diverting attention away from 'real politics' (the politics of redistribution and class analysis) or of complicating or contaminating class analysis with other 'specialised', 'peripheral' concerns. The implication is that there is only so much revolutionary zeal to go round and that class politics has been exhausted by the demands of other, central, more marginal struggles. Trump pursues his programme of 'authoritarian kleptocracy', usefully defined by Sarah Kendzior (2017) – literally seizing the apparatus of democratic governance and funnelling it towards his own oligarchical family under a legitimating banner of 'America first', built on racism and xenophobia. On announcing a snap General Election on 18 April 2017, Theresa May promised to 'crush the sabateurs'[6] – those figures in the House of Commons and the House of Lords who voiced their desire to bring the advisory referendum result through the parliamentary channels of accountability. The decision to leave the European Union was allegedly driven by a desire to 'restore' British sovereignty; although its execution (in the form of the 2017 Repeal Bill) has been somewhat at odds with this, proposing to use antiquated law to bypass Parliament entirely.[7] The first rumbles of authoritarianism are always in the name of 'the people'.

This book has sought to examine the cultural mechanisms through which widening class inequality, rising poverty and the erosion of social solidarity have been legitimated. Cultural studies scholars argue that we cannot understand the grip of authoritarian populism (and our disinclination to revolt against it) without attending to *both* the material and practical obstacles of neoliberal capitalism, *and* – importantly – the ideological dimensions that persuade us that neoliberalism is inevitable. Neoliberal culture works both to secure consent and to generate political inertia. 'Good parenting', as this book has sought to show, provides a direction for hopeful activity – busily packing children full of value, resilience, grit, skills and character, in the hope that they will succeed in an increasingly cruel landscape of competitive individualism – while eclipsing any embryonic motivation to do things differently.

Such a project of change requires that we start meaningfully to unpick the binaries of 'good' and 'bad' parenting – and specifically, as we have seen across this book, 'good' and 'bad' mothering, the moral landscape of mothering that holds women to punishing ideals. Our twin fascination with and denigration of mothers works in two contradictory ways. On the one hand, we glamourise and fetishise fertility and domesticity. On the other hand, we police and punish mothers who are held to be 'undeserving'. This is a complex tapestry. It must be unravelled, if we are to find our way back to social solidarity and to think imaginatively about how to value, recognise and support the labour of social reproduction and the work of care.

Notes

[1] James Frayne (2016) of right-wing think-tank Policy Exchange defined the JAMs as C1 and C2 voters; provincial English families, homeowners, heavily dependent on public services like state schools and the NHS, not having significant disposable income and without resilience to withstand economic shocks. Frayne described the JAMs as 'middle class' – 'but a long way from the stereotype of the middle class' – and estimated that they include just under half of the UK population. David Finch (2016), of the centre-left think-tank the Resolution Foundation, defined the JAMs in narrower terms: low- and middle-income households of working age, in paid work and not reliant on benefit payments (though certainly perhaps claiming some), and now twice more likely to rent housing than to own it. Finch estimated that a third of UK households could be described as JAMs and proposed that what unites the group is the additional costs of having children. Theresa May has never said which definition is correct, or offered her own elaboration.

[2] The German Chancellor Angela Merkel is also widely known in Germany as 'Mutti' (Mummy).

[3] Bailey (2013) defines 'misogynoir' as a specific form of racialised misogyny which targets black women.

[4] Thatcher famously began a speech in Plymouth on 22 May 2001 with a joke about how her appearance had been heralded by a local cinema billboard that was advertising *The Mummy Returns*.

[5] The full amendment is listed as 2017 No 376 'The Social Security (Restrictions on Amounts for Children and Qualifying Young Persons) Amendment Regulations 2017'.

[6] The phrase 'Crush the Sabateurs' was used by the *Daily Mail* in its full-page splash headline on 19 April 2017.

[7] Known popularly as the 'Henry VIII law', this was originally intended to allow King Henry VIII to dissolve his marriage without parliamentary approval.

References

Adams, S. and Womack, S. (2007) 'Bringing Up Baby is "dangerous"', say experts', *The Telegraph*, 16 October

Adonis, A. (2013) *5 Days in May: The Coalition and Beyond* London: Biteback Publishing

Ahmed, S. (2010) *The Promise of Happiness*, Durham: Duke University Press

Aitkenhead, D. (2006) 'You've been very, very naughty', *The Guardian*, 22 July

Aitkenhead, D. (2007) 'Playtime's over', *The Guardian*, 8 September

Allen, K. (2016) 'Top Girls Navigating Austere Times: interrogating youth transitions since the "crisis"', *Journal of Youth Studies*, vol 19, no 6, pp 805–20

Allen, G. and Duncan Smith, I. (2008) *Early Intervention: Good Parents, Great Kids, Better Citizens*, London: Centre for Social Justice and Smith Institute

Allen, K. and Bull, A. (forthcoming) 'Following Policy: A network ethnography of the UK character education community', *Sociological Research Online*

Allen, K. and Taylor, Y. (2012) 'Placing Parenting, Locating Unrest: failed femininities, troubled mothers and riotous subjects', *Studies in the Maternal*, vol 4, no 2, [online] https://www.mamsie.bbk.ac.uk/articles/abstract/10.16995/sim.39/

Allen, K., Tyler, I. and de Benedictis, S. (2013) 'Thinking with "White Dee": The gender politics of "austerity"', *Sociological Research Online* 19, 3, 2, www.socresonline.org.uk/19/3/2.html

Andrejevic, M. (2004) *Reality TV: The work of being watched*, London/New York: Rowman and Littlefield Publishers

Andrews, D. (2010) '"I'm Claiming £50,000 of Benefits I Don't Need": Shameless Mother of Ten Admits to Fiddling the System – but Says She Will NEVER Stop while the Government Make it this Easy', *Mail Online*, 29 May, www.dailymail.co.uk/femail/article-2151202/Im-claiming-50k-benefits-I-dont-need-Shameless-mother-admits-fiddling–says-NEVER-stop.html#ixzz34K7GwyNx

Apple, R. (2006) *Perfect Motherhood: Science and Childrearing in America*, New Brunswick, New Jersey and London: Rutgers University Press

Arlidge, J. (2003) 'Cruelty TV?', *The Guardian*, 18 May

Ashcroft, M. and Oakeshott, I. (2016) *Call Me Dave: The unauthorised biography of David Cameron*, London: Biteback Publishing

Atkins, L. (2009) 'Should you treat your children like dogs?', *The Guardian*, 7 December

Back, L. (2007) *The Art of Listening*, Oxford and New York: Berg

Bagehot (2016) 'May's Revolutionary Conservatism', *The Economist*, 8 October

Bailey, M. (2013) 'New Terms of Resistance', *Souls: A Critical Journal of Black Politics, Culture & Society*, vol 14, pp 341–3

Baraitser, L. (2009) *Maternal Interruptions: The ethics of interruption*, London and New York: Routledge

Baraitser, L. (2017) *Enduring Time*, London: Bloomsbury Academic

Barlow, A., Duncan, S. and James, G. (2002) 'New Labour, the Rationality Mistake and Family Policy in Britain' in Carling, A., Duncan, S. and Edwards, R. (eds) *Analysing Families: Morality and rationality in policy and practice*, London: Routledge

Barrett, M. and McIntosh, M.(1982) *The Anti-Social Family*, London: Verso

Bassel, L. and Emujulu, A. (2017) *Minority Women and Austerity: Survival and resistance in France and Britain*, Bristol: Policy Press

Bauman, Z. (2003) *Wasted Lives: Modernity and its outcasts*, Cambridge: Polity

Baumberg, B., Bell, K. and Gaffney, D. (2012) 'Benefits Stigma in Britain', London: Elizabeth Finn Care/Turn2us, www.turn2us.org.uk/PDF/Benefits%20Stigma%20in%20Britain.pdf

Beck, U. (1992) *Risk Society: Towards a new modernity*, London: Sage

Beck, U. and Beck-Gernsheim, E. (2002) *Individualization: Institutionalised individualism and its social and political consequences*, London: SAGE

Becker, R. (2006) 'Help is on the Way! Supernanny, Nanny 911 and the neoliberal politics of the family' in Heller, D. (ed) *The Great American Makeover*, New York: Palgrave Macmillan, pp 175–91

Ben-Galim, D. and Gambles, R. (2008) 'The "public" and "private" of work-family reconciliation: Unsettling gendered notions and assumptions' in Seelib-Kaiser, M. (ed) *Welfare state transformations*, Basingstoke: Palgrave

Berlant, L. (1997) *The Queen of America Goes to Washington City*, Duke University Press

Berlant, L. (2011) *Cruel Optimism*, Durham: Duke University Press

Beveridge, W. (1942) *Social Insurance and Allied Services*, London: HM Stationery Office

Bevir, M. (2005) *New Labour: A critique*, London: Routledge

Bhattacharyya, B. (2015) *Crisis, austerity and everyday life: Living in a time of diminishing expectations*, London: Palgrave

Birch, K. (2015) *We Have Never Been Neoliberal*, Winchester: Zero Books

Biressi, A. and Nunn, H. (2008) 'The Bad Citizen: Class politics in lifestyle television' in Palmer, G. (ed) *Exposing Lifestyle Television: the big reveal*, Ashgate, pp 15-24

Biressi, A. and Nunn, H. (2010) 'Picturing the Underclass After Thatcherism' in Hadley, L. and Ho, E. (eds) *Thatcher and After*, London: Palgrave Macmillan, pp 137-57

Biressi, A. and Nunn, H. (2013) *Class and Contemporary British Culture*, London: Palgrave Macmillan

Blair, T. (1999) 'Beveridge Lecture' delivered at Toynbee Hall, London, 18 March

Blair, T. (2006) 'Tony Blair writes for the Sun', *The Sun*, 6 November

Blum, L. (1999) *At the Breast: Ideologies of Breastfeeding and Motherhood in the Contemporary United States*, Boston: Beacon Press

Blyth, M. (2013) *Austerity: The History of a Dangerous Idea*, Oxford: Oxford University Press

BMA (British Medical Association) (2017) 'BMA ratifies position on the shameful "rape clause"', [online] https://www.bma.org.uk/news/media-centre/press-releases/2017/july/bma-ratifies-position-on-the-shameful-rape-clause

Bourdieu, P. (1979) *Distinction: A social critique of the judgement of taste*, London: Routledge & Kegan Paul

Bousted, M. (2009) 'Don't blame parents when it's teachers who are failing', *The Guardian*, 5 April

Bowcott, O. (2005) 'The Guardian profile: Louise Casey', *The Guardian*, 9 September

Bowlby, J. (1951) *Maternal Care and Mental Health*, Geneva: World Health Organisation

Bramall, R. (2013) *The Cultural Politics of Austerity: Past and Present in Austere Times*, London: Palgrave Macmillan

Brien, S. (2010) 'Make Work Pay – for All', *The Spectator*, 11 March

Briggs, D. (2012) *The English Riots of 2011: A summer of discontent*, London: Waterside Press

Bristow, J. (2009) *Standing Up to Supernanny*, Exeter: Societas

Bristow, J. (2014) 'Who Cares for Children? The problem of generational contact' in Lee, E., Bristow, J., Faircloth, C. and Macvarish, J. (eds) *Parenting Culture Studies*, London: Palgrave Macmillan

Broadhurst, K., Hall, C., Wastell, D., White, S. and Pithouse, A. (2010) 'Risk, instrumentalism and the humane project: Identifying the informal logics of risk management in children's statutory services', *British Journal of Social Work*, vol 40, no 4, pp 1046-64

Buckingham, D. (2011) *The Material Child: Growing Up in Consumer Culture*, Cambridge: Polity

Budig, M. (2014) 'The Fatherhood Bonus and the Motherhood Penalty: Parenthood and the gender gap in pay', Washington, DC: Third Way, [online] www.thirdway.org/report/the-fatherhood-bonus-and-the-motherhood-penalty-parenthood-and-the-gender-gap-in-pay

Burney, E. (2005) *Making People Behave: Anti-Social Behaviour, Politics and Policy*, Cullompton: Willan Publishing

Burney, E. (2006) 'No Spitting: Regulation of offensive behaviour in England and Wales' in A. von Hirsch and A.P. Simester (eds) *Incivilities: Regulating offensive behaviour*, Oxford: Hart Publishing

Burrows, R. and Loader, B. (1994) *Towards a Post-Fordist Welfare State?* London: Routledge

Busby, R. (2009) *Marketing the Populist Politician: The demotic democrat*, Basingstoke: Palgrave Macmillan

Byrne, B. (2006) *White Lives: The interplay of race, class and gender in everyday life*, London: Routledge

Byron, T. (2006) *Little Angels: The essential guide to transforming your life and having more time with your children*, Harlow: Educational Publishers LLP

Byron, T. (2008) *Your Child, Your Way*, London: Penguin Group

Calam, R., Miller, C. and Sadhnani, V. (2008) 'Second Great Parenting Experiment: Effects of Media-based Delivery of Parenting Advice', University of Manchester Research Report, [online] http://dera.ioe.ac.uk/8594/1/ACF453.pdf

Calhoun, A. (2005) 'Supercalanormalistic', *The New York Times*, 16 October

Cameron, D. (2006) Speech to Conservative Party Conference, delivered in Bournemouth, 4 October

Cameron, D. (2010a) 'Building the Responsible Society', Speech given at Demos Headquarters, London, 11 January

Cameron, D. (2010b) 'Help us stop 1.5 billion pounds benefits scroungers', *The Sun*, 11 August

Cameron, D. (2011a) 'PM statement on violence in England', Speech delivered in the House of Commons, 11 August

Cameron, D. (2011b) Speech on the fight-back after the riots, delivered in Witney, 15 August

Cameron, D. (2011c) Speech on Troubled Families, Sandwell Christian Centre, Oldbury, 15 December

Campbell, J. (2001) *Margaret Thatcher: The Grocer's Daughter*, London: Pimlico

Carlomagno, M. (2011) *Live More, Want Less*, North Adams, Massachusetts: Storey Publishing

Casey, E. (2013) '"Urban Safaris": Looting, Consumption and Exclusion in London 2011', *Sociological Research Online*, 18(4), 8, [online] http://www.socresonline.org.uk/18/4/8.html

Catton, P. and Suntree, C. (2009) *Be Thrifty: How to live better with less*, New York: Workman Publishing

Centre for Social Justice (2006) *Breakdown Britain: Interim report on the state of the nation*, London: Social Justice Policy Group

Chambers, D. (2000) 'Representations of Familialism in the British Popular Media', *European Journal of Cultural Studies*, vol 3, no 2, pp 195-214

Chambers, D. (2001) *Representing the Family*, London: SAGE

Chapman, J. (2010) 'A Life Without Work: 1.5 million Britons Have Never Worked a Day in their Lives', *MailOnline*, 14 September, [online] www.dailymail.co.uk/news/article-1311789/1–5m-Britons-havent-job-left-school.html

Childers, M. and hooks, b. (1990) 'A conversation about race and class' in M. Hirsch and E. Fox Keller (eds) *Conflicts in Feminism*, New York: Routledge, Chapman & Hall

Chorley, M. (2014) 'Revealed: How 10 Families on Benefits Were Paid More on Average Each Week than Someone with a Salary of £85,000', *MailOnline*, 13 May, [online] www.dailymail.co.uk/news/article-2627028/Revealed-How-10-families-benefits-paid-average-week-salary-85–000.html

Chua, A. (2011) *Battle Hymn of the Tiger Mother*, London: Bloomsbury

Clarke, J. (2008) 'Living With/In and Without Neoliberalism', *Focaal*, vol 51, pp 135-47

Clarke, J. and Newman, J. (2012) The alchemy of austerity, *Critical Social Policy*, 32, 3, 299-319

Collier, H. (2014) 'Channel 4's Benefits Street claims 4.3 million viewers', *The Guardian*, 7 January

Collins, P.H. (1994) 'Shifting the center: Race, class, and feminist theorizing about motherhood', in Bassin, D., Honey, M. and Kaplan, M. (eds) *Representations of Motherhood*, New Haven, CT: Yale University Press

Coontz, S. (1992) *The Way We Never Were: American families and the nostalgia trap*, New York: Basic Books

Cooper, V. and White, D. (2017) *The Violence of Austerity*, Chicago: University of Chicago Press

Corner, J. and Pels, D. (2003) *Media and the Restyling of Politics: Consumerism, Celebrity and Cynicism*, London: SAGE

Correll, S. and Barnard, S. (2005) 'Getting a job: is there a motherhood penalty?', *American Journal of Sociology*, vol 112, no 5, 1297-338

Couldry, N. (2010) *Why Voice Matters: Culture and Politics After Neoliberalism*, London: Sage

Cromby, J. (2011) 'The Greatest Gift? Happiness, Governance and Psychology', *Social and Personality Psychology Compass*, vol 5, no 11, pp 840-52

Cronin, A. (2000) 'Consumerism and compulsory individuality: women, will and potential' in Ahmed, S., Kilby, J., Lury, C. and McNeil, M. (eds) *Thinking Through Feminism*, London: Routledge

Crossley, S. (2016) 'Realising the (troubled) family: crafting the neoliberal state', *Families, Relationships and Societies* vol 5, no 2, pp 263-79

Crossley, S. (2017) *In Their Place: The imagined geographies of poverty*, London: Pluto Press

Cruikshank, B. (1996) 'Revolutions Within: Self-Government and Self Esteem' in Barry, A., Osbourne, T. and Rose, N. (eds) *Foucault and Political Reason: Liberalism, Neo-Liberalism and the rationalities of government*, Chicago: University of Chicago Press

Cunningham, H. (1995) *Children and Childhood in Western Society Since 1500*, London and New York: Routledge

Cunningham, H. (2006) *The Invention of Childhood*, London: BBC Books

Cvetkovich, A. (2003) *An Archive of Feelings: Trauma, Sexuality and Lesbian Public Cultures*, New York: Duke University Press

Dally, A. (1982) *Inventing Motherhood: The Consequences of an Ideal*, London: Burnett Books

Das, L. (2013) 'Why Super Nanny is considering adoption', *Daily Mail*, 1 March, [online] www.dailymail.co.uk/femail/article-2285962/Why-super-nannys-considering-adoption-Jo-Frost-says-shes-busy-baby.html

Davies, C. (2011) 'Boris Johnson heckled in Clapham Junction over London riots', *The Guardian*, 9 August

De Beauvoir, S. (1949) *The Second Sex*, Paris: Gallimard

de Benedictis, S. (2012) 'Feral Parents: austerity parenting under neoliberalism', *Studies in the Maternal*, vol 4 (2), [online] https://www.mamsie.bbk.ac.uk/articles/abstract/10.16995/sim.40/

de Benedictis, S., Allen, K. and Jensen, T. (2017) 'Portraying poverty: the economic and ethics of factual welfare television', *Cultural Sociology*, vol 11, no 3, pp 337-58

Department for Business, Innovation and Skills (2015) *Pregnancy and Maternity-Related Discrimination and Disadvantage: First Findings*, BIS Research Paper No. 235, IFF Research, [online] https://www.equalityhumanrights.com/sites/default/files/pregnancy-and-maternity-related-discrimination-and-disadvantage_0.pdf

Department for Education (DfE) (2003) *Every Child Matters*, Crown Copyright

Department for Education and Skills (DfES) (2007) *Every Parent Matters*, London: TSO

Department for Work and Pensions (DWP) (2012) *Benefit Cap (Housing Benefit) Regulations 2012: Impact assessment for the benefit cap*, 16 July, DWP.

Department for Work and Pensions (2013) *Universal Credit and Your Claimant Commitment*, London: The Stationery Office

Department for Work and Pensions (2015) *Universal Credit at Work*, London: The Stationery Office

Dermott, E. (2008) *Intimate Fatherhood: A Sociological Analysis*, Routledge: London and New York

DiQuinzio, P. (1999) *The Impossibility of Mothering: Feminism, individualism and the problem of mothering*, New York: Routledge

Dodd, V. (2014) 'Mark Duggan's family lose attempt to overturn inquest verdict', *The Guardian*, 14 October

Doherty, K. and Coleridge, G. (2008) *Seven Secrets of Successful Parenting*, Bantam Press

Dolan, A. and Bentley, P. (2013) 'Vile Product of Welfare UK: Man Who Bred 17 Babies by Five Women to Milk Benefits System is Guilty of Killing Six of Them', *MailOnline*, 3 April, www.dailymail.co.uk/news/article-2303120/Mick-Philpott-vile-product-Welfare-UK-Derby-man-bred-17-babies-milk-benefits-GUILTY-killing-six.html

Donzelot, J. (1979) *The Policing of Families*, New York: Random House

Douglas, S. and Michaels, M. (2005) *The Mommy Myth: The idealisation of motherhood and how it has undermined all women*, Free Press: New York

Dovey, J. (2000) *Freakshow: First person media and factual television*, London: Pluto Press

Drake, P. and Higgins, M. (2006) 'I'm a celebrity, get me into politics: the political celebrity and the celebrity politician', in Holmes, S. and Redmond, S. (eds) *Framing Celebrity: New Directions in Celebrity Culture*, London: Routledge

Duell, M. and Tomlinson, S. (2013) 'Child-killer Mick Philpott received the equivalent of £100,000 salary', MailOnline, 4 April ,[online] http://www.dailymail.co.uk/news/article-2303881/Mick-Philpott-got-100k-benefits-wages-wife-Mairead-lover-Lisa-Willis-paid-HIS-account.html

Duerden, N. (2007) 'Jo Frost: Nanny state', *The Independent*, 7 September

Duncan, S. and Edwards, R. (1999) *Lone Mothers, Paid Work and Gendered Moral Rationalities*, London: Palgrave Macmillan

Duncan-Smith, I. (2013) 'I'm proud of our welfare reforms', *The Guardian*, 28 July

Easton, M. (2011) 'England Riots: The Return of the Underclass', BBC News, 11 August, [online] www.bbc.co.uk/news/uk-14488486

Edwards, H. (2005) 'Super Nanny or Demonic Mary Poppins?', *The Sydney Morning Herald*, 24 April

Edwards, R. and Gillies, V. (2013) 'Where are the parents?' Changing parental responsibilities between the 1960s and the 2010s' in C. Faircloth, D. Hoffman and L. Layne (eds) *Parenting in Global Perspective: Negotiating ideologies of kinship, self and politics*, London: Routledge

Ehrenreich, B. (2010) *Smile or Die: How positive thinking fooled the world* London: Granta Publications

Ehrenreich, B. and English, D. (1978) *For Her Own Good: 150 years of the experts' advice to women*, New York: Anchor Press

Ehrenreich, B. and English, D. (2005) *For Her Own Good: 150 years of the experts' advice to women* (2nd edn), New York: Anchor Press

English, R. (2006) 'If your kids are behaving badly, treat them like a dog', Mail Online, 29 August [online] www.dailymail.co.uk/news/article-1049499/If-kids-behaving-badly-treat-like-dog-says-expert.html

Equalities and Human Rights Commission (2016) *Pregnancy and Maternity-Related Discrimination and Disadvantage*, London: IFF Research

Equalities Review (2007) *Fairness and Freedom: The Final Report of the Equalities Review*, London: Crown Copyright

Etzioni, A. (1995) *New Communitarian Thinking: Persons, virtues, institutions, and communities*, Charlottesville: University Press of Virginia

Faircloth, C. (2014) 'Intensive parenting and the expansion of parenting' in Lee, E., Bristow, J., Faircloth, C. and Macvarish, J. (eds) *Parenting Culture Studies*, London: Palgrave Macmillan

Faludi, S. (1993) *Backlash: The undeclared war against American women*, London: Vintage

Fawcett Society (2012) *The Impact of Austerity on Women*, London: Fawcett Society

Ferguson, I., Lavalette, M. and Mooney, G. (2002) *Rethinking Welfare: A Critical Perspective*, London: SAGE

Field, F. (2010) *The Foundation Years: Preventing poor children becoming poor adults: The report of the Independent Review on Poverty and Life Chances*, London: Cabinet Office

Finch, D. (2016) *Hanging On: The stresses and strains of Britain's 'just managing' families*, Resolution Foundation, [online] www.resolutionfoundation.org/app/uploads/2016/09/Hanging-On.pdf

Finlayson, A. (2010) 'The Broken Society Versus the Social Recession', *Soundings*, vol 44, no 13, pp 22-34

Firestone, S. (1970) *The Dialectic of Sex: The case for feminist revolution*, New York: Morrow

Fisher, M. (2009) *Capitalist Realism: Is there no alternative?*, Winchester: Zero Books

Flanagan, C. (2005) 'Becoming Mary Poppins: P.L. Travers, Walt Disney and the making of a myth', *The New Yorker*, 19 December

Ford, G. (1999) *The Contented Little Baby Book*, London: Vermillion

Foster, P. (2007) 'TVs toughest nanny and the string of qualifications that do not exist', *The Times*, 27 October

Foucault, M. (1975) *Discipline and Punish: The birth of the prison*, New York: Random House

Foucault, M. (1978) *The Birth of Biopolitics: Lectures at the Collège de France* (translated by Graham Burchell), New York City: St Martins Press

Foucault, M. (1982) 'The Subject and Power', *Critical Inquiry*, vol 8, no 4, pp 777–95

Fraser, N. (2013) *Fortunes of Feminism: From state-managed capitalism to neoliberal crisis*, London: Verso

Frayne, J. (2015) *Overlooked But Decisive: Connecting with England's Just About Managing Classes*, Policy Exchange, London: Heron, Dawson and Sawyer

Friedan, B. (1963) *The Feminine Mystique*, London: Victor Gollancz Ltd

Friedli, L. and Stearn, R. (2013) 'Whistle While You Work (For Nothing): Positive Affect as Coercive Strategy – The Case of Workfare', Centre for the Medical Humanities, December, [online] http://centreformedicalhumanities.org/whistle-while-you-work-for-nothing-positive-affect-as-coercive-strategy-the-case-of-workfare

Frost, J. (2006) *Ask Supernanny: What Every Parent Wants to Know*, New York City: Hyperion Books

Gabriel, D. (2017) 'The othering and objectification of Diane Abbott MP' in *Election Analysis: Personality Politics and Popular Culture*, [online] www.electionanalysis.uk/uk-election-analysis-2017/section-8-personality-politics-and-popular-culture/the-othering-and-objectification-of-diane-abbott-mp/

Gallie, M. (1994) 'Are the Unemployed an Underclass? Some Evidence from the Social Change and Economic Life Initiative', *Sociology*, vol 28, no 3, pp 755-56

Gambles, R. (2010) 'Going Public? Articulations of the personal and political on Mumsnet.com', in Mahony, N., Newman, J. and Barnett, C. (eds) *Rethinking the Public: Innovations in Research, Theory and Politics*, London: Sage

Ganesh, J. (2012) *The Austerity Chancellor*, London: Biteback Publishing

Gatrell, C. (2005) *Hard Labour: The Sociology of Parenthood*, Open University Press, Buckingham

Gentleman, A. (2011) 'Being liberal is fine, but we need to be given the right to parent', *The Guardian*, 10 August

Gentleman, A. (2015) 'Labour vows to reduce reliance on food banks if it comes to power', *The Guardian*, 17 March

Gewirtz, S. (2001) 'Cloning the Blairs: New Labour's programme for the re-socialization of working-class parents', *Journal of Education Policy*, vol 16, no 4, pp 365-78

Giddens, A. (1991) *Modernity and Self-Identity: Self and society in the late modern age*, Cambridge: Polity

Giddens, A. (1992) *The Transformation of Intimacy: Sexuality, love and eroticism in modern societies*, Oxford: Polity Press

Gilbert, J. (2013) 'What kind of thing is neoliberalism?', *New Formations*, no 80/81, pp 7-22

Gill, R. (2007) 'Post-feminist Media culture: Elements of a sensibility', *European Journal of Cultural Studies*, vol 10, no 2, pp 147-66

Gill, R. (2015) 'Postfeminist sexual culture' in C. Carter, L. Steiner and L. McLaughlin (eds) *The Routledge Companion to Media & Gender*, London and New York: Routledge, pp 589-99

Gillies, V. (2005) 'Raising the "Meritocracy": parenting and the individualization of social class', *Sociology*, vol 39, no 5, pp 825-53

Gillies, V. (2007) *Marginalised Mothers: Exploring working-class experiences of parenting*, London: Routledge

Gillies, V. (2011) 'From Function to Competence: Engaging with the New Politics of Family', *Sociological Research Online*, 16, 4, [online] www.socresonline.org.uk/16/4/11.html

Gilroy, C. (2011) 'Paul Gilroy speaks on the riots', Speech given at community meeting in Tottenham, http://dreamofsafety.blogspot.co.uk/2011/08/paul-gilroy-speaks-on-riots-august-2011.html

Gilroy, P. (2013) '1981 and 2011: From Social Democratic to Neoliberal Rioting', *South Atlantic Quarterly*, vol 112 (3), pp 550-8

Gingerbread (2013) *Paying the Price: Single parents in the age of austerity*, London: Gingerbread

Glennerster, H. (2007) *British Social Policy 1945 to the Present*, Oxford: Blackwell

Goodhart, D. (2011) 'The riots at the end of history', *Prospect Magazine*, 9 August

Gramsci A. (1971) *Selections from the Prison Notebooks*, London: Lawrence & Wishart

Grant, J. (1998) *Raising Baby by the Book: The education of American mothers*, New Haven and London: Yale University Press

Griffiths, S. (2014) 'Ofsted boss says mixed schools are better', *The Sunday Times*, 28 September

Grindstaff, L. (2002) *The Money Shot: Trash, Class, and the Making of TV Talk Shows*, Chicago: University of Chicago Press

Grover, C. (2011) 'Social Protest in 2011: Material and Cultural Aspects of Economic Inequalities', *Sociological Research Online* 16(4), 18, [online] www.socresonline.org.uk/16/4/18.html

Groves, J. (2010) '"Sam and I are part of the sharp-elbowed middle classes" claims Cameron as he defends cuts to Sure Start', *Daily Mail*, 11 August

Hacking, I. (1990) *The Taming of Chance*, Cambridge University Press

Hall, S. (1979) 'The Great Moving Right Show', *Marxism Today*, January, 14-20

Hall, S. (1987) 'Gramsci and Us', *Marxism Today*, June, 1-8

Hall, S. (1997) *Representation: Cultural representations and signifying practices*, London/Thousand Oaks, California: Sage

Hall, S. (1998) 'Notes on deconstructing the popular' in Storey, J. (ed) *Cultural Theory and Popular Culture*, London: Prentice Hall, pp 442–53

Hall, S. (2003) 'Marx's notes on "method": a "reading" of the "1857" introduction', *Cultural Studies* , vol 17, no 2, pp 113–49

Hall, S. (2016) 'Family Relations in Times of Austerity: Reflections from the UK' in Punch, S. and Vanderbeck, R. (eds) *Families, Intergenerationality, and Peer Group Relations: Geographies of Children and Young People*, 5, Springer

Hall, S., and O'Shea, A. (2013) 'Common-sense neoliberalism', *Soundings*, no 55, pp 9–25

Hall, S., Critcher, C., Jefferson, T., Clarke, J. and Roberts, B. (1978/2013) *Policing the Crisis: Mugging, the State and Law and Order*, London: Palgrave Macmillan

Hall, S., Massey, D. and Rustin, M. (2014) *After Neoliberalism? The Kilburn Manifesto*, London: Lawrence & Wishart

Hancock, A. (2004) *The Politics of Disgust: The public identity of the welfare queen*, New York: New York University Press

Hancock, L. and Mooney, G. (2013) '"Welfare Ghettos" and the "Broken Society": Territorial Stigmatization in the Contemporary UK', *Housing, Theory and Society*, vol 30, no 1, pp 46-64

Hardman, I. (2014) 'A Tricky Balance between Church and State', *The Telegraph*, 20 February

Hardyment, C. (1995) *Perfect Parents: Baby-care advice past and present*, Oxford: Oxford University Press

Hardyment, C. (2007) *Dream Babies: Childcare advice from John Locke to Gina Ford*, London: Frances Lincoln Ltd.

Harris, J. (2006) 'Blue Sky Thinking – or just plain barmy?', *The Guardian*, 15 June

Harvey, D. (2007) *A Brief History of Neoliberalism*, Oxford: Oxford University Press

Hayes, S. (2010) *Radical Homemaking: Reclaiming Domesticity from Consumer Culture*, New York: Left to Write Press

Haylett, C. (2000) 'Illegitimate Subjects? Abject whites, neoliberal modernisation and middle class multiculturalism', *Environment and Planning*, 19, 3, 351-70

Hays, S. (1996) *The Cultural Contradictions of Motherhood*, Yale University Press

Hayton, R. (2010) 'Conservative Party Modernisation and David Cameron's Politics of the Family', *The Political Quarterly*, vol 81, no 4, pp 492-500

Hendrick, H. (2016) *Narcissistic Parenting in an Insecure World*, Bristol: Policy Press

Henricson, C. (2008) 'Governing parenting:is there a case for a policy review and statement of parenting rights and responsibilities', *Journal of Law and Society*, vol 35, no 1, pp 150-65

Hills, J. (2015) *Good Times, Bad Times: The Welfare Myth of Them and Us*, Bristol: Policy Press

Hilsenrath, R. (2017) 'Letter to Damian Hinds', [online] https://www.equalityhumanrights.com/sites/default/files/letter-to-damian-hinds-child-tax-credits-rape-clause-21-april-2017.pdf

HL Paper 117/HC Paper 81 (2003) *The UN Convention on the Rights of the Child: Tenth Report of Session 2002-03*, London: The Stationery Office

Hochschild, A. (1997) *The Time Bind: When work becomes home and home becomes work*, New York: Metropolitan Books

Hoff-Sommers, C. (1994) *Who Stole Feminism? How women have betrayed women*, New York: Simon and Schuster

Holmes, S. and Jermyn, D. (2004) *Understanding Reality Television*, Abingdon, Oxon: Routledge

Holt, A. (2008) 'Room for Resistance? Parenting orders, disciplinary power and the production of 'the bad parent'' in Squires, P. (ed) *ASBO Nation*, Bristol: Policy Press

Home Office (1998) *Supporting Families: A consultation document*, London: TSO

Home Office (2006) *Respect Action Plan*, London: TSO

House of Lords (2011a) *Hansard*, 23 November, col GC421, [online] https://publications.parliament.uk/pa/ld201011/ldhansrd/text/111123-gc0001.htm

House of Lords (2011b) *Hansard*, 21 November, col GC367, [online] https://publications.parliament.uk/pa/ld201011/ldhansrd/text/111121-gc0002.htm

Howarth, G. (2013) House of Commons, Debate, 13 May, *Hansard*, col 388, [online] https://publications.parliament.uk/pa/cm201314/cmhansrd/cm130513/debtext/130513-0002.htm

Hughes, B. (2006) 'Keynote Speech for launch of *Daddy Dearest: Public policy and active fatherhood*', delivered on 19 October at the Institute for Public Policy Research

Hulbert, A. (2003) *Raising America: Experts, parents and a century of advice about children*, New York: Alfred A. Knopf

Humphrys, J. (2004) 'Take This Oath: first, do no harm', MacTaggart Lecture delivered at the Edinburgh Television Festival, 27 August

Huntingdon, R. (2004) *The Nanny State*, London: Jot Publishing

Hurst, G., Sylvester, R. and Thomson, A. (2014) 'Fine parents who don't read to their children' *The Sunday Times*, 17 June

Illouz, E. (2007) *Cold Intimacy: The making of modern capitalism*, Cambridge: Polity Press

Ipsos-Mori (2006) 'Happy Families?', [online] https://ems.ipsos-mori.com/researchpublications/researcharchive/348/Happy-Families.aspx

Jamieson, L. (1999) 'Intimacy Transformed? A critical look at "the pure relationship"', *Sociology*, vol 33, no 3, pp 477-94

Jensen, T. (2010) *Beyond the Naughty Step: The intersections of class and gender in parenting culture*, awarding body: Open University, [online] http://ethos.bl.uk/OrderDetails.do?uin=uk.bl.ethos.527445

Jensen, T (2012) 'Tough Love in Tough Times', *Studies in the Maternal*, vol 4(3), [online] https://www.mamsie.bbk.ac.uk/articles/abstract/10.16995/sim.35/

Jensen, T. (2013) 'Riots, Restraint and the new Cultural Politics of Wanting', *Sociological Research Online*, 18(4), 7, www.socresonline.org.uk/18/4/7.html

Jensen, T. (2014) 'Welfare Commonsense, Poverty Porn and Doxosophy', *Sociological Research Online*, 19(3), 3, www.socresonline.org.uk/19/3/3.html

Jensen, T. and Tyler, I. (2012) 'Austerity Parenting: New Economies of Parent-Citizenship', *Studies in the Maternal*, vol 4(2), [online] https://www.mamsie.bbk.ac.uk/articles/10.16995/sim.34/

Jensen, T. and Tyler, I. (2015) '"Benefits broods": The cultural and political crafting of anti-welfare commonsense', *Critical Social Policy*, vol 35, no 4, pp 470-91

Jessop, B. (2010) 'Cultural Political Economy and Critical Policy Studies', *Critical Policy Studies*, vol 3, no 3-4, pp 336-56

Jessop, B. (2014) 'A Specter is Haunting Europe: A Neoliberal Phantasmagoria', *Critical Policy Studies*, vol 8, no 3, pp 352-55

Jessop, B. (2015) *The State: Past, Present and Future*, Cambridge: Polity

Jones, C. and Novak, T. (1999) *Poverty, Welfare and the Disciplinary State*, London: Routledge

Jones, R., Pykett, J. and Whitehead, M. (2011) 'The Geographies of Soft Paternalism in the UK: the rise of the avuncular state and changing behaviour after neoliberalism', *Geography Compass*, vol 5, pp 50-62

Jorsh, M. (2012) '50K Spongers: Blame the Government', *Daily Star*, 31 May

Kavka, M. and West, A. (2004) 'Temporalities of the Real' in Holmes, S. and Jermyn, D. (eds) *Understanding Reality Television*, London: Routledge

Keay, D. (1987) 'Interview with Margaret Thatcher', *Woman's Own*, 23 September

Kempson, E. (1996) *Life on a Low Income*, York: Joseph Rowntree Foundation.

Kendzior, S. (2017) 'Welcome to the Authoritarian Kleptocracy Parts I-XVIII' series of essays, sarahkendzior.com

Key, E. (1909) *The Century of the Child*, New York and London: GP Putnam

Krugman, P. (2012) *End this Depression Now!*, New York City: W.W. Norton

Kynaston, D. (2007) *Austerity Britain: 1945–51*, London: Bloomsbury

Ladd-Taylor, M. (1994) *Mother-work: Women, child welfare and the state 1890–1930*, University of Illinois Press

Ladd-Taylor, M. and Umansky, L. (1998) *Bad Mothers: The Politics of Blame in 20th Century America*, New York: New York University Press

Lammy, D. (2011) *Out of the Ashes: Britain After the Riots*, London: Guardian Books

Langan, M. (1994) 'Series Editor's Preface', in Burrows, R. and Loader, B. (eds) *Towards a Post-Fordist Welfare State?*, London: Routledge, xi–xiii

Lareau, A. (2003) *Unequal Childhoods: Class, race and family life*, Oakland: University of California Press

Lawler, S. (2000) *Mothering the Self: Mothers, Daughters, Subjects*, London: Routledge

Laws, D. (2016) *Coalition: The inside story of the Conservative-Liberal Democrat Coalition Government*, London: Biteback Publishing

Lawson, V. (1999) *Mary Poppins, She Wrote: The life of P.L. Travers*, London: Aurum Press

Layard, R. (2005) *Happiness: Lessons from a New Science*, London: Penguin Press

Lee, E. (2014) 'Experts and Parenting Culture' in E. Lee, J. Bristow, C. Faircloth and J. Macvarish (eds) *Parenting Culture Studies*, London: Palgrave

Lee, E., Bristow, J., Faircloth, C. and Macvarish, J. (2014) *Parenting Culture Studies*, London: Palgrave Macmillan

Levitas, R. (1998) *The Inclusive Society: Social Exclusion and New Labour* London: Palgrave

Levitas, R. (2005) *The Inclusive Society? Social Exclusion and New Labour* (2nd edn), Hampshire and New York: Palgrave Macmillian

Levitas, R. (2012) 'There may be "trouble" ahead: what we know about those 120,000 "troubled" families, *Poverty and Social Exclusion*, Policy Series Working Paper 3, [online] www.poverty.ac.uk/system/files/WP%20Policy%20Response%20No.3-%20%20%27Trouble%27%20ahead%20(Levitas%20Final%2021April2012).pdf

Lewis, P., Roberts, D. and Newburn, T. (2011) *Reading the Riots: Investigating England's summer of disorder*, London: Guardian Shorts

Lexmond, J. and Reeves, R. (2009) *Building Character*, London: Demos, [online] https://www.demos.co.uk/files/Building_Character_Web.pdf

Lexmond, J. and Grist, M. (2011) *The Character Inquiry*, London: Demos [online] https://www.demos.co.uk/files/Character_Inquiry_-_web.pdf?1304696626

Linn, S. (2004) *Consuming Kids: The hostile takeover of childhood*, New York: The New Press

Lister, R. (1996) 'Charles Murray and the Underclass: The Developing Debate', *Choice in Welfare*, IEA Health and Welfare Unit, 33

Lister, R. (2006) 'Children (but not women) first: New Labour, child welfare and gender', *Critical Social Policy*, vol 26, no 2, pp 315–35

Littler, J. (2013) 'The rise of the "yummy mummy": popular conservatism and the neoliberal maternal in contemporary British culture', *Communications, Culture and Critique*, vol 6, no 2, pp 227-43

Littler, J. (2017) *Against Meritocracy: Culture, power and myths of mobility*, London: Routledge

Livingstone, S. and Sefton-Green, J. (2016) *The Class: Living and Learning in the Digital Age*, New York: NYU Press

Lowe, R. (2005) *The Welfare State in Britain since 1945*, London: Palgrave Macmillan

Lupton, D. and Barclay, L. (1997) *Constructing Fatherhood: Discourses and Experiences*, London: Sage

Macauley, S. (2010) 'Jo Frost interview', *The Telegraph*, 28 January

MacDonald, M. (2004) 'Is this the new Dr Spock?', *Evening Standard*, 23 July

Macdonald, R., Shildrick, T. and Furlong, A. (2014) 'In search of "intergenerational cultures of worklessness": Hunting the Yeti and shooting zombies', *Critical Social Policy*, vol 34, no 2, pp 199-220

Macnicol, J. (1987) 'In pursuit of the underclass', *Journal of Social Policy*, vol 16, no 3, pp 293-318

MacVarish (2014) 'The politics of parenting' in E. Lee, J. Bristow, C. Faircloth and J. Macvarish (eds) *Parenting Culture Studies*, London: Palgrave

Mason, R. and Dominiczak, P. (2013) 'David Cameron: Philpott Case Does Raise "Wider Questions" about the Welfare System', *The Telegraph*, 5 April

Maternity Action (2013) *Overdue: a plan of action to address pregnancy discrimination now*, [online] https://www.maternityaction.org.uk/wp-content/uploads/2013/12/Overdue.pdf

Maternity Action (2015) *Making a Difference: Fifth Anniversary Impact Report 2009–2014*, Maternity Action: London, [online] www.maternityaction.org.uk/wp-content/uploads/2014/11/Fifth-Anniversary-Impact-Report-for-website.pdf

May, T. (2011) 'Statement to the House of Commons', Speech delivered in the House of Commons, 11 August, [online] https://www.gov.uk/government/speeches/riots-theresa-mays-speech-on-11-august-2011

May, T (2016) 'Statement from the new Prime Minister Theresa May', Speech delivered outside 10 Downing Street, London, 13 July, [online] https://www.gov.uk/government/speeches/statement-from-the-new-prime-minister-theresa-may

Mayo, E. and Nairn, A. (2009) *Consumer Kids: How big business is grooming our children for profit*, London: Constable

McCoy, J. (2009) *Miserly Moms: Living Well on Less in a Tough Economy*, Bloomington, Minnesota: Bethany House Publishers

McRobbie, A. (2004) 'Notes on *What Not To Wear* and post-feminist symbolic violence', in Adkins, L. and Skeggs, B. (eds) *Feminism After Bourdieu*, Oxford: Blackwell

McRobbie, A. (2013) 'Feminism, the family and the new 'mediated' maternalism', *New Formations* vol 80, pp 119-137

Mendelsohn, F. (2008) *Rhetorics of Fantasy*, Middletown, CT: Wesleyan University Press

Mendes, E., Saad, L. and McGeeney, K. (2012) 'Stay-at-home moms report more depression, sadness, anger', *The Gallup Poll*, Washington: Pew Research Centre

Merrick, J. and Brady, B. (2010) 'The Mother of All Elections', *The Independent*, 14 March

Miller, T. (2010) *Making Sense of Fatherhood: Gender, Caring and Work* Cambridge: Cambridge University Press

Millett, K. (1971) *Sexual Politics*, New York: Columbia University Press

Millie, A. (2008) *Anti-Social Behaviour*, Maidenhead: Open University Press

Modleski, T. (1991) *Feminism Without Women: Culture and criticism in a 'post-feminist' age*, Routledge: London

Mooney, G. (2009) 'The "broken society" election: class hatred and the politics of poverty and place in Glasgow East', *Social Policy and Society*, vol 8, no 4, pp 437-50

Moseley, R., Wheatley, H. and Wood, H. (2016) *Television for Women: New Directions*, Abingdon: Routledge

Muir, H. (2006) 'Childcare expert threatens to have website shut down', *The Guardian*, 8 August

Mumsnet (2007) 'Live Chat with Tanya Byron', 6 September, https://www.mumsnet.com/onlinechats/tanya-byron

Mungham, S. and Lazard, L. (2010) 'Virtually experts: exploring constructions of mothers' advice seeking in online parenting forums', *Radical Psychology*, vol 9, no 2, [online] http://oro.open.ac.uk/49711/2/49711.pdf

Munt, S. (2007) *Queer Attachments: The cultural politics of shame*, Abingdon: Routledge

Murkoff, H. (2000) 'The real parenting expert is … you', *Newsweek*, Fall–Winter, pp 20-1

Murkoff, H. (2002) *What to Expect When You're Expecting*, New York: Workman Publishing

Murray, C. (1990) 'The Emerging British Underclass', *Choice in Welfare*, IEA Health and Welfare Unit, 2, London: Civitas

National Institute of Economic and Social Research (NIESR) (2016) *National Evaluation of the Troubled Families Programme*, Crown Copyright

Neate, P. (2013) 'Reports of Mick Philpott's Awful Crime Omit the Phrase "Domestic Violence"', *The Guardian*, 4 April

Negra, D. (2009) 'Time Crisis and the Postfeminist Heterosexual Economy' in Negra, D. (ed) *Hetero: Queering Representations of Straightness*, Albany, NY: SUNY Press

Negra, D. and Tasker, Y. (2014) *Gendering the Recession: Media and Culture in an Age of Austerity*, Duke University Press

Neil, B. (2010) 'Meet the two Mumsnet founders, the women who could decide the next General Election mumsnet election', *The Mirror*, 26 January

Nelson, M. (2010) *Parenting Out of Control: Anxious parents in uncertain times*, New York and London: New York University Press

Nunn, H. (2011) 'Investing in the "Forever Home": From Property Programming to "Rereta TV"', in B. Skeggs and H. Wood (eds) *Reality Television and Class*, London: BFI Books

Oakley, A. (1974) *The Sociology of Housework*, Oxford, New York: Basil Blackwell

O'Hara, M. (2015) *Austerity Bites*, Bristol: Policy Press

Oppenheim, C. and Harker, L. (1996) *Poverty: The Facts*, London: Child Poverty Action Group

Osborne, G. (2010) 'Comprehensive Spending Review', Speech presented to House of Commons, 20 October [online] https://publications.parliament.uk/pa/cm201011/cmhansrd/cm101020/debtext/101020-0001.htm#10102049000003

Ouellette, L. and Hay, J. (2008) *Better Living Through Reality TV: Television and post-welfare citizenship*, Maldon, MA: Blackwell Publishing

Page, R. (2007) *Revisiting the Welfare State*, New York/Maidenhead: McGraw Hill/Open University Press

Palmer, S. (2006) *Toxic Childhood: How the Modern World is Damaging our Children and What We Can Do About It*, London: Orion Books

Parkinson, J. (2009) 'Pledge Watch, Supernannies', BBC News, [online] http://news.bbc.co.uk/1/hi/uk_politics/8236967.stm

Parton, N. (2006) 'Every child matters: the shift to prevention whilst strengthening protection in children's services in England', *Children and Youth Services Review*, vol 28, no 2, pp 976-92

Patrick, R. (2017) *For Whose Benefit? The everyday realities of welfare reform*, Bristol: Policy Press

Pearson, A. (2013) 'Mick Philpott, a Good Reason to Cut Benefits', *The Telegraph*, 3 April

Peck, J. and Theodore, N. (2010) 'Recombinant Workfare, across the Americas: Transnationalizing "Fast" Social Policy', *Geoforum*, 41, 195-208

Peck, J. and Theodore, N. (2015) *Fast Policy: Experimental Statecraft at the Threshold of Neoliberalism*, Minneapolis: University of Minnesota Press

Peev, G. (2010) 'Britain's Benefits Bonanza: How 100,000 Households Rake in More Than Average Wage in Welfare Every Year', *Daily Mail*, 7 August

Perkins Gilman, C. (1903) *The Home: Its Work and Influence*, New York: McClure, Phillips, & Co

Philby, C. (2013) 'Jo Frost: I've had some real head-on situations with the fathers', *The Independent*, 10 March

Phibbs, H. (2011) 'More rights for women has led to fewer jobs in this recession', *Daily Mail*, 12 January

Pietras, E. (2014) 'Supernanny Jo Frost reveals the time may finally be right to have children of her own', *The Mirror*, 22 April

Piketty, T. (2014) *Capital in the Twenty-First Century*, Paris: Harvard University Press

Platell, A. (2010) 'They're the Family with the Mercedes in the Drive Getting £42,000 a Year in Benefits. Scroungers?', *MailOnline*, 16 April, www.dailymail.co.uk/news/article-1266649/Theyre-family-Mercedes-drive-getting-42–000-year-benefits-Scroungers-AMANDA-PLATELL-meets-them.html

Plummer, K. (2003) *Intimate Citizenship: private decisions and public dialogues*, Seattle: University of Washington Press

Porter, R. (2012) 'Gordon Brown's poisonous legacy lives on', *The Telegraph*, 5 April

R v Philpott, Philpott and Moseley (2013) Nottingham Crown Court, sentencing remarks of Mrs Justice Thirlwall

Rabindrakumar, S. (2013) *Paying the Price: Single parents in an age of austerity*, Gingerbread, www.gingerbread.org.uk/uploads/media/17/8737.pdf

Rapping, E.(1996) *The Culture of Recovery: Making sense of the self-help movement in women's lives*, Ann Arbor, MI: Beacon Press

Reay, D. (1997) 'The Double-Bind of the working class feminist academic: the success of failure or the failure of success?', in Mahoney, P. and Zmroczek, C. (eds) *Class Matters: 'Working class' women's perspectives on social class*, London: Routledge

Reay, D. (1998) *Classwork: Mothers' involvement with the children's primary schooling*, London: UCL Press

Reddy, W. (2001) *The Navigation of Feeling: A Framework for the History of Emotions*, New York: Cambridge University Press

Reimer, V. and Sahagian, S. (2015) *The Mother-Blame Game*, Ontario: Demeter Press

Reynolds, T. (2005) *Caribbean Mothers: Identity and experience in the UK*, London: Tufnell Press

Rich, A. (1976) *Of Woman Born: Motherhood as Experience and Institution*, New York: Norton

Riddell, M. (2011) 'The London Riots: the underclass lashes out', *The Telegraph*, 8 August

Riots Communities and Victims Panel (2012) *After the Riots: The final report of the Riots Communities and Victims Panel*, Crown Copyright

Roberts, A. (2007) 'From Supernanny to Superbrand', *Evening Standard*, 11 September

Roberts, D., Lewis, P. and Newburn, T. (2011) *Reading the Riots: Investigating. England's Summer of Disorder*, London: Guardian Shorts 37.

Robinson, J. (2004) 'Pap – or "porn with a purpose"', *The Guardian*, 18 July

Rodger, J. (2003) 'Social solidarity, welfarism and post–emotionalism', *Journal of Social Policy*, vol 32, no 3, pp 403-21

Rose, N. (1990) *Governing the Soul: The shaping of the private self*, London and New York: Free Association Books

Rose, N. (1996) *Inventing Ourselves: Psychology, Power and Personhood*, Cambridge: Cambridge University Press

Ross, A. (2009) *Nice Work if You Can Get it*, New York: New York University Press

Rottenberg, C. (2013) 'The Rise of Neoliberalism', *Journal of Cultural Studies*, vol 28, no 3, pp 418-37

Rutherford, J. and Shah, H. (2006) *The Good Society*, London: Compass

Savage, M. (2000) *Class Analysis and Social Transformation*, Milton Keynes: Open University Press

Sayer, A. (2002) 'What Are You Worth? Why class is an embarrassing subject', *Sociological Research Online*, 7, 3, www.socresonline.org.uk/7/3/sayer.html

Sayer, A. (2014) *Why We Can't Afford the Rich*, Bristol: Policy Press

Scammell, M. (2017) 'Theresa May for Britain: a personal brand in search of personality', in *Election Analysis: Personality Politics and Popular Culture*, [online] www.electionanalysis.uk/uk-election-analysis-2017/section-8-personality-politics-and-popular-culture/theresa-may-for-britain-a-personal-brand-in-search-of-personality/

Schor, J. (2004) *Born to Buy: The commercialised child and the new consumer culture*, New York: Scribner

Segal, L. (1994) *Straight Sex: Rethinking the politics of pleasure*, Virago: London

Segal, L. (1997) *New Sexual Agendas*, London: MacMillan

Seldon, A. and Snowdon, P. (2016) *Cameron at 10: The inside story 2010–2015*, London: William Collins

Sennett, R. and Cobb, J. (1972) *The Hidden Injuries of Class*, New York: Alfred A. Knopf

Shields, R. (2009) 'Tough Love: the good parent's guide', *The Independent on Sunday*, 8 November

Shildrick, T., Macdonald, R., Webster, C. and Garthwaite, K. (2012) *Poverty and Insecurity: Life in Low-Pay, No-Pay Britain,* Bristol: Policy Press

Silverstone, R. (1994) *Television and Everyday Life*, London: Routledge

Sims, P. (2010) 'Why Work When I Can Get £42,000 in Benefits a Year AND Drive a Mercedes?', *MailOnline*, 13 April, www.dailymail.co.uk/news/article-1265508/Peter-Davey-gets-42-000-benefits-year-drives-Mercedes.html

Skeggs, B. (1997) *Formations of Class and Gender: Becoming Respectable*, London: Sage

Skeggs, B. (2004) *Class, Self, Culture*, London: Routledge

Skeggs, B. and Wood, H. (2012) *Reality Television and Class*, London: BFI Books

Skeggs, B., Wood, H. and Thumim, N. (2008) '"Oh goodness, I *am* watching reality TV": how methods make class in audience research', *European Journal of Cultural Studies*, vol 2, no 1, pp 5-24

Skenazy, L. (2009) *Free Range Kids: Giving our children the freedom we had without going nuts with worry*, San Francisco: Jossey-Bass

Slater, T. (2011) 'From "criminality" to marginality: rioting against a broken state', *Human Geography: A New Radical Journal*, vol 4, no 3, pp 106-15

Slater, T. (2013) 'The Myth of "Broken Britain": Welfare Reform and the Production of Ignorance', *Antipode*, vol 46, no 4, pp 948-69

Smith, A. (2006) 'The right lessons?', *The Guardian*, 31 July

Smith, A. (2008) '"New Man" or "Son of the Manse"? Gordon Brown as a Reluctant Celebrity Father', *British Politics*, vol 3, no 4, pp 556-75

Spock, B. and Needlman, R. (2004) *Dr Spock's Baby and Childcare*, London: Simon & Schuster, Ltd

Squires, P. (ed) (2008) *ASBO Nation*, Bristol: Policy Press

Standing, G. (2011) *The Precariat: The New Dangerous Class*, London: Bloomsbury

Starkey, P. (2000) 'The Feckless Mother: Women, Poverty and Social Workers in Wartime and Post-war England', *Women's History Review*, vol 9, no 3, pp 539-57

Starkey, P. (2001) *Child welfare and social action in the nineteenth and twentieth centuries - international perspectives*, Liverpool: Liverpool University Press

Steedman, C. (2009) *Labours Lost: Domestic Service and the Making of Modern England,* Cambridge: Cambridge University Press

Stone, J. (2016) 'Government must look to end working age benefits freeze, Iain Duncan Smith says', *The Independent*, 7 November

Stuckler, D. and Basu, S. (2013) *The Body Economic: Why austerity kills*, New York: Basic Books

Sylvester, R. and Thomson, A. (2007) 'State Supernanny lays down the law', *The Telegraph*, 2 June

Tansel, C.B. (2017) *States of Discipline: Authoritarian Neoliberalism and the Contested Reproduction of Capitalist Order*, London: Rowman & Littlefield

Tapsfield, J. (2013) 'David Cameron backs George Osborne in Philpott Welfare Row', *The Independent*, 5 April

Taylor, J., Layne, L. and Wozniak, D. (2004) *Consuming Motherhood*, New Brunswick, NJ and London: Rutgers University Press

Taylor-Gooby, P.F. (2013) *The Double Crisis of the Welfare State and What We Can Do About It*, Basingstoke: Palgrave

Terazono, E. (2005) 'Shed agrees £30m purchase of group behind Supernanny', *Financial Times*, 26 November

Thatcher, M. (1996) 'Liberty and Limited Government', Keith Joseph Memorial Lecture, Speech given at Swiss Bank House, London, 11 January 11, [online] https://www.margaretthatcher.org/document/108353

References

The Sun Says (2013) 'In the Gutter', *The Sun*, 4 April

Thomson, R., Kehily, M., Hadfield, L. and Sharpe, S. (2011) *Making Modern Mothers*, Bristol: Policy Press

Thompson, S. and Yates, C. (2017) 'Maybot, Mummy or Iron Lady? Loving and loathing Theresa May' in *Election Analysis: Personality Politics and Popular Culture*, [online] www.electionanalysis.uk/uk-election-analysis-2017/section-8-personality-politics-and-popular-culture/maybot-mummy-or-iron-lady-loving-and-loathing-theresa-may/

Timmins, N. (2001) *The Five Giants*, London: Harper Collins

Tincknell, E. (2005) *Mediating the Family: Gender, culture and representation*, London: Hodder Arnold

Tobin, L. (2013) *Ausperity: Live the life you want for less*, London: Heron Books

Tyler, I. (2007) 'The Selfish Feminist: Public Images of Women's Liberation', *Australian Feminist Studies*, 22, 53, 173–90

Tyler, I. (2008) Chav Mum Chav Scum: class disgust in contemporary Britain, *Feminist Media Studies*, vol 8, no 1, pp 17–34

Tyler, I. (2009) 'Why Study the Maternal Now', Editorial, *Studies in the Maternal*, 1(1), [online] https://www.mamsie.bbk.ac.uk/articles/abstract/10.16995/sim.167/

Tyler, I (2013) 'The riots of the underclass? Stigmatisation, mediation and the government of poverty and disadvantage in neoliberal Britain' *Sociological Research Online* 18(4), [online]www.socresonline.org.uk/18/4/6.html

Tyler, I. (2015) 'Classificatory Struggles: class, culture and inequality in neoliberal times', *The Sociological Review,* vol 63, no2, pp 493–511

UNICEF (2007) *Child poverty in perspective: An overview of child well-being in rich countries*, Innocenti Report Card 7, Florence: UNICEF Innocenti Research Centre

Wacquant, L. (2009) *Punishing the Poor: The neoliberal government of social insecurity*, Durham and London: Duke University Press

Wacquant, L. (2010) 'Crafting the Neoliberal State: Workfare, Prisonfare, and Social Insecurity', *Sociological Forum*, vol 25, no 2, pp 197–220

Walkerdine, V. (2003) 'Reclassifying upward mobility: femininity and the neo-liberal subject', *Gender and Education*, vol 15, no 3, pp 238–48

Walkerdine, V. and Lucey, H. (1989) *Democracy in the Kitchen: Regulating Mothers and Socialising Daughters*, London: Virago Press

Warner, J. (2006) *Perfect Madness: Motherhood in the Age of Anxiety*, New York: Vermillion

Warner, J. (2015) *The Emotional Politics of Social Work and Child Protection*, Bristol: Policy Press

Weaver, T. (2015) *Blazing the Neoliberal Trail: Urban political development in the US and UK*, Philadelphia: University of Pennsylvania Press

Weeks, K. (2011) *The Problem with Work*, Durham: Duke University Press

Welshman, J. (2006) 'The concept of the unemployable', *Economic History Review*, vol 59, no 3, pp 578-606

Welshman, J. (2013) *Underclass: A History of the Excluded since 1880*, London: Bloomsbury

Wheatley, H. (2016) *Spectacular Television: Exploring Televisual Pleasure*, London: I.B.Tauris

Wilcox, B. and Nock, S. (2006) '"Her" Marriage after the Revolution, *Sociological Forum*, vol 22, no 1, pp 103–110

Williams, F. (1994) 'Social Relations, Welfare and the Post-Fordism Debate', in Burrows, R. and Loader, B. (eds) *Towards a Post-Fordist Welfare State?*, London: Routledge, pp 49-73

Williams, F. (2004) *Rethinking Families*, London: Calouste Gulbenkian Foundation

Williams, R. (1961) *The Long Revolution*, London: Chatto & Windus

Williams, R. (1977) *Marxism and Literature*, Oxford and New York: Oxford University Press

Winlow, S. and Hall, S. (2013) *Rethinking Social Exclusion*, London: SAGE

Wintour, P. (2006) 'No more misbehaving', *The Guardian*, 26 July

Wolf, J. (2007) Is Breast Really Best? Risk and total motherhood in the national Breastfeeding Awareness campaign, *Journal or Health Politics, Policy and Law*, vol 32, no 4, pp 595-636

Women's Budget Group (2012) 'The Impact on Women of the Budget 2012', [online] https://wbg.org.uk/wp-content/uploads/2016/12/The-Impact-on-Women-of-the-Budget-2012-FINAL.pdf

Wood, H. (2009) *Talking with Television: Women, Talk Shows and Modern Self-Reflexivity*, Chicago: University of Illinois Press

Wong, A. (2016) *Baby Cobra*, Netflix Comedy Special (directed by Jay Karas)

Wurtzel, E. (1999) *Bitch: In praise of difficult women*, London: Quartet Books

Yates, C. (2015) *The Play of Political Play, Emotion and Identity*, London: Palgrave Macmillan

YouGov (2013) 'Welfare Reform: Who, Whom?', [online] https://yougov.co.uk/news/2013/01/07/welfare-reform-who-whom/

Zelizer, V. (1994) *Pricing the Priceless Child: The changing social value of children*, Princeton: Princeton University Press

Index

Note: Page numbers followed by an n refer to end-of-chapter notes.
Page numbers in *italics* indicate figures.

Index